The Civil Code Controversy in Meiji Japan

THE CIVIL CODE CONTROVERSY IN MEIJI JAPAN

The Struggle to Modernize the Nation

Michał A. Piegzik

LEIDEN UNIVERSITY PRESS

Cover design: Andre Klijsen
Cover illustration: Ola Piegzik
Lay-out: Crius Group

ISBN 9789087284503
e-ISBN 9789400604902 (e-PDF)
https://doi.org/10.24415/9789087284503
NUR 820

Printed and bound by CPI Group UK Ltd Croydon CR0 4YY

CONTENTS

INTRODUCTION

This book presents the Civil Code Controversy in Japan, which emerged between two factions of Japanese jurisprudence from 1889 to 1892. The first of the parties, the so-called decisive faction, consisted of the French School of legal scholarship representatives, who advocated the newly drafted Civil Code and its entry into force on 1 January 1893, the date initially set by the cabinet. The second group, the postponement faction, comprised the English School of legal jurisprudence representatives. Unlike their adversaries, they called for delaying the entry into force of the Civil Code to reconsider its principles and introduce multiple formal amendments. Both parties had a different vision of the first national Civil Code for Japan from the beginning to the end of the Controversy, which made the compromise highly improbable. Despite the initial criticism of the Civil Code draft, it was promulgated by Aritomo Yamagata's cabinet in two parts. Property Law, Security and Evidence constituting Books Two, Three (part), Four and Five were published in April 1890, followed by Personal and Succession Law forming Books One and Three (part) in October 1890. The challenged Civil Code was drafted in 1879–1889 by Gustave E. Boissonade, a French legal adviser to the Meiji government and the Ministry of Justice, and a team of Japanese jurists, the French School graduates, working under his supervision. The democratically elected Imperial Diet eventually settled the Controversy in May and June 1892. It ended with the postponement faction's unexpected but unquestionable victory, which resulted in delaying the entry into force of the Civil Code to enable comprehensive revision to be carried out in the following years.

An important issue that deserves special attention in the introduction is using the correct terminology related to the Civil Code Controversy in Japan. Since this subject is a relatively new research field in Western legal scholarship, I decided to adopt the widely recognized nomenclature in Japanese legal history, even though Japanese scholars also used different terms in the past. The Civil Code Controversy is often closely linked to the parallel discussion on the Commercial Code. It is not uncommon that Japanese scholars refer to the more general description of the "dispute over the codes", yet a particular group of scholars use different kanji characters for the word "dispute". Because Japanese legal history witnessed several disputes about different codes in the last 150 years, Japanese scholars introduced the more precise term 民法転論争; *Mimpōten Ronsō* – the Civil Code Controversy – to unambiguously identify the distinction between the postponement and decisive factions. In the 1940s, Tōru Hoshino, a recognized researcher of Japanese private law, promoted this nomenclature, which became the standardized indication of the events in 1889–1892. To adequately transplant the *Mimpōten Ronsō* term to Western legal scholarship, it must be remembered that it contains two nouns without a connecting particle (の; *no*), characteristic of the Japanese language. The indication of the subject (論争; *Ronsō* – a dispute or controversy) and the object (民法典; *Mimpōten* – the Civil Code) is possible due to the specific order of kanji characters. Therefore, the most natural translation of this term in English is *the Civil Code Controversy*.

The time frames of the Controversy are inseparably connected to the legislative process and the discussion on the Civil Code. It was initiated by the Association of Jurists, which published its opinion on the Civil Code draft in April 1889. After three years of intensive exchange of views between the two Japanese jurisprudence factions, the Imperial Diet settled the dispute. The bill delaying the entry into force of the Civil Code was passed at the end of May 1892 by the House of Representatives and then approved by the House of Peers in June. Although the cabinet initially planned to challenge the parliament's decision using its political power, the bill was upheld and entered into force in November 1892, formally ending the Controversy.

This book portrays the causes, course, effects and importance of the Civil Code Controversy for the codification of Japanese private law during the Meiji era. It also answers additional questions that need detailed clarification to understand the nature of the dispute – reasons for which the Civil Code, drafted in 1879–1889 by G. Boissonade and a team of Japanese jurists and published in two parts in 1890, did not enter into force on 1 January 1893. At the time of the promulgation of the Constitution of Japan in 1889, private law was the last uncodified branch of the Japanese legal system, whose reform was publicly announced by Emperor Meiji himself as early as 1868. The Civil Code, the cornerstone for regulating the most critical issues related to economic and personal relations between citizens in a modern state governed by the rule of law, became the subject of a fierce dispute between two factions of Japanese jurisprudence. The postponement of the date of entry into force of the Civil Code was a direct result of the Controversy, which lasted over three years. To answer the initial question, it is necessary to identify and categorize the most critical objections of the postponement faction against the Civil Code and the counterarguments of the decisive faction. Since the dispute went beyond ordinary debate between members of the Japanese jurisprudence, the extra-legal factors that influenced the decision to delay the date of entry into force of the Civil Code must also be considered. Additionally, the book will provide findings on the issues related to the Civil Code that did not become the subject of dispute despite the overall rivalry between the two factions.

The primary legal research methodology adopted in the book is based on qualitative analysis of Japanese jurisprudence's opinions presented during the Civil Code Controversy. Since they were drawn up in the Japanese language characteristic of the Meiji era, i.e. with traditional writing and archaic grammatical forms compared to modern Japanese, I used a linguistic method that allows us to understand not only the basic meaning of legal opinions but also their historical and cultural nuances resulting from Japan's centuries-old belonging to the circle of Eastern civilization. Additionally, discussing the systematics of the Civil Code and the content of some of its provisions criticized by the postponement faction required the adoption of the doctrinal legal research methodology.

Although broadly understood Japanese-related legal and political topics have grown in popularity, Japanese private law and its history remain a relatively unknown field in Western legal scholarship. They have been analysed to varying degrees in the works published by H. Oda,[1] Y. Noda,[2] H. Tanaka,[3] R. Ishii and W.J. Chambliss[4], K. Takayanagi[5] and M. Dean.[6] Special mention must also be given for the papers by S. Ono,[7] K. Hatoyama,[8] P. Van den Berg,[9] S. Kanamori[10] and T. Hayashi.[11] The most notable research in English was provided in 2005 by W. Röhl, who published a monograph concerning the history of Japanese law since 1868. For the first time in Western legal scholarship, he outlined the development of the Japanese Civil Code over 20 years, also covering the Civil Code Controversy in a separate subchapter.[12] Yet, W. Röhl's work depicts the entire Japanese legal system throughout the last 150 years without focusing on drafting the Civil Code. Therefore, the 1912 monograph by N. Hozumi, one of the three fathers of the revised Civil Code and a Civil Code Controversy participant, continues to be the most comprehensive account of the Japanese private law codification in the 19th century.[13]

Important publications on Japanese private law history have also been published in French. The reception of French law into the Japanese legal system

[1] Oda, 2009.
[2] Noda (ed.), 1976.
[3] Tanaka (ed.), 1976.
[4] Ishii, Chambliss, 1969.
[5] Takayanagi, 1931, pp. 1–21.
[6] Dean, 2002.
[7] Ono, 1996, pp. 27–45.
[8] Hatoyama, 1902, pp. 354–370.
[9] Van den Berg, 2018, pp. 69–87.
[10] Kanamori, 1999, pp. 93–95.
[11] Hayashi, 2008, pp. 15–26.
[12] Röhl, 2005. W. Röhl is also the author of an article on the history of Japanese law in German: Röhl, 2002, pp. 185–207.
[13] Hozumi, 1912.

in the Meiji era was presented by Y. Noda,[14] Y. Horie,[15] J. Robert[16] and B. Jaluzot.[17] Furthermore, the Civil Code Controversy was described in short by Y. Ōkubo,[18] a distinguished Japanese legal scholar famous for research on the Old Civil Code and G. Boissonade's activity in Japan.

A more general review of Japanese private law history, including the codification process in the 19th century, was addressed in German by H.P. Martuschke,[19] C. Steenstrup,[20] C. Sokolowski[21] and J.M. Jehle, V. Lippa and K. Yamanaki, who edited a collection of speeches from the Göttingen – Kansai symposium.[22]

In other European languages, Japanese private law history remains unpopular, yet the following articles, loosely related to Japanese legal history or Japanese law in general, require honourable mention: F.L. Ramaioli in Italian,[23] H. Bocken in Dutch,[24] A. Kość,[25] L. Leszczyński,[26] L. Górnicki,[27] T. Karaś and T. Suzuki[28] in Polish, W.N. Yeremin[29] and N.P. Zarubina[30] in Russian, M. Frolík in Czech,[31] L.R. Marković and R.M. Đurović in Serbian,[32] and T. Hayashi,[33] F.V. Rodríguez[34] and R. Domingo[35] in Spanish.

The non-Japanese-language works mentioned above present issues related to the history of Japanese private law to a limited extent. The description of the codification process usually focuses on its basic stages, outlining the circumstances of employing foreign jurists as advisers to the Ministry of Justice and identifying the most important political and linguistic problems, which emerged during the drafting of the Civil Code and the Commercial Code, without referring to the broad legal,

14 Noda, 1963. pp. 543–556.
15 Horie, 2014, pp. 49–59.
16 Robert, 1994, pp. 49–62.
17 Jaluzot, 2015, pp. 121–146.
18 Ōkubo, 1991, pp. 389–405.
19 Martuschke, 2009.
20 Steenstrup, 1990, pp. 37–47.
21 Sokolowski, 2010.
22 Jehle, Lipp, Yamanaka (ed.), 2008.
23 Ramaioli, 2015, pp. 443–469.
24 Bocken, 1985, pp. 81–144.
25 Kość, 2001.
26 Leszczyński, 1995; Leszczyński, 1996.
27 Górnicki, 2012, pp. 77–155.
28 Karaś, Suzuki (ed.), 2008.
29 Jeriemin, 2010.
30 Zarubina, 2016.
31 Frolík, 2009.
32 Marković, Đurović, 2016.
33 Hayashi, 2009, pp. 9–21.
34 Rodríguez, 2011, pp. 97–126.
35 Domingo, 2003, pp. 263–279.

social and historical aspects of the legislative undertaking. Most of the cited works do not even contain references to the crucial Civil Code Controversy in 1889–1892, thus completely omitting its course and participants from three distinctive schools of legal jurisprudence. This fact allows for the assertion that the history of Japanese private law is still an unknown area for Western legal scholarship. The few available publications mostly depict the characteristics of the Meiji Civil Code (1898), which could be assessed as the most important work of Japanese jurisprudence in the field of private law, yet it only marked the culmination of about 30 years of codification work. Marginalizing or ignoring the events leading to the creation of the revised Civil Code, including the Civil Code Controversy, could hinder understanding the nature of Japanese private law and some of its norms which remain unchanged to this day.

Considering the relatively modest literature on the subject in Indo-European languages, I was motivated to research the Japanese archival sources and works to analyse thoroughly the Civil Code Controversy. In Japanese legal scholarship, this topic is part of *kindai hōseishi* – modern legal history – as part of the section devoted to the process called *hōten no hensan* – drafting the codes. The Civil Code Controversy is discussed to varying degrees in collective studies on the history of Japanese private law development. Special mention goes to the following: Y. Kawaguchi,[36] K. Kumagai,[37] K. Nakamura,[38] H. Iwamura,[39] H. Asako, T. Itō, N. Ueda and F. Jimbo,[40] and C. Takatani and Y. Koishikawa.[41] The challenged Civil Code was also the subject of in-depth research by M. Niida,[42] A. Iwata,[43] T. Hoshino,[44] K. Harada,[45] R. Ishii,[46] Y. Tezuka,[47] Y. Ōkubo and Y. Takahashi,[48] and M. Ikeda.[49] Additionally, T. Hoshino researched the Civil Code Controversy from the perspective of the family law system in Japan.[50]

The above list does not cover the wide range of other Japanese studies and articles concerning the codification of Japanese private law, the development of legal scholarship in Japan, the jurists involved in the codification process and the

[36] Kawaguchi, 2014.
[37] Kumagai, 1955.
[38] Nakamura, 1956; Nakamura, 1967.
[39] Iwamura, 1996.
[40] Asako, Itō, Ueda, Jimbo, 2010.
[41] Takatani, Koishikawa, 2018.
[42] Niida, 1943.
[43] Iwata, 1928.
[44] Hoshino, 1943.
[45] Harada, 1954.
[46] Ishii, 1979.
[47] Tezuka, 1990; Tezuka, 1991.
[48] Ōkubo, Takahashi, 1999.
[49] Ikeda, 2011.
[50] Hoshino, 1949.

Controversy, as well as historical and economic aspects related to the analysed matter. Thus, I also investigated the works published by N. Hozumi,[51] K. Sakamoto,[52] Y. Ōkubo,[53] M. Fukushima[54] and M. Itō.[55]

Regardless of the extensive study of the Japanese works related to the history of private law, I based my research mostly on archival sources and legal opinions from the period of the Civil Code Controversy. The analysed documents can be found in *Kokuritsu Kokkai Toshokan* – the National Diet Library – and *Kokuritsu Kōbunshokan* – the National Archives. The archival resources concerning the drafting of the Code can be divided into two collections including materials covering: (1) the drafting of the Code by the Civil Law Codification Department and its formal successor, the Law Research Committee in 1881–1887, and (2) the analysis of the completed draft of the Code by the Law Research Committee, the Chamber of Elders and the Privy Council in 1887–1890, which marked the final preparations for the legislative procedure and promulgation of the Code. The cited archival materials include approved drafting plans, legal opinions, procedural resolutions, and minutes of official meetings of various Japanese institutions, which discussed issues related to the content of individual provisions of the Civil Code. Although this book does not focus on the process of drafting the Code, my goal was also to demonstrate some details about the work on its provisions and the legislative procedure to better understand the doubts which arose during the Controversy.

Due to the fact that over 300 legal opinions concerning the Civil Code (and the related Commercial Code) were published in various Japanese journals in 1889–1892, selecting the most representative texts, which would reflect the nature of the Controversy, was a difficult task. Thanks to a thorough analysis of legal opinions provided by Tōru Hoshino and Kazuhiro Murakami, this scope was narrowed down to over 100 opinions. To avoid quoting identical arguments of Japanese jurists, I discussed 50 legal opinions, which covered all key aspects of the dispute and helped me to answer my research questions. When selecting legal opinions, I tried to maintain a balance between the views of two opposing factions in each of the three stages of the Controversy. Although the issue of the entry into force of the Civil Code and the Commercial Code also became the subject of a lively debate among Japanese entrepreneurs, politicians, economists, scholars and journalists in 1891–1892, I concentrated on the legal aspects of the dispute, namely those aspects related to theory and philosophy of law, theory of private law and legal history.

[51] Hozumi, 1890; Hozumi, 1980.

[52] Sakamoto, 2004.

[53] Ōkubo, 1977.

[54] Fukushima, 1988.

[55] Itō, 1966.

This book consists of this introduction, seven chapters and a conclusion. Chapter One presents the historical and political background and the legal history of Japan until the collapse of the Tokugawa shogunate and the Meiji Revolution. It also depicts the reasons for the codification of Japanese private law and discusses the similarities and differences between the Japanese and European legal cultures, which became a model for the Meiji government during the reform of the state. Chapter Two briefly describes all attempts to draft the Civil Code in 1868–1889. It presents the various periods covering the first failed translation projects of the Ministry of Justice, the drafting of a Civil Code imitating the French Civil Code, and finally the establishment of the drafting team led by G. Boissonade, who submitted the Civil Code for the legislative procedure. Chapter Three outlines the schools of legal scholarship in Japan during the Meiji era, preserving the chronology of their establishment and the hierarchy of influence in the Ministry of Justice. Along with the general characteristics of the French, English and German Schools of legal scholarship, the chapter covers a short history of their most important academic centres and a description of two factions, the main participants in the Civil Code Controversy. Chapter Four focuses on the first stage of the Controversy between April 1889 and April 1890. The time limits of the first stage are marked by the critical opinion of the Association of Jurists on the draft Civil Code, publicly announced and presented to Prime Minister Kiyotake Kuroda, and the publication part of the Civil Code regarding Property Law, Security and Evidence by A. Yamagata's cabinet. Chapter Five presents the second stage of the Controversy, which lasted from May 1890 to March 1891. During this transitional period, A. Yamagata's cabinet promulgated the missing part of the Civil Code regarding Personal and Succession Law. It was also distinctive of the first victory of the postponement faction during the Imperial Diet's first meeting[56] when the date of entry into force of the Commercial Code was extended by two years, until 1 January 1893.[57] Chapter Six describes the last stage of the Controversy from April 1891 to June 1892. Due to numerous publications of both parties before the Imperial Diet's second and third meetings, the dispute escalated from a scholarly debate between jurists to a crucial national matter discussed by various influential circles. Finally, the Civil Code Controversy (including the issues related to the Commercial Code) was resolved by the Imperial Diet's third meeting at the turn of May and June 1892. The House of Peers and the House of Representatives passed a bill postponing the date of entry into force of both codes by another four years, until

[56] The term meeting is used to refer to the period in which the Imperial Diet debated bills; this often lasted two to three months. The term session is used to refer to the particular day when they met and discussed specific agenda items.

[57] Meiji 23-nen 12-gatsu 27-nichi Hōritsu Dai 108-gō: Shōhō oyobi Shōhō Shikō Jōrei Shikō Kigen Hōritsu.

31 December 1896.[58] Chapter Seven summarizes the Controversy, and the book then ends with a conclusion based on analysed legal opinions and events in parliament. The bibliography and the summary in Japanese are attached after the last chapter.

As a consequence of the choice of a topic related to Japanese legal history, I needed to systematize the Japanese terminology throughout the book. For the spelling of names, places, given names and surnames in Japanese, I used the old Hebon-Shiki rōmaji – the traditional version of the Hepburn Transcription, which allows writing kanji, hiragana and katakana characters in the Latin alphabet with specific diacritics characterizing Japanese pronunciation. The exceptions are geographical names or terms that appear in English in a commonly recognized changed form. These include words such as Tokyo, Kyoto, Osaka, Kobe, Kyushu, Hokkaido, shogun, daimyo and Shinto. For practical reasons, I adopted the method of referencing people by giving initials/names followed by surnames, deliberately departing from the rules of East Asian languages. In the case of people who are mentioned for the second and subsequent times, I kept the first letter of a name to correctly identify people bearing the same surname in Japanese. My intention was also to include in the main text some words or fragments of statements in Japanese to promote new terms from an unknown field in Western legal scholarship.

I would like to express my gratitude to my long-term academic supervisor, Professor Leonard Górnicki, for pushing me on the track of researching Japanese private law and for constant support in my academic development. In a present-day world which often rejects the role of authorities, he is my genuine mentor, fully respecting my identity and academic integrity.

Drafting the book would not have been possible without the financial and organizational support of the Ministry of Education of Japan (MEXT), which provided me with a scholarship for foreign researchers in 2020–2022. The research programme was supervised by Professor Fumiaki Okesha, the head of the Department of Civil Law at the Faculty of Law of the Tokyo Metropolitan University. Professors Ryōhei Sakuuchi and Takenori Tsutsumi were also the first readers of the Japanese version of the book and authors of many valuable comments during long discussions.

Finally, my acknowledgements could not miss my beloved wife and my dearest life companion, Ola. She has always been the most supportive person to me, including my academic career full of hardship and doubts. Ola was also the first critical yet kind reader of the book, who had a significant influence on its final shape. Thank you and I love you.

Sagamihara 2022 – Edinburgh 2023

[58] Meiji 25-nen 11-gatsu 24-nichi Hōritsu Dai 8-gō: Mimpō oyobi Shōhō Shikō Enchōki Hōritsu.

日本語の要旨

本書は、5年間の間ポーランド、ヴロツワフ大学及び東京都立大学で行われた1889年から1892年にかけて起こった大日本帝国における民法典論争の研究をまとめたものである。ヨーロッパの法学において、日本の法学の民法典論争は未知の研究領域である。そのため、本書では日本の私法を研究するポーランドの法学者の目線から、ヨーロッパの法学者に日本法制史の一部を明らかにし、その研究成果を発表する。なお、本書の原本はポーランド語及び日本語で執筆され、エディンバラ・ネイピア大学のプロジェクト下で英語に翻訳されたものである。

本書は、目次、序論、7つの章に分けられた本論、結論で構成されており、結論後に参考文献が提示される。本書は研究目標を含め、民法典論争の時系列に沿って構成されている。主な研究目標は、日本における民法典論争の原因、経緯、影響を提示し、1893年に旧民法が施行しない理由を検討すること、また、民法典論争を研究することにより日本の明治期（1968年から1912年までに）における民法編纂の過程を発表することである。。

序論では、日本における民法典論争の概要を説明し、3つのテーゼを成立する。第一テーゼでは、明治時代においてフランス民法の継受、又はフランス民法典のもとで日本の民法典が編纂された可能性は低いことを明らかにする。第二のテーゼでは、民法典論争が民法の編纂に重大な影響を及ぼし、明治民法の基盤となったことを証明する。また、第三テーゼでは、民法典論争が日本法学の発展に寄与するのみならず、独立の日本法学の誕生につながったことを提示しる。

以上に述べたテーゼを検討するために、次の3つの研究課題を考査した。まず、第一課題は、なぜ1890年に山縣内閣が公布した旧民法を施行しなかったのだろうか。第二課題は、なぜ旧民法は日本に適わない法律として評価されたのだろうか。第三課題はなぜ元々影響力を持たない延期派が、民法典論争において勝利を収めたのだろうか。また、序論ではポーランドと日本に限らず、ヨーロッパにおける民法典論争についての研究状況を評価する。

民法典論争に関する外国語の文献が極めて少ないため、本研究は日本語の資料に基づくものである。また、研究方法として、民法典論争に関する60以上の断行派・延期派の法的な意見書及び第1回・第2回・第3回帝国議会での演説の研究分析を行った。意見書の研究では、旧民法と対象となる延期派の疑問及び断行派の立場が明らかにし、民法典論争の概略とその本義を提示する。なお、旧民法に関する意見と議会の演説を分析し、議論の進行具合とその激化を把握する。

第1章では、幕末から明治維新にかけての日本の法制史及び政治的背景の概要を説明する。これは、民法典論争の本質を理解するためには、日本の民法編纂に関連する政治、法、社会的な改革を説明する必要があるからである。そして、当時の日本とその近代化を特徴付けしつつ、なぜ明治政府はフランス民法を採用したのか、その事由を考査するなお、民法編纂の理由の中には、日本法制度の統一、資本主義に基づく国民国家の成立、不平等条約を改正する政策などが提示される。

第2章では、明治維新における民法を編纂する全ての事業の概要を説明し、明治初期に司法省が失敗したフランス民法典を和訳する箕作麟祥の事業だけなく、フランス民法典を模倣する日本の民法典を編纂するプロジェクトも紹介する。こうした6つのプロジェクトが失敗に繋がったため、当時のドイツ帝国における民法典を編纂する政策と比較された概要も紹介する。また、10年間にわたってギュスターヴ・エミール・ボアソナードとフランス法派に所属した日本の法学者によって草案された旧民法とその特性を説明する。旧民法を編纂する方法及びボワソナードとその法的経験についてもまとめる。

第3章では、明治期において、フランス法派・イギリス法派・ドイツ法派という民法典論争に参加した3つの法学派の発展と各派の旧民法に対する見解を紹介する。フランス法派はついては、ボワソナードの見解を中核とし、理想な民法典を編纂する進行を明らかにする。イギリス法派は、フランス法派との対立のみならず、民法典編纂における固有な慣習法を保護する論拠も説明する。ドイツ法派に関しては、団体主義に基づく民法典を促進する見解がまとめられる。さらに、以上に述べた3つの法学派の紹介と共に、その民法典論争に対する立場及びその主な大学を表示する。

第4章では、1889年4月から1890年4月までに繰り広げられた、民法典論争の第1段階に焦点を当て、黒田総理大臣宛に提出された旧民法に関する法学士会の意見書及び、その内容を徹底的に解釈する。これは、法学士会の意見書は、民法典論争を引き起こしたため、その全文を解説することが必要であるからである。また、イギリス法派は旧民法を非難したものの、1890年4月に山縣内閣がボワソナードによって草案された民法典の財産編を公布することに至った粗筋も紹介する。さらに、この章では民法典論争の第1段階における延期派が発表した11の意見も解釈した。

第5章では、民法典論争が第2段階（1890年5月から1891年3月）に移行する伴い、山縣内閣が1890年10月にフランス法派によって草案された人事編及び相続法を公布した状況を明らかにする。第2回帝国議会において、民法典及び商法典をめぐる議論した結果、商法典の施行日が延期され、延期派は予想外の勝利を収めたこと、そのため、翌年に民法典論争が激しくなった概要も説明する。また、第5章では、民法典論争の第2段階における延期派・断行派が発表した8つの意見書及び議会での演説も解釈する。また議会演説の解釈では帝国議会の演説中に旧民法に対する延期派の議論に留意する。

第6章では、1891年4月から1892年6月までに繰り広げられた民法典論争の最終段階を紹介する。当時、延期派は挑発的な見解を発表したため、（具体例：穂積八束の「民法出テ、忠孝亡フ」という意見）民法典論争が日本社会の注目を集め、重要な主題になった粗筋を紹介する。また、民法典論争の激化に対応して断行派の法学者は統合し、何としても旧民法を守ろうとしたが、第2回衆議院議員総選挙に干渉しようとした結果松方内閣及び田中不二麿率いる司法省の政治的影響力が減退した内容もまとめる。さらに、断行派の一部は、政治の敗北の影響により旧民法の弁護を嫌うようになった。第3回帝国議会において、旧民法と旧商法をめぐる議論が開始され、断行派及び延期派が劇的議論した結果、貴族院及び衆議院は旧民法及び旧商法の施行日を延長し、1896年12月31日までに両法典を改正することに至る経歴も明らかにする。特に焦点を当てた議会演説は、大木文部大臣の「天賦人権」をめぐる貴族院の議論（「舌禍事件」というもの）であり、5月27日に富井男爵が行った画期的な演説である。なお、研究内容には、第3回帝国議会における、他の断行派・延期派が発表した旧民法に関する22つの意見書もある。

第7章では、民法典論争を要約し、1893年から1898年にかけて行われた明治民法を編纂する法典調査会の作業の概要を説明する。また、法典調査会の組織だけなく、妥協の民法典が草案するために方法を説明した。民法典論争のまとめとしては、旧民法に対する断行派・延期派の議論を表示し、大きなカテゴリーに(旧民法の理念・体裁・立法上の手続き)分け、延期派が勝利を収めた理由を明らかにする。この勝利の理由として、延期派の見解で提示する日本社会に与えた影響、旧民法の理念、旧民法と大日本帝国憲法の間に多数な矛盾、旧民法の実用的な欠陥、内閣及び司法省が弱体化した政治的影響力などを論述する。

結論では、民法典論争のまとめを発表する。本書はポーランドに限らず、ヨーロッパにおいて日本民法編纂に関する最初の研究論文であり、民法典論争の経緯とその意義を初解釈したものである。なお、旧民法をめぐる議論と民法典論争における両法派の見解が明らかにする。

本図書の参考文献は、歴史資料、江戸時代及び明治時代の法律、民法典論争の意見、帝国議会の演説、300以上の論文で構成する。研究した歴史資料は、国立国会図書館及び国立公文書館に所属している。旧法及び議会の演説は、オンラインデータベースにより検討した。民法典論争の法的意見は、日本に出版された資料編集をもって手に入った。なお、300以上の論文は、日本語、英語、ポーランド語、フランス語、ドイツ語、ロシア語、スペイン語、オランダ語、チェコ語を集めた書籍である。

CHAPTER ONE

THE HISTORY OF THE JAPANESE LEGAL SYSTEM

Abstract

This chapter focuses on the historical and political background and the legal history of Japan until the collapse of the Tokugawa shogunate (bakumatsu period) and the Meiji Revolution (Meiji ishin). It also depicts the reasons for the codification of Japanese private law and discusses the similarities and differences between the Japanese and European legal cultures, which became a model for the Meiji government during the reform of the state.

Keywords: history of Japan, bakumatsu, shogunate, Meiji Japan, unequal treaties

"As long it was a painful experience, the arrival of black ships also made us to reform the state".

—Bakumatsu administration clerk comment on the Perry's expedition after over 40 years.

1.1. Edo-Era isolation (1639–1854)

The Japanese law codification process, which began during the reign of Emperor Meiji (1868–1912), was preceded by over two centuries of restrictive isolation of Japan, significantly limiting diplomatic and trade contacts with the rest of the world (1639–1854). This confinement, commonly known as *sakoku*, resulted from two critical events that had a decisive impact on the history of Japan. The first was the end of a long-lasting civil war (1467–1603),[1] which concluded in the decisive victory of Ieyasu Tokugawa, a shogun and one of the most notable domain leaders.

[1] There are some significant differences in Japanese and Western historiography in the assessment of the beginning and end of the civil war era in Japan. Most historians agree that the Onin War of 1473 (Ōnin no ran) was the beginning, but the end remains an open question. It is generally accepted that the era of civil war ended with the unification of Japan by Hideyoshi Toyotomi (1587), the decisive battle of Sekigahara won by the Tokugawa family (1600), or Ieyasu Tokugawa assuming the post of Great Shogun (1603). In this book, the Imperial Rescript on the Great Shogun of 1603, which recognized the administrative and military supremacy of I. Tokugawa, was used as a landmark event.

Despite the initial setbacks, he defeated all internal enemies and captured the last opposing stronghold in Osaka, securing unquestioned rule over the united country in 1615.[2] His crushing military triumph also consolidated the shogun's superior political power and authority to decide on domestic policy, eventually superseding the already impaired yet still sacred *ten'nō sei* – the emperor system. Consequently, the end of the civil war led to the emergence of an entirely new political system (also called *Edo no bakufu* – the Edo-era shogunate), which survived with minor changes until the mid-19th century.[3]

An equally important event that significantly influenced the course of Japanese history in the 17th century was the establishment of political and commercial contacts with European countries, which tried to extend their sphere of influence to East Asia during the era of great geographical discoveries. Portuguese sailors were the first to reach Japanese islands, arriving in Kyushu in 1543. They established close trade relations with the Japanese, soon confirmed in the agreement to open an international port in Nagasaki. In the following years, ships sent by Lisbon regularly brokered the exchange of goods and enslaved people between Japan, China and Korea, taking advantage of the lack of any official concessions. The merchants were followed by Catholic missionaries, supported first by the Jesuits and later by the Dominicans and Franciscans, who also appeared in Japan in 1549. Fundamental cultural differences between Europeans and Japanese substantially stalled the Christianization process, given the original plans of the papacy to anchor permanently in Japan. Still, despite mediocre progress in conversion, Catholic clergy emphasized that the Japanese were "good people who could be persuaded to change their religion".[4]

After more than three decades of failed attempts to promote the new faith, the activities of the Portuguese and Spanish missionaries finally began to bring the first tangible results. Due to the focus on smaller agricultural and commercial centres, the Japanese community of *Kirishitan*, which is what Christians were called, already numbered about 130,000 in 1579.[5] Most *Kirishitan* lived in Kyushu, envisaged as the bridgehead for further expansion into Japan. Having reached the point of managing the financial transactions from trade and receiving donations, the Catholic community in Kyushu acquired Buddhist and Shinto temples, transforming them into temples of their denomination. Notably, among the *Kirishitan* group were also several daimyos – feudal lords – who significantly raised the status of the new religion in Japan, previously associated only with the lower social class.

[2] Nakamura, 1965, p. 492.

[3] Matsudaira, 1919, pp. 1–3.

[4] Ellis, 2003, pp. 155–169.

[5] Walker, 2002, pp. 44–62.

The spread of the new religion to daimyos was one of the reasons why Hideyoshi Toyotomi, the most famous shogun in Japanese history, became keenly interested in Christianity at the end of the 16th century. He feared a rapid increase in Christian population, especially among the influential elites with financial resources, and thus, on 24 July 1587, he promulgated Bateren Tsuihōrei – the Bateren Edict.[6] The Criminal Law Act, comprising 11 articles, prohibited *namban bōeki* – trade with Portugal and Spain – and missionary activity. At the same time, H. Toyotomi ordered all missionaries to leave Japan.[7] Although the Bateren Edict was amended in 1596, and further restrictions were added, officials, merchants and clergy ignored these provisions. As W.N. Yeremin argued, the persecution of Christians in Japan was a short-lived phenomenon. The Russian scholar also referred to K. Yoshio, who stated, "Japan hardly experienced what was common in Western Europe: brutal religious repressions such as 'witch-hunts' and trials of heretics; fierce religious wars such as the Crusades or the Thirty Years' War."[8]

American historians claim that H. Toyotomi's anti-Christian edicts were administrative measures to stave off unknown social unrest linked to religious fanaticism. The shogun regularly received reports of armed groups supported by Christian daimyos who attacked Buddhist temples or Shinto shrines.[9] Responding to the San Felipe incident, 26 Christians were sentenced to death and crucified.[10] This decision shocked Europeans, though they did not break the official contact with Japan. In addition to internal security policy, H. Toyotomi tried to solve the issue of the slave trade of Japanese people, which brought considerable profits to Christian merchants. The shogun initially thought that the problem would gradually disappear under the pressure of missionaries, yet they did not condemn any European activity in Japan. Although slavery was banned in the Bateren Edict, he did not have sufficient resources to control all Japanese ports sufficiently.

The ascending anti-Christian policy did not prevent Japan from maintaining political and commercial relations with four European countries at the beginning of the Edo era: Portugal, Spain, England and the Netherlands.[11] I. Tokugawa expanded trade with the Portuguese and opened the country to contact with the Spanish-ruled Philippines. The shogun, however, remained sceptical of the growing influence of the Roman Catholic Church. At the beginning of the 17th century, the number of

[6] The date is given according to the Gregorian calendar; in the Japanese calendar, the Bateren Edict was issued on 18 June, the 15th year of the Tenshō era [1587].

[7] Yamamoto, 2015, pp. 100–102.

[8] Yeremin, 2010, p. 22.

[9] Kanda, 2010, pp. 158–165.

[10] Jansen, 2000, p. 68.

[11] Japan–Netherlands relations were formally established in 1609, but the first Dutch merchant ship, *De Liefde*, arrived in Japan in 1600.

Christians in Japan exceeded 300,000, becoming the first religious minority group in Kyushu.[12] Taking advantage of the growing anxiety in the shogun's administration, English and Dutch merchants intended to eliminate competitors by spreading rumours about a Spanish plan to use the Roman Catholic Church to colonize Japan gradually. The English and Dutch also declared readiness to give up any missionary activity in Japan in exchange for receiving exclusivity in trade.

The rivalry of Europeans for a privileged position in Japanese trade was not purely based on false backdoor propaganda. Indeed, while reassuring the shogun about the purely peaceful intentions, the Spanish and Portuguese probed the possibility of an intervention by the allied fleet stationed in Manila. Both Iberian countries also secretly supplied firearms and gunpowder to Roman Catholic daimyos, who wanted to establish a self-defence force in case of the forcible removal of the missionaries and merchants from Japan. Yet, the Tokugawa clan could not entirely ignore the presence of troops loyal to European newcomers. The Edo government could not overlook the fact that 86 Japanese feudal lords had officially converted to Christianity by 1620. Additionally, a large group of daimyos did not abandon their traditional beliefs but openly declared sympathy with the new religion.[13]

The growing threat from the Roman Catholic Church and repeated incidents involving Christians persuaded Hidetada Tokugawa, son of Ieyasu, to ban the entire Christian activity. All missionaries were ordered to leave Japan. The reasons for such a sudden turnaround were outlined in the justification for the new law: "Christians have finally made it to Japan. They sent merchant ships to exchange goods and spread a harmful idea to deceive honest people into overthrowing the government and taking over the country. This would be a great catastrophe. There's nothing we can do but stop it."[14] Based on materials edited and published by Hirokazu and Yūmio Shimizu, Christians were also accused of breaking government regulations, discrediting Shinto and traditional law, violating public order and corrupting morality.[15]

As a direct result of the edict, more than half of the missionaries left in the first year after the ban was introduced. There were some plans for armed resistance, but the real strength of Christians in Japan was limited to local self-defence groups. The immediate intervention of the Spanish fleet from the Philippines turned out to be impossible. Even if the ships could arrive in Japan, the outcome of the military mission was uncertain. Therefore, the clergy recommended refraining from provoking the authorities, hoping for a change in policy in the following years. The

12 Jansen, 2010, p. 79.

13 Abe, Rejaunier, 1998, ch. 16–17.

14 Higashibaba, 2002, p. 139.

15 Shimizu, Shimizu, 2002, p. 264.

shogun's view, however, did not soften at all. Until his abdication in 1623, the bakufu consistently suppressed any attempts to spread the new religion.

Hidetada's successor, Iemitsu, continued not only his father's anti-Christian policy but also organized a bureaucratic system whose task was to persecute dissenters. Public executions and interrogation torture led to mass local unrests of the Christian peasantry against local daimyos. On 11 December 1637, after the assassination of a provincial tax collector, one of the riots escalated into an organized uprising against the shogunate. It differed from previous rebellions as almost 40,000 people joined it. Notably, the insurgency command established its headquarters in a fortified castle.[16]

Iemitsu gathered over 125,000 men, led by trusted daimyos, to suppress the rebellion. In the spring of 1638, his army secured the last points of enemy resistance, bringing the uprising to a brutal end. Although from a military point of view, the rebels did not have a chance to threaten the shogun's power, the large-scale riots finally convinced him that coexistence with Christians was futile, also in economic relations. In 1639, he issued an act forbidding Portuguese ships to dock at Japanese ports. The Dutch were the only Europeans allowed to continue trading, provided they used a designated harbour and refrained from any missionary activity.

Even though historians agree that 1639 marked the symbolic beginning of more than 200 years of Japan's isolation, contact with foreigners had been gradually limited in the previous decade. As early as 1624, the English were the first to withdraw from precarious trade with the Japanese.[17] A year later, the Tokugawa shogunate undermined diplomatic relations with Madrid by denying Spanish ships access to ports. From 1633 to 1639, Iemitsu issued five "Isolation Acts", banning foreigners from staying in Japan and Japanese people from leaving the country. Violating those rules resulted in the death penalty with no means of appeal. Trade contact with the outside world considered vital for the shogunate was managed through *yottsu no kuchi* – four gates – vividly described by the Japanese as "mouths" to their country.

As previously mentioned, the only Europeans allowed to enter Japanese ports were the Dutch, who were given the right to use the island of Dejima off Nagasaki. Trade with China, which was crucial to the Japanese economy, was also carried out through Nagasaki. The exchange of goods with Korea was supervised by the Sō clan from the Tsushima domain. The Matsumae clan served as agents in contact with the Ainu people living in Hokkaido. The last trading partner of the Japanese was the subjugated Ryūkyū Kingdom (present-day Okinawa Prefecture). Trade with Ryūkyūans was made through the Shimazu clan from the Satsuma domain.[18]

16 Kanda, 2005, pp. 14–18.

17 Iwao, 2005, pp. 326–333.

18 Asada, 2000, pp. 27–46.

The shogunate intended to adhere to the policy of isolation consistently. Even one exception could lead to a situation where foreign countries might exploit the breach to enforce their national interests. In 1641, the Dutch left most of their trading posts, including the most important one in Hirado, and moved to Nagasaki. Two years later, Maarten G. Vries, a Dutch explorer and cartographer, docked in the port of Yamada in north-eastern Japan during a terrible storm. The locals initially welcomed him. Officials, however, soon forced him to set off and threatened severe punishment for breaching the ban. In 1647, two Portuguese ships attempted to re-establish diplomatic relations, but the Nagasaki port was blocked by 900 Japanese vessels. To prevent similar incidents in the future, the Edo government soon decided to reinforce patrols in the southwestern waters of Kyushu. The English merchant ship *Return* tested the Japanese vigilance and received a permanent ban on dropping anchor in Nagasaki in 1673.[19]

Successive shoguns from the Tokugawa clan consistently followed the acts of isolating Japan introduced by Iemitsu. Although a Russian expedition visited Honshu for a short time in 1738 and was warmly greeted by the local population, the shogunate's views on trade with unauthorized nations remained relentless.[20] Pavel Lebedev-Lastochkin, a Yakutsk merchant who arrived in Hokkaido in 1778 with a request to establish trade relations, also experienced strict isolation. The Japanese initially seemed cordial and accepted his gifts, but the answer to his offer of a stable exchange of goods was unequivocally negative.[21] In 1825, due to increasingly frequent attempts to circumvent the imposed bans, shogun Iesada Tokugawa issued Ikokusen Chiharairei – the Act Concerning the Deterrence of Foreign Ships. It authorized the governors of the coastal provinces to shell foreign merchant ships if they tried to enter Japanese ports without consent. The police also received new competencies and could arrest or kill any foreigner encountered aground without warning or interrogation.[22] The American merchant ship *Morrison* learned about the effectiveness of the new law: she was shot at while approaching the shore in 1837 and soon turned back.[23]

[19] Asaji, 2009, pp. 37–38.

[20] Barratt, 1981, pp. 35–37.

[21] Rossijskij Gosudarstwiennyj Archiw Driewnich Aktow (RGADA), F.7, op. 1, d. 2539, Zapiska brigadira Niemcowa ob otprawlenii ekspiedicyj na Kurilskije ostrowa. 5 diekabria 1779 goda, pp. 13–14.

[22] Ikokusen Uchiharairei (Foreign Ship Deterrence Act), http://archives.pref.yamaguchi.lg.jp/user_data/upload/File/ags/3-3-6-010.pdf, [access: 25.09.2020].

[23] Cullen, 2003, pp. 158–178.

1.2. Bakumatsu period and the Meiji Restoration (1854–1868)

Protected for more than two centuries, the isolation of Japan was a unique phenomenon in history. Yet, it could not endure during the Industrial Revolution era and the colonial powers' domination. In 1842, due to the First Opium War, China was forced to open its ports to foreign trade. Economic and political penetration of East Asia had begun. European governments sought opportunities to expand their influence. Japanese islands were also one of the areas of interest for Western newcomers, as they were located directly on the trade route connecting China and Korea with the west coast of North America. The shogunate's policy of strict isolation not only deprived American and European trading companies of additional profits but also caused additional inconvenience during the journey through the western part of the Pacific Ocean. Previous attempts to open Japan had failed, so the governments of the Western powers concluded that the most effective method of securing economic and political interests would be using military force, which worked perfectly in relations with an equally tenacious China.

A threat as a political instrument was first used by the Americans in the early 1850s, who explored the possibilities of stepping into East Asia. The *sakoku* ended with the US Navy expedition to Japan led by Commodore Matthew C. Perry. In 1853–1854, American warships twice entered Edo Bay (now Tokyo Bay) and, through a military demonstration, forced the shogunate to establish trade and diplomatic relations. Signed in Yokohama on 31 March 1854, the Japan–US Treaty of Peace and Amity (*Nichibei Washin Jōyaku*), also known as the Kanagawa Treaty, was a turning point in Japanese history, as it set the grounds for the decline of the Tokugawa shogunate and the restoration of imperial power, the foundation of a modern capitalist state, and the gradual increase of the country's importance on the international arena to become one of the world powers.

The 12-article Japan–US Treaty of Peace and Amity granted Americans the right of free trade in the ports of Shimoda and Hakodate and allowed US citizens to stay in Japan in specially designated zones.[24] An extension of the relations established under the threat of force was the Treaty of Amity and Commerce (*Nichibei Shūkō Tsūshō Jōyaku*), signed on 29 July 1856. Comprised of 14 articles, it provided for, among other things, the creation of extraterritorial diplomatic posts and the opening of the ports of Nagasaki, Kanagawa, Niigata and Hyōgō to American merchants with the right to freedom of religion and the construction of temples within its

[24] Nichibei Washin Jōyaku (Japan–US Treaty of Peace and Amity), https://www.ndl.go.jp/modern/img_t/002/002-003tx.html [access: 24.10.2020].

boundaries.[25] The American breach in the *sakoku* policy was soon followed by the European colonial powers. By the end of 1858, the United Kingdom, France, the Netherlands and Russia signed treaties with the shogunate, obtaining trade and diplomatic privileges analogous to the Americans.[26]

The sudden arrival of foreigners, even in relatively small numbers, caused civil unrest in Japan's conservative society. In 1858, the shogunate administration suppressed several local incidents related to assaults on newcomers. The assailants' pretext for the attacks varied depending on the period, including accusations of responsibility for the cholera epidemic, which claimed the lives of about 100,000 people in Edo alone. Additionally, the increased exchange of goods and uncontrolled circulation of money led in 1860 to the collapse of the Japanese monetary policy based on the parity of gold, silver and copper.[27] The Edo government attempted to intervene by redenominating money, yet failed to contain the natural effects of opening up to more developed external markets, such as rising unemployment and galloping inflation. A common reaction to the economic crisis that hit the lower class was blaming foreigners. Some people also expressed concern that religious beliefs could explain the recent adversities – the gods were punishing Japanese society for violating the traditional order protected for centuries. This notion became even more widespread when three successive natural disasters, the so-called Ansei great earthquakes of 1854–1855, affected the Tōkai, Nankai and Kantō regions, bringing death and large-scale destruction.[28]

Increased contact with Europeans and Americans revealed the enormous backwardness of Japan in all areas that shaped the 19th-century state. Still, the shogunate and all clans were well aware of the unprecedented situation they found themselves in. For the first time in 220 years, Japanese neutrality was violated by force. There was nothing the Tokugawa family could do to return to the past policy of isolation. Ordinary people noticed the weakness of the Edo government. The authority crisis resulted in the popularization of the slogan *sonnō jōi* – restore the emperor, expel the barbarians – which soon resounded in Japanese streets among all social classes.[29] In a short time, this catchy phrase became part of the

[25] Nihonkoku-Meriken Gasshūkoku Shūkō Tsūshō Jōyaku (Japan–US Treaty of Amity and Commerce), Hōrei Zenshū, 1912, p. 285.

[26] Nichiei Shūkō Tsūshō Jōyaku (Anglo-Japanese Treaty of Amity and Commerce); Nichiro Washin Jōyaku (Treaty of Commerce and Navigation between Japan and Russia); Nichiran Shūkō Tsūshō Jōyaku (Treaty of Amity and Commerce between the Netherlands and Japan); Nichifutsu Shūkō Tsūshō Jōyaku (Treaty of Amity and Commerce between France and Japan), *Hōrei Zenshū*, 1912, p. 6.

[27] Metzler, 2006, p. 15.

[28] Hammer, 2006, p. 65.

[29] Popularization of the slogan *sonnō jōi* during the bakumatsu period is attributed to the Mito school from Kōdōkan (present-day Ibaraki Prefecture). It was not a new expression at that time but

political programme of influential and progressive clans from the Satsuma and Chōshū domains, known for their critical attitude towards the Tokugawa regime. The erosion of the shogunate system was hastened by Emperor Kōmei, who actively followed the situation in the country and decided to rupture the centuries-old custom of the emperor's non-intervention in domestic politics. On 11 March 1863, he issued *Jōi chokumei* – the Order to Expel Barbarians. It was to come into force within two months.[30] The shogunate, however, never intended to enforce this act, although the explicit will of the emperor encouraged some clans to take independent action. The central government gradually was losing control in the western and southern parts of the country. In 1864–1865 alone, two bloody uprisings broke out in western Japan. The insurgents called for the restoration of imperial power and the expulsion of foreigners. The pacification of the rebellious domains, especially Satsuma, was a massive military and economic problem for the Edo government. In the meantime, due to the Chōshū's unprovoked attack on foreign merchant ships, the United States, the United Kingdom, France and the Netherlands intervened in the domestic affairs of Japan by dispatching their warships to bombard the ports of Shimonoseki and Kagoshima.[31]

Social unrest provoked by the *Jōi chokumei* slogan ended with the recognition of the treaty rights of the Western powers and payment of compensation for the damage caused by the rebels. Skirmishes with the enemy fleet revealed the Japanese armed forces' and the country's backwardness. Since Iemochi Tokugawa could no longer ignore the military weakness, he sent a delegation to Europe to acquire the latest technology and knowledge, thus lifting the official ban on people leaving the country. Despite the shogun's efforts to consolidate power and regain his authority, the second pacification expedition against the Chōshū domain in June 1866 ended in a compromising defeat. Iemitsu's 100,000-strong army lost to the 3,000-strong rebellious detachment equipped with modern firearms and artillery purchased in the West. Unexpectedly, the 20-year-old shogun died of a heart attack in August 1866. Soon after, due to the smallpox epidemic, 36-year-old Emperor Kōmei died in January 1867. His anti-Western attitude was the last obstacle to the country's modernization. As Sir Ernest Satow, a British diplomat in Japan, argued,

expressed a specific political programme to which the opponents of the shogunate had been referring since the 17th century. The *sonnō* part called for disobedience towards the Tokugawa shogunate and allegiance to the emperor as the rightful and divine ruler of Japan. The *jōi* part initially referred only to the expulsion of Christians, but after breaking the sakoku policy, it was extended to all foreigners. Imai, Setani, Bitō, 1973, pp. 558–559.

30 Jōi Chokumei.

31 Medzini, 1971, pp. 44–46, Denney, 2011, pp. 189–191; Inoue, 2006a, pp. 126–128.

the assumption of the Japanese throne by Kōmei's minor son was a historical moment that presented an excellent opportunity to carry out thorough reforms.[32]

Only 14 years old, Emperor Meiji, known also as Mutsuhito, was under the tutelage of advisers from the Satsuma, Chōshū and Tosa domains. Iemitsu's legacy as a shogun was taken over by Yoshinobu Tokugawa, who wanted to overcome the crisis of the shogunate and proposed to his opponents a major political reform to reconcile the interests of both sides. In exchange for establishing a government under the emperor's formal supervision as a head of state, the shogun demanded to keep his leading role in the executive. In Japanese historiography, this idea was called the *kōbu gattai* – the unification of the imperial system and the shogunate.[33] However, Yoshinobu's offer did not receive a positive response since his authority was irretrievably lost within both the elites and lower classes. Despite significant differences of opinion, at Shikō Kaigi – the Conference of Four Daimyos – held in May 1867 in Kyoto, the prominent hard-liners from Satsuma and Chōshū domains chose to defy the Tokugawa shogunate openly and expressed their readiness to launch military operations. Upon learning of the preparations of the enemy, on 9 November 1867, Yoshinobu, probably under the influence of his advisers, issued *Taisei Hōkan* and agreed to "be the instrument for carrying out" imperial will. Ten days later, he also resigned as the shogun but remained in effective control of the Tokugawa domain, in particular the administrative capital of Edo. Some observers of the Japanese political scene at that time emphasized that it was only a tactical move aimed at consolidating his forces and spying on the opponent's reaction. The Tokugawa family still had many allies among the Japanese clans, some with personal connections to the imperial court. Yoshinobu's detailed strategy remains unknown, yet some sources claim that he hoped Emperor Meiji would convey the general assembly of daimyos, supporting his candidacy for the highest position in the newly formed executive.[34]

As a result of Yoshinobu's formal resignation as the shogun, the highest level of Japanese government lost its political leader. The Japanese executive needed an immediate substitution to replace this nominal void to maintain the continuity of state authorities' decision-making and contact with foreign diplomatic missions. On 3 January 1868, Emperor Meiji issued in Kyoto *Ōsei Fukko no Dai Kōrei* – the Restoration of Imperial Power Great Order – publicly announcing the shogun's resignation and the restoration of imperial rule over Japan.[35] The shogunate was formally dissolved, followed by the regency, the office of supreme adviser to the

[32] Keene, 2002, pp. 94–96.

[33] Sasaki, 1998, p. 72.

[34] Satow, 1968, pp. 282–285.

[35] Sakamoto, 2004, pp. 122–126.

emperor, and the police and administrative institutions of the shogunate in Kyoto: Shugoshoku and Shoshidai.[36]

Yoshinobu's first reaction to Emperor Meiji's Grand Order was inaction. Some of his subordinates and enemies understood it as tacit consent. Still, in the following weeks, probably after receiving promising military intelligence from western Japan disclosing the significant numerical disadvantage of the emperor's forces, he launched the campaign to restore his supreme position. On 17 January, the former shogun demanded that Emperor Meiji revoke the Great Order he had issued two weeks before. Since the emperor categorically refused, Yoshinobu's 100,000-strong army set off from Edo to capture Kyoto, controlled by the Satsuma and Chōshū forces. These moves opened hostilities, which lasted less than a year and a half and went down in history as the Boshin War. In January 1868, the shogunate army was defeated in the decisive battle of Toba-Fushimi near Kyoto. In the following months, Yoshinobu gradually lost his allies and control of central and eastern Japan. In July, the emperor's army seized Edo, and at the end of November, the most important ally of the former shogun, the Aizu clan, was eliminated from the war. The defeat of the Tokugawa clan was complete. According to Katsuo Inoue, a recognized Japanese historian of the *bakumatsu* period, the shogun failed for four main reasons: his army was insufficiently equipped with modern firearms and artillery; he lacked a strategic and tactical plan; his troops had lower morale and were unaware of the common goals of the war; and some of the most prominent clans betrayed him.[37]

Better organized and more determined progressive forces supporting the emperor became the winning side of the Boshin War. The defeated Yoshinobu recognized Mutsuhito's supremacy and was removed from Japanese political life. Yet, for practical and personal reasons, he retained the title of daimyo and avoided the death penalty. Neighbouring countries quickly recognized the new regime. Despite different visions of the future shape of the government, both sides of the civil war desired to secure a declaration of neutrality from the Western powers. The non-intervention policy in Japan's internal affairs during the Boshin War was crucial in shaping future diplomatic relations. It should be mentioned, however, that the United Kingdom and the United States sympathized with Mutsuhito, while the Tokugawa clan and France were bound by military and economic agreements concluded by Yoshinobu. The collapse of the shogunate and the Meiji Revolution marked the birth of a new political system in Japan, which survived with minor changes until 1945. Having received the support of the Satsuma, Chōshū and Tosa domains, Mutsuhito faced the vital task of reforming the state from long-lasting

36 Hōrei Zenshō, https://dl.ndl.go.jp/info:ndljp/pid/787948/9, [access: 12.10.2020].

37 K. Inoue cited the reasons in the context of the battle of Toba-Fushimi, but they can be applied to the entire civil war. Inoue, 2006b, pp. 76–78.

stagnation. The restoration of imperial power made the *sonnō jōi* programme suddenly irrelevant, at least in part related to the criticism of the central government. A new political vision of Japan was soon expressed in the maxim *fukoku kyōhei* – enrich the country and strengthen the army – focusing all-out effort to catch up with the Western powers.[38]

1.3. The Japanese legal system until the Meiji-era codification

The most important feature of the Japanese legal system at the beginning of the Meiji era was a strongly outlined particularism deriving from the historical and political background. Over the centuries, it comprised several hundred separate *kanshū hōsei* – customary law systems. They were in force in clan domains, the formal capital of the country in Kyoto, and the territory governed directly by the shogun. In addition to broadly respected *dōtoku* – morality – and traditions resulting mainly from Buddhist and Shinto rules, Japanese customary law was strongly influenced by *judō* – Confucian ethics – which promoted social obedience, public safety and stable state income.[39]

The dominance of customary law in the Japanese legal system did not preclude the existence of statutory acts promulgated by the central government, binding throughout the state territory.[40] Unambiguous identification of the first Japanese statutory act (and therefore the code) is impossible due to a lack of sources. The Japanese Chronicles, dating back to 720, was the only source indicating that during Empress Suiko's reign, the so-called Seventeen Articles Constitution (*Jūshichi-jō Kempō*) came into force in 604. The Constitution, known only from a general description, was undoubtedly influenced by Buddhist philosophy. It outlined moral values to officials and subjects, which helped the efficient functioning of the state. Subsequently, the Japanese Chronicles quoted the 22-volume Ōmi Code (*Ōmi-ryō*) of 669, which was supposed to contain only the norms of administrative law compiled by Fujiwara no Kamatari following the order of Emperor Tenji.[41] Although many Japanese scholars challenged the authenticity of those two legal acts, some believe they deserve honourable mention in legal history monographs as an example of early codification works.[42]

38 Suzuki, 2006, pp. 525–526.

39 Kość, 2001, p. 75.

40 Depending on the period, the law was promulgated by the emperor or the shogunate.

41 Kitabatake, 2020, http://www.j-texts.com/chusei/rek/jinno.html, [access: 26.09.2020].

42 Ōtsu, 2011, p. 4.

The first universally recognized Japanese statutory law, the so-called *Asuka Kiyomihara-ryō* – Asuka Kiyomihara Code – was promulgated in 689. Like the Ōmi Code, it comprised 22 volumes and governed the relations between state officials and ministers to the emperor, retaining a purely administrative character.[43] Since *Asuka Kiyomihara-ryō* provisions were gradually published over nearly two decades, Japanese legal historians refuse to call it a code of law.[44]

The first Japanese code of law confirmed by historical sources was *Taihō Ritsuryō* – the Taihō Code – promulgated in 701 and entered into force a year later. It was a set of rules implemented into the legal system from the translated Chinese codes of the Tang dynasty.[45] The Taihō Code consisted of 11 volumes of *ryō* – administrative law – and six volumes of *ritsu* – criminal law. All volumes were adapted to Japan's local customs and social conditions.[46] The administrative and criminal parts also contained numerous provisions of private law. However, their enforcement by state authorities remains unknown.[47] The Taihō Code was supplemented by *Yōrō Ritsuryō* – the Yōrō Code – promulgated in 717. It took more than four decades to come into force and eventually consisted of ten administrative and ten criminal law volumes.[48]

Even though the Japanese ruling elites highly appreciated the achievements of Chinese legislators and the implemented codes were carefully studied and commented on, *ritsuryōsei* – the ritsu-ryō system – did not have a long career in Japan. Due to vast social and cultural differences, direct reception of Chinese law proved impossible. At the end of the eighth century, many provisions of the Tang were seen as obsolete. Some criminal law norms were never enforced, and over time multiple administrative law norms became good practices for Japanese officials.[49] Although none of the promulgated codes was derogated from in the following centuries, their writing in official Chinese characters made practical application difficult, leading to a natural withdrawal from their use.[50]

In the following centuries, the ritsu-ryō system was gradually replaced by customary law and the laws published by the imperial court, reflecting moral imperatives.[51] The famous samurai code, better known as *bushido*, also mainly comprised the customary law. To protect the central government's interest and

43 Yeremin, 2010, pp. 65–67; Farris, 1998, p. 104.
44 Ōtsu, 2011, p. 4.
45 Chen, 1966, p. 9.
46 Kość, 2001, p. 61.
47 Hozumi, 1933, p. 11.
48 Takayanagi, Rizō, 1995, p. 976.
49 Yeremin, 2010, pp. 72–73; Leszczyński, 1995, p. 88.
50 Sogabe, 1995, pp. 11–20.
51 Sakamoto, 2004, pp. 122–124.

maintain the feudal system of dependencies, some of its rules were written down as *Goseibai Shikimoku* – the Jōei Code – promulgated in 1232. The code comprised 51 articles and applied only to the samurai class, yet it was the first attempt to codify customary feudal law.[52] As A. Kość emphasized, the Jōei Code was distant from present-day positive law and based on the *jōri* principle, which could be compared to equity in the common law system.[53] Additionally, according to T. Nagamata, the Jōei Code significantly influenced the development of Japanese law, as it strengthened the role of customary law and precedent.[54]

In 1615, the Tokugawa shogunate promulgated *Buke Shohatto* – the Samurai Public Law – and *Kuge Shohatto* – the Imperial Court Law. They both soon became the cornerstone of the Edo shogunate's two most influential social groups. *Buke Shohatto* consisted of 13 articles which indicated the rules of conduct in private life and guidance regarding marriage and formal dress code for daimyos. It was primarily intended to prevent feudal lords from forming local alliances and maintaining a larger army. As an additional measure to secure the *sakoku* policy, it forbade the construction of seagoing ships and the propagation of Christianity. In the more private sphere, it also strictly regulated the rules for daimyos having an audience at the shogun's Edo court. *Buke Shohatto* was later amended and supplemented with additional provisions in 1629, 1635, 1663, 1683 and 1710. The final version of the code comprised 17 articles, which were confirmed as the binding law until 1859 by subsequent shoguns.

At first sight, *Kuge Shohatto* was much less wordy than *Buke Shohatto*. In reality, it became the foundation of Japan's political system in 1615–1868.[55] The code limited the personal freedom of the emperor and the court aristocracy and forbade them from leaving the capital city of Kyoto. Even residential life in the city was limited to the Imperial Palace, its utility buildings and the routes connecting them. *Kuge Shohatto* contained, among others, the rules for nominating the most critical positions at the court, the selection of appropriate clothes and the policy of promotions. Court officials were subjected to the restrictive military control justifying routine surveillance from Edo. The distinctive set of rules also bound the emperor himself. According to Article 1, his most important duty was to study science and cultivate traditional arts, poetry and calligraphy.[56]

52 Ishii, 1972, p. 40.

53 Kość, 2001, p. 69.

54 Nagamata, 2017, pp. 130–132.

55 The full name of the legislation in Japanese is *Kinchū Narabi ni Kuge Shohatto*. Shin Nihonshi shiryōshū, 1999, pp. 183–184.

56 Pałasz-Rutkowska, 2012, p. 35.

The last code preceding the period of reform of Japanese law in the second half of the 19th century was *Kujikata Osadamegaki* – the Conduct in Official Matters Code. Promulgated by shogun Yoshimune Tokugawa in 1742, the code consisted of two parts: the provisions of criminal and administrative law, and criminal and civil procedure principles based on judicial decisions.[57] The rules on civil procedure principles, however, were not entirely private law in nature, as they were only guidelines for the courts in criminal matters.[58]

During the transition from the Tokugawa shogunate to the Meiji government, customary law based on Shinto and Buddhist ethics or Chinese codes implemented by the administration offices centuries ago still dominated the Japanese legal system. National and local customary law was supplemented by statutory law, which focused on ensuring the stable functioning of the country and maintaining public order. In addition to restrictive rules concerning contacts with neighbouring countries, the purpose of introducing the statutory law was to guarantee the daimyos' obedience to the shogun, excluding the emperor from the decision-making process and establishing a basic framework for the courts and local offices strictly subordinated to the central authority in Edo. The law enacted at that time was understood primarily as the norms of administrative and criminal law, considered crucial to implementing the Confucian idea of a harmonious society. Albeit in the 17th century, Japanese statutory law gradually began to distinguish the norms of private law (substantive and procedural, emphasizing procedural); economic and family relations between people were still based on customary law.[59]

When analysing the development of Japanese law from the earliest times to the Meiji era, it should be stated that four factors, listed in chronological order, had the most significant impact on its shape: (1) Chinese administrative and criminal law, (2) legislation of central government on matters related to the court and samurai class, (3) limited influence of judicial decisions, (4) and the gradual increase in the importance of local customary law in matters not covered by regulation and court decisions. Compared to the European model, the Japanese maintained historical continuity over the centuries, despite numerous changes in the central government and political system. The phenomenon of continuity was possible for three reasons: (1) there were no significant conflicts with neighbouring countries nor permanent

[57] Hōseishi Gakkai Hen, 1961, pp. 11–141.

[58] Takanagi, 1942, pp. 5–8.

[59] Despite the lack of any Japanese civil code, various types of private law contracts and a few norms resulting from them were widely known during the feudal era. In the literature of the Tokugawa shogunate period, in addition to the norms regarding the conclusion of marriage, divorce and adoption, Japanese legal historians found detailed characteristics of contracts of sale, pawnbroker purchase, lease, renting, exchange, storage of rice, or loans granted by financial institutions. Asako, Itō, Ueda, Jimbo, 2010, pp. 191–209; Nakada, 1923, pp. 4–35.

changes in borders (so-called geopolitical stability); (2) the country avoided large-scale migration during the medieval age and there was a relatively early formation of a cohesive Japanese nation (so-called homogeneity of society); and (3) there was a lack of significant internal social unrest related to ideological and religious issues. The above-mentioned aspects primarily result from Japan's insular geography. Yet, the historical and legal continuity was also strongly influenced by the specific mentality of the Japanese people, which W.N. Yeremin described as "a passion for constant revision with respect for the old".[60]

1.4. The Importance of law codification for the birth of contemporary nations

European legal scholars defined codification as gathering legal provisions from a specific branch of law into a single, structured, written legal document based on which legal norms can be deducted. The term codification derives directly from the Latin word *codex*, which could mean book, list or action.[61] L. Górnicki also noted that *codex* was initially understood in ancient Rome as a set of two or more joint wooden tablets used to write down a particular text. The wooden tablets were later replaced by parchment sheets sewn together to form a *codex*, a book more convenient to use than a rolled papyrus biblion.[62] Referencing the code of law as legal work, S. Grzybowski explained that "acts created through codification are the most comprehensive and highest formal expression of the rule of statutory law",[63] giving them a unique role in the present-day state governed by the rule of law.

It is generally believed that the oldest code of law known in human history was the Code of Ur-Nammu, written on tablets in the Sumerian language c. 2100–2050 BCE.[64] However, the codification of law and the term *codification* itself are relatively new in legal history.[65] The term *code*, known since the Middle Ages, was widely used without reference to legal matters until the beginning of the 19th century.[66] The codification postulates came to the attention of legislators in the second half of the 18th century, following the development of Enlightenment rationalism and the natural law doctrine.[67] The most famous advocate of the law codification of

[60] Yeremin, 2010, pp. 21–22.

[61] Sójka-Zielińska, 2009, p. 31.

[62] Górnicki, 2012, p. 79.

[63] Grzybowski, 1981, p. 166.

[64] The Code of Ur-Nammu, despite its name and significance, was not a code of law in the modern sense.

[65] Sawczuk, Konarski, 2011, pp. 133–146.

[66] Górnicki, 2012, p. 80.

[67] Radwański, 2009, pp. 131–142.

that period was Jeremy Bentham, an English jurist, philosopher and economist known for his critical attitude towards the natural law doctrine.[68] As a precursor of legal positivism, in his monumental work *General View of a Complete Code of Laws*, he outlined the requirements for a set of laws to be called a code of law. According to Bentham, the code of law should be stable, complete, without gaps, yet concise. Norms constituting a code of law should be general enough for state authorities to apply them to the specific issue properly. From the systematics point of view, it should be divided into a general part, containing a binding glossary of legal terms, and a second part comprising abstract norms. Additionally, it had to be established under proper legislative technique, by which Bentham understood a legal act written in a language understandable to ordinary people, built of short sentences devoid of unnecessary phrases and ambiguous words. To increase the comprehension of the code as a legal text, he suggested the introduction of a harmonious arrangement and distinguishing individual areas of law, branches of law, and the separation of substantive law from procedural law.[69]

Although J. Bentham's beliefs concerning codification did not affect the British and American common law systems he criticized,[70] they were applied to a greater or lesser extent in continental Europe. By his death in 1832, the old continent experienced eight main codifications from various branches of law.[71] As for private law, the *Code Civil des Français* of 1804, known as the Napoleonic Code, significantly influenced future law codification. In the following decades, it became a model for subsequent codes of law until the German *Bürgerliches Gesetzbuch* was promulgated in 1896.[72]

By the overthrow of the Tokugawa shogunate and the Meiji Revolution, European jurisprudence also witnessed a dispute between the supporters of codification and representatives of the Historical School of Jurisprudence, which took place in Germany. Opposing the Enlightenment ideas and legal positivism, especially the Napoleonic Code introduced in Germany during the Napoleonic Wars, supporters of natural law doctrine emphasized that the codification of law in the shape proposed

[68] Harrison, 1995, pp. 85–88.

[69] Bowring, 1843, pp. 155–210.

[70] In 1811, Bentham wrote a letter to the President of the United States, James Madison, in which he unsuccessfully offered to draft a code of law that would free Americans from "the yoke of which in the wordless, as well as boundless, and shapeless shape of common, alias Unwritten law, remains still about your necks" (Morriss, 1999, pp. 355–370).

[71] By eight codes of law, I mean: (1) the *Codex Maximilianeus Bavaricus Civilis* of 1756, (2) the *Theresiana* of 1766, (3) the Joseph's Civil Code (*Allgemeines Bürgerliches Gesetzbuch*) of 1786, (4) the Prussian Landrecht of 1794, (5) the Civil Code for Western Galicia of 1797, (6) the Napoleonic Code of 1804, (7) the French Penal Code of 1810, and (8) the Austrian Civil Code of 1811.

[72] Górnicki, 2012, p. 87. The Napoleonic Code and the *Bürgerliches Gesetzbuch* were referred to as model codes of law.

by the positivists overlooked the social conditions and national spirit. According to representatives of the Historical School of Jurisprudence, authoritarian and mechanical legislation was supposed to stop the law development and make it a foreign element in the nation. Therefore, they argued that codification should not be based on the arbitrary creation of legal norms but on understanding the national spirit and strengthening the law shaped during the historical process. Additionally, they generally understood the law as a historical phenomenon having its source in "the will of the people", not the legislator's will, as the positivists believed.[73]

Although the German Historical School of Jurisprudence ultimately lost the dispute regarding codification, it should be noted that the arguments presented by its representatives were considered in the codification process of Japanese law. Despite the Japanese elites' decision to adopt the positive law system by codifying all areas and branches of law from scratch, ignoring common law and Japanese customary law was criticized even by supporters of radical reforms. Notably, some postulates of the German Historical School of Jurisprudence have not lost their relevance in the 20th and 21st centuries. Setting the codes in the historical and social context is described by the jurisprudence as "the substantive autonomy of the code", explained in more detail by S. Grzybowski: "each code of law corresponds, to a greater or lesser extent, to specific individual conditions prevailing in the society in which it is applied. These conditions include social and economic relations, the level of social, economic, technical and cultural development, and the outcomes of historical events, which all together create a complex picture of the society, leading to the so-called substantive autonomy of the code."[74]

It is worth noting that Japanese jurists also recognize the significant influence of the German Historical School of Jurisprudence on the codification process of the Meiji era. According to Y. Suzuki, this influence is reflected in the career of the German lawyer and economist Hermann Roesler, a supporter of the Historical School of Jurisprudence, who in 1878 was invited by the Meiji government as an expert on international law at the Ministry of Foreign Affairs. In 1884, Roesler was promoted to the cabinet's legal adviser. He was soon asked by the Japanese Prime Minister, Hirobumi Itō, to assist Kowashi Inoue in drafting numerous bills, including a new constitution, which went down in history as the Meiji Constitution of 1889. Additionally, Roesler also participated in drafting the Commercial Code, which finally came into force in 1899.[75]

Regardless of European legal scholars' influence on legislative policy in other countries, the codification of civil law in Japan was an independent and unique

[73] Savigny, 1964, pp. 50–59.

[74] Grzybowski, 1981, p. 165.

[75] Suzuki, Siemes, 1941, pp. 53–87.

process lasting more than three decades. N. Hozumi, one of the three drafters of the Meiji Civil Code, claimed that the codification of private law helped the Japanese legal system ultimately transition from outdated Chinese law to the modern Roman law model, thus joining the group of developed countries.[76]

1.5. Internal and external motives for codifying Japanese civil law

The motives for codifying Japanese civil law should be understood as all reasons that influenced the Meiji elites to codify private law based on the civil (continental) law system.[77] They were mainly identical to the general motives for the codification of law in Japan at that time, with the difference that private law was primarily intended to shape the relationship between citizens, as opposed to public law, which was to determine the relationship between the citizens and the state.

Japanese legal history scholars distinguish the internal motives (*naiteki yōin*) and external motives (*gaiteki yōin*) for codifying Japanese civil law. Internal causes were related to the state's domestic policy and the government's commitment to exert specific power in the public sphere to carry out social and economic reforms in the longer term. By contrast, the external motives were linked to the international position of the Empire of Japan after the *kaikoku* – opening of the country to contact with the world – also envisaging that the strategy would influence diplomatic relations, especially with Western powers. Since Japanese scholars did not provide a hierarchical and closed catalogue of motives for codifying civil law, *The Struggle to Modernize the Nation* presents only the most important ones, keeping the traditional division into internal and external motives.

1.5.1. Internal motives

1) Breaking with the existing legal tradition and establishing a new legal system

Undoubtedly, the essential internal motive for the codification of Japanese law was included in *Gokajō no Goseimon* (formerly known as *Goseimon*), the so-called Charter Oath announced by Emperor Meiji on 6 April 1868. The five-section

[76] Hozumi, 1912, p. 19.

[77] In Japanese legal history, the terms *gen'in*, *yōin* and *dōki* are used interchangeably, which should be properly translated as "cause", "primary factor" and "motive". Being aware of those discrepancies, I adopted the word "motive" as that sounds the most natural in English yet differs from the terminology adopted by the distinguished Japanese legal history scholar, R. Ishii, in his monumental monograph on the codification of Japanese civil law (see Ishii, 1979, p. 3).

declaration was made at the Imperial Palace in Kyoto as part of a solemn ceremony of enthronement and power transfer to the emperor, then publicly announced throughout Japan. Kimimasa Yuri of the Fukui domain prepared the draft in January 1868. It was then revised by Takachiki Fukuoka of the Tosa domain and Takayoshi Kido of the Chōshū domain in March.[78] Finally, through Michitomi Higashikuze of the imperial court, the draft was submitted to the Vice President of *Gijō* – the Supreme Council[79] – Tomomi Iwakura, who presented it to the emperor to receive his sanction, formally ending the legislation process.

In the Charter Oath, Emperor Meiji outlined a political programme concerning the restoration of imperial power. Point four presented his attitude towards the existing Tokugawa shogunate's legal system and political thought. The emperor called for a break from the "bad habits of the past" and wanted to establish "justice based on the laws of nature".[80] Japanese historiography presented several interpretations of the exact meaning of "evil customs of the past" and "justice based on the laws of nature", yet legal scholars agree that he criticized the existing legal system based on the Tokugawa family's orders, supplemented by the ancient Chinese laws implemented centuries ago.[81] The negative axiological assessment of the existing law foreshadowed establishing a legal system based on statutory law, which would be drafted and enacted in new political and social conditions.[82] The reform aimed to revise public and private law, which had not been significantly revised since the early Middle Ages and was mainly based on customary law. The plan to introduce the radical changes was designed to break up ties with the classical Chinese legal model, the backbone of Japanese criminal and administrative law that had been in place for several ages.

2) Support for political and social reforms (abolition of feudalism)

Despite the clearly outlined vision to modernize Japan, Emperor Meiji and the clans supporting him faced substantial difficulties carrying out the new programme. After

[78] Inoue, 2006b, pp. 101–103; Tanaka, 2007, p. 68.

[79] The Supreme Council was established on 3 January 1868 and was the first Meiji government entity. It initially consisted of ten members chosen from the imperial family, court nobility and daimyos, and was later expanded to include four additional members. The Council was dissolved on 15 August 1869 with the establishment of *Dajōkan* – the Grand Council of State.

[80] Dajōkan Nikki, 1876, p. 39.

[81] The pre-war historian T. Osatake defined the "bad habits of the past" as a policy of isolation and the expulsion of foreigners. In contrast, post-war historians S. Sasaki, M. Matsuo and M. Inada, based on research on the private correspondence of influential Meiji-era politicians and the diaries of Emperor Meiji, argue that the correct interpretation should also include the intention to abolish feudalism and the legal particularism.

[82] Kawaguchi, 2014, p. 83; Takayanagi, 1931, pp. 4–5.

centuries of feudal fragmentation, the country had to be unified and its political system thoroughly reformed. Inherited from the Tokugawa shogunate, *bakuhan taisei* – the bakuhan/domain system – was characterized by a strongly decentralized model of exercising power. More than 260 years after its introduction, it was outdated compared to countries that had undergone the Industrial Revolution. Japanese and Western historians described the Empire of Japan at the beginning of the Meiji era as *hōkenshugi no kuni* – a feudal country – considering both the political and socio-economic aspects. In the mid-19th century, Japan was one of the last feudal states in the world, having the well-preserved mechanisms of the feudal society. The feudal administration and economy, founded on the principles of ancient relations of production, was developed to a perfection that could no longer function effectively in a world dominated by the capitalist economy.[83] For this reason, the formal and actual abolition of all forms of feudalism was one of the most important goals of the codification of the Japanese legal system, particularly private law.[84]

The emergence of a new centre of power focused around Emperor Meiji required abolishing 270 separate clan law systems and introducing a national one, effective in all domains despite remarkable regional differences.[85] The ultimate goal of this policy was apparent unification of the country and strengthening of the emperor's position, who hitherto had been a passive observer of the political scene. The Meiji reformers were also aware that it was impossible to create the foundations of a modern nation without establishing a unified legal system.[86] The need to promote modern Japanese nationhood was explicitly mentioned in sections two and three of the Charter Oath. They called for the admission of all classes to govern the state and the abolition of the traditional division into social classes and traditional roles assigned to them.[87] This programme met with some opposition from radical traditionalists. Still, most clans accepted the erosion of the Tokugawa shogunate and voluntarily transferred their legislative and jurisdictional powers to the central government.[88]

[83] Svetlov, 1934, p. 6.

[84] The beginning of Japanese feudalism dates to the Kamakura era (1185–1333), and then in the following 400 years, it evolved into *senseiteki na keisatsu kokka* – the autocratic police state. Some historians classify Japanese feudalism as an Asian form of feudalism (bureaucratic feudalism), significantly different from the European model of feudalism. Amino, 1988, p. 72.

[85] Ishii, 1979, p. 3.

[86] Tomii, 1922, pp. 63–64. The direct effect of the codification of law in Japan was also its unification. For more on the differences between unification and codification, see Górnicki, 2012, p. 107.

[87] Dajōkan Nikki, 1876, p. 39.

[88] Hozumi, 1912, pp. 3–4; Takatani, Koishikawa, 2018, p. 194. The formal abolition of domains as local centres of power and the establishment of regular administrative units of the state (prefectures and cities with special rights) was not executed until 29 August 1871. Meiji Shōchokushū, 1893, p. 18.

The general positive attitude of the Meiji-era reformers to the idea of introducing the codes was best expressed by S. Etō, one of the activists supporting political and social change, who argued that the unification of national law was of great importance. According to him, the codification addressed the slogan "enrich the country, strengthen the army". He was also to be convinced that the social position of a citizen in the modern state should be correctly regulated by codified civil law.[89]

3) Building a capitalist state governed by the rule of law

Witnessing the end of 250 years of the strict policy of isolation, Japanese elites suddenly faced the critical issue of preserving the political and economic independence of the country in a world dominated by Western colonial powers. The overthrow of the Tokugawa shogunate, the Meiji Restoration, and re-joining the international market allowed Japan to carry out fundamental economic reform. An early debate on the scope of changes led to the conclusion that the only way to surmount the feudal backwardness of Japan was by establishing the modern capitalist state.[90]

Although capital protection and property rights were known in the Edo era, the Japanese domestic market and legal system were not adapted to 19th-century international trade and the large-scale circulation of money. Introducing the latest technological achievements of the Industrial Revolution to Japan, namely the iron railway and ships, followed by the construction of shipyards, factories and railway network, required substantial financial investment. The development of Japanese industry was also impossible without establishing a modern banking system and private and state commercial companies.

A well-functioning free market economy, based on the free flow of capital and respect for private property, required the codification of private law as a supervisory tool.[91] The shift into the capitalist state was also not possible without abolishing the key feature of feudalism: serfdom.[92] As shown by N. Hozumi, the Japanese industrial and economic revolution resulted in a social change that affected virtually every sphere of human life. Therefore, the reform could not omit the codification of private law, which had to replace the hitherto unwritten and fragmented branch of law.[93]

[89] Ishii, 1979, pp. 6–7.

[90] Kość, 2001, p. 77.

[91] Toshitani, 2013, p. 23.

[92] Fukushima, 1988, p. 21.

[93] Hozumi, 1912, pp. 4–5.

1.5.2. External motives

1) Revision of unequal treaties

The most crucial external motive for codifying Japanese law, including private law, was the political programme to revise *fubyōdō jōyaku* – unequal treaties. Japanese historiography views *Ansei Jōyaku* – the Ansei Treaties – as unequal, signed under the threat of force by the Tokugawa shogunate in 1858 with five *bum'meikoku* (civilized countries): the United States, the United Kingdom, France, the Netherlands and Russia.[94] Since ratification, the Ansei Treaties regulated diplomatic and trade relations with Western powers and became a pretext for multiple interventions in Japan's domestic affairs. In addition to guaranteeing foreigners the right to reside and trade in the designated ports of Edo, Kobe, Nagasaki, Niigata and Yokohama, all five Western nations were granted: unilateral most-favoured-nation provision; the system of extraterritoriality with consular courts independent of Japanese law; and fixed, low import/export duties subjected to international control that impinged on Japanese sovereignty.[95]

Extraterritoriality, understood as excluding foreign residents from the jurisdiction of Japanese courts and placing them under consular courts, was a characteristic element of 19th-century relations between Western powers and colonized countries.[96] Once Japan opened its borders to the world, it witnessed unavoidable law violations by foreigners. The inability to prosecute them, including those who committed unquestionable crimes, negatively impacted the views of Japanese society on newcomers and the authority of the Edo/Meiji government.[97] Even foreigners sometimes criticized the extensive application of the law of extraterritoriality, calling it a preposterous privilege that damaged diplomatic relations between countries. Still, the particular interests of colonial powers became a rationale to support the existing inequalities.[98]

From an economic point of view, unequal treaties set low import/export duties for foreign companies, giving them an advantage over competing domestic businesses. Too low fiscal burdens of foreign entities also significantly decreased revenue for the state treasury. When the Edo government ratified the Ansei Treaties, it was not fully aware of the importance of tariffs for the proper functioning

[94] Asako, Itō, Ueda, Jimbo, 2010, p. 252.

[95] Kimura, 1891, pp. 1–18.

[96] Kashimi, 2014, pp. 106–139.

[97] Nakamura, 1956, pp. 2–3.

[98] Suzuki, 2018.

of the economy and finances of the state, but soon it realized its own mistake.[99] Although the Tokugawa shogunate had managed to increase the tariffs to 16% by 1864 through numerous treaty loopholes,[100] the Western powers took advantage of domestic unrest in Japan to introduce a fixed 5% tariff in 1866. Therefore, in the early years of the Meiji era, revenue from duties accounted for only 4% of the total income of the treasury. In contrast, the share of customs duties in the revenue of the British Treasury at that time was more than six times higher.[101]

Once they assumed power over the country in 1868, the Meiji elites unequivocally determined that revising unequal treaties was one of the most critical points of their new political programme.[102] During official meetings with foreign diplomats, the Japanese repeatedly presented demands to reconsider the existing treaties, but each time they received a negative answer. As the reason for maintaining the old order, Western powers indicated the need for an institutionalized legal system and a judiciary that could impartially settle potential disputes between Japanese citizens and foreigners based on the existing law. Despite establishing a central government dedicated to modernizing the country, Europeans and Americans referred to incidents from the end of the Tokugawa shogunate, which led to military intervention and the forceful restoration of order under international treaties. The Japanese soon realized that the codification of public and private law, surpassing even European countries to some extent, was the quickest and most effective way to revise the Ansei Treaties.[103]

2) Strengthening the position of the country in the international arena

Although the Meiji elites initially did not see a close relationship between having a codified legal system and the position of the country in the international arena, this view rapidly changed in the early 1870s when they sent an expedition to the United States and Europe to explore the civilizational differences between Japan and world powers. The Japanese noticed that some continental European countries still struggled with the codification or did not have a civil code. One of T. Iwakura's conclusions was the inevitability of adopting a constitution and codifying the entire legal system in Japan.[104] His view was based on observing the unification movements and trends among European legislators. Regardless of the degree of development of

[99] Ishii, 2010, pp. 275–277.
[100] Inoue, 2006a, p. 132.
[101] Okamoto, 2010, p. 285.
[102] Arano, 2009, pp. 158–172.
[103] Hoshino, 1943, p. 7.
[104] Iwamura, 1996, pp. 18–19.

private law in individual countries, the French Civil Code, the Austrian Civil Code, and the Italian Civil Code were presented as innovative works of centralized governments, which successfully led their nations through the Industrial Revolution. T. Iwakura's thorough analysis helped the Meiji government to realize that codified private law would strengthen its position in domestic politics. Equally important, it would promote Japan internationally, especially among other Asian countries, by outpacing developed states like Germany, Spain and Switzerland, which still did not have national civil codes.

CHAPTER TWO

JAPANESE ENDEAVOURS TO CODIFY CIVIL LAW, 1868–1889

Abstract

This chapter describes all attempts of the Meiji government to draft the Civil Code in 1868–1889. It presents the various periods covering the first failed translation projects of the Ministry of Justice, the drafting of a Civil Code imitating the French Civil Code, and finally the establishment of the drafting team led by G. Boissonade, who submitted the Civil Code for the legislative procedure.

Keywords: Japanese Civil Code, Codification in Japan, Japanese and French law, Meiji Japan

"The inheritance of property by the eldest son in Japanese [succession] law cannot be revised."

—S. Etō's opinion on the law of primogeniture

The years from 1868 to 1889 in Japanese legal history saw seven separate initiatives to draft the first national Civil Code. These attempts resulted from the decision of the Meiji government to codify the Japanese legal system, including private law. Japanese legal historians distinguished six failed projects and the seventh, the successful, project to draft the Civil Code. The first codification endeavours from 1868 to 1879 did not bring the expected outcome and led to a complete revision of the legislative policy of the Ministry of Justice. From 1879 to 1889, a new draft of the Civil Code was developed and eventually submitted for legislative procedure. After acquiring all required approvals, the Civil Code was published by the cabinet in two separate parts in April and October 1890, despite existing criticism in the conservative group of jurisprudence not engaged in the drafting process. Notwithstanding the subsequent Controversy and the Imperial Diet's decision to postpone its entry into force in June 1892, it became the first Civil Code in the history of Japanese private law.

2.1. The first unsuccessful attempts to draft the Civil Code (1868–1879)

2.1.1. Drafting the Civil Code under Shimpei Etō's leadership (1869–1873)

The most crucial decision the Meiji government made in 1868 concerned choosing an adequate legal system, which would become a role model for the Japanese jurists responsible for drafting the new codes. As emphasized by W.N. Yeremin, the Japanese political elites openly acknowledged the legal achievements of other countries and intended to use their experiences to establish the entirely new legal system from scratch. The adoption process, however, was not a mindless borrowing of the entire branches of law. The Meiji government made a strict selection from existing legal systems, endorsing options suitable for the Empire of Japan and its political goals. Additionally, every element of the foreign culture that did not contradict domestic culture was designed to be transferred to Japan to such an extent that the initial implementation would enable integration with the existing set of standards known as "Japanese spirit".[1]

Despite genuine admiration for the industrial and economic power of the British Empire and the United States, the Meiji government never considered adopting the common law systems from these countries. Apart from the lack of sufficiently developed scholarship on Japanese judicial decisions and legal education among the elites, a system upholding domestic customary law would not support the unification of the country and the strengthening of the central government authority.

The Japanese investigation of continental law systems started in 1862 when the Tokugawa shogunate sent barons Mamichi Tsuda and Amane Nishi to the Netherlands to study politics, economics and law.[2] During the *rangaku* (Western sciences) course, they paid particular attention to the French system of statutory law, which included five Napoleonic codes, tested in practice and acknowledged as outstanding works by global jurisprudence. Japanese jurists soon recognized the excessive influence of French law on the shape of other European codes,[3] particularly in the field of criminal and civil law.[4] Notably, France had a reputation as a highly developed country in Japan that had quickly and successfully transformed from a feudal to a capitalist state.[5] The Meiji government believed adopting French law would help their country to follow a similar path.[6] Although the core of French law

1 Yeremin, 2010, pp. 22–23.

2 Itō, 1966, p. 184.

3 Ushiomi, Toshitani, 1975, p. 18.

4 Makino, 1949, p. 57.

5 Tōyama, 1951, p. 60.

6 Makino, 1949, p. 16.

incorporated the natural law doctrine, the Japanese elites saw it as an opportunity to overcome the "bad habits of the past" and promote modern Japanese nationhood in accordance with the declarations of the Charter Oath. T. Hoshino also stressed that cordial diplomatic relations between the two countries, which had already been established in the final years of the Tokugawa shogunate, were a significant factor in the positive views on the reception of French law. Despite internal friction between supporters of the shogun and Emperor Meiji, Napoleon III pursued a friendly foreign policy towards Japan,[7] successfully promoting France in the Japanese political establishment by respecting the Japanese language and culture.[8]

Regardless of the Japanese notions about France, the decision to adopt the French legal system was profoundly influenced by the personal experience of the shogunate delegation, which took part in *Exposition Universelle* – the International Exposition of 1867. One of the emissaries, Jōn Kurimoto, acted as a plaintiff in a claim of the Japanese government against the French government regarding a US$6 million loan agreement that the Edo government believed had been effectively concluded. J. Kurimoto was undoubtedly the first Japanese citizen to act as a litigant in French civil proceedings. Having a chance to experience the civil procedure, he expressed an extremely positive opinion on French civil law and the judiciary in his official report from the visit to Paris, published in 1868.[9] J. Kurimoto compared five French codes to two excellent Confucian books and recommended that they be translated into Japanese.[10]

The Meiji government was impressed with J. Kurimoto's testimony and in early 1869 decided to translate all five codes into Japanese.[11] At that time, the administration branch office responsible for preparing a new Japanese civil code was the Bureau of Procedural Proceedings at the Grand Council of State, led by Shimpei Etō.[12] On 9 July 1871, the Bureau was transformed into *Shihōshō* – the Ministry of Justice – which took over the task to codify the Japanese legal system. Since that time, the Minister of Justice has had an undue influence on decisions concerning codification policy and solving issues related to specific legal provisions.[13]

One of S. Etō's first decisions as the head of the Bureau of Procedural Proceedings was entrusting the translation of the French Civil Code to 23-year-old Rinshō Mitsukuri.[14] Despite the young age of the assistant, this choice was not accidental. R.

7 Iwata, 1928, p. 176; Ushiomi, Toshitani, 1975, p. 42.

8 Nabatsu, 2018, p. 43.

9 French legal history scholars present J. Kurimoto as a Francophile. Jaluzot, 2015, p. 123.

10 Kurimoto, 1868, p. 6.

11 Takayanagi, 1976, pp. 168–169.

12 Hoshino, 1943, p. 15.

13 Since the establishment of the Ministry of Justice, the post of Minister of Justice had been vacant, and S. Etō assumed the post on 31 May 1872.

14 Kumagai, 1955, p. 146.

Mitsukuri belonged to a distinctive family of scholars previously employed in the Tokugawa shogunate administration and already held a degree in Western sciences. He participated in the International Exhibition of 1867 as one of the members of the Japanese delegation. There is no doubt that R. Mitsukuri had a unique opportunity to take a closer look at France and its legal system, which was supposed to become a role model for Japan.[15] Worth noting, he also had practical experience translating legal texts as Tanetomi Soejima, Emperor Meiji's adviser, told him in August 1869 to translate the French Penal Code.[16] Thanks to R. Mitsukuri's excellent French language skills, he completed the work in January 1870, and the Japanese edition of the French Penal Code was published the following month.[17]

Notwithstanding R. Mitsukuri's exceptional talent and experience, he faced more severe challenges while translating the French Civil Code. Unexpectedly to him and other Japanese jurists, enormous difficulties arose with legal terminology. Many French private law concepts did not have their equivalents in the Japanese legal system, and thus he had to invent them in his native language intuitively. Still, he was uncertain whether the new words correctly reflected the meaning in the original code. For example, such terms as *kenri* (right, entitlement), *gimu* (obligation), *gimu sōsai* (set-off), *dōsan* (movable property) and *fudōsan* (immovable property), which were fundamental to private law, did not exist in the Japanese language and had to be conceived.[18] R. Mitsukuri honestly admitted the linguistic and interpretative barriers he encountered while preparing the Japanese edition of the French Civil Code in his keynote address during the inauguration of the academic year at the Law Department of the Meiji Law School in September 1887:

> I had tremendous problems with the translation, [...] in 1870, when a man called Shimpei Etō held a head position in the Bureau of Procedural Proceedings at the Grand Council of State, I translated two or three pages [of the French Civil Code] and brought them to a meeting of the Bureau to present the results. It was a coincidence, but that's how I became the founder of the Civil Law Council of Japan. At that time, I translated the original French *droits civils* as *minken* – civil rights – but soon I provoked a dispute as to whether the *min* – citizens – could have any *ken* – right/power/authority – and what it meant in practice. I did my best to defend my interpretation but met with stubborn opposition. Fortunately, Chairman Etō explained the meaning of the term for me and thus cut off further debate.[19]

15 Ushiomi, Toshitani, 1975, pp. 3-5.

16 Ōtsuki, 1907, p. 100; Sakamoto, 2004, p. 178.

17 Mitsukuri, 1870.

18 Ōtsuki, 1907, p. 101.

19 Ōtsuki, 1907, pp. 102–103.

The discussion recalled by R. Mitsukuri was one of the reasons why S. Etō established *Mimpō Kaigi* – the Civil Law Council – on 18 September 1870, which consisted of 14 permanent members and seven advisers.[20] Its main task was to conduct an in-depth study of French law and use it as a basis to draft the Japanese Civil Code.[21]

The quoted discussion also revealed the lack of understanding of the new legal terminology among some Japanese jurists and their conservative views on citizens possessing any rights.[22] As for private law rights, the Civil Law Council members wanted to be sure they would not be confused with power or authority attributed only to the emperor.[23] Their confusion, however, was not a peculiar thing. R. Ishii tried to defend the discussion participants. He showed that even the Old Civil Code, which took almost 20 years to write, also contained significant terminology errors, as it did not clearly distinguish civil rights and private law rights. However, despite the project failing, the process of writing that did give jurists experience that could be used in the future.[24]

Regardless of linguistic and legal issues, some Japanese legal history researchers highlighted that S. Etō directly told R. Mitsukuri to translate the French Civil Code "as quickly as possible, without worrying about errors".[25] The ready code was to be implemented immediately by replacing the adjective "French" with "Japanese".[26] R. Mitsukuri, still struggling with many interpretation issues, completed the translation in early 1871. The result of his work, divided into 16 volumes, was released in May of the same year by Nankō University's small publishing company.[27]

Despite the original intention to apply the French Civil Code directly, the Civil Law Council faced more critical issues than only presenting a comprehensive

[20] For a full list of permanent members and advisers of the Civil Law Council, see Kobayakawa, 1944, pp. 212–213.

[21] Sakamoto, 2004, p. 202.

[22] The issue of misunderstanding completely new legal terms, which were *jukugo* (new words created by combining two basic kanji characters), is described in more detail in Hozumi, 1980, p. 213.

[23] The refusal to guarantee numerous civil rights in the new civil code (like France) resulted from the fear of possible disobedience of the people towards the emperor. Hirano, 1948, p. 181.

[24] Ishii, 1979, p. 23.

[25] "Goyaku mo mata samatagezu, tada sokuyakuseyo." – S. Etō's order was cited many years later by his biographer, H. Tekino, and then disseminated by N. Hozumi. Some Japanese researchers questioned its authenticity. Matono, 1914, p. 107; Hozumi, 1980, p. 212; Sakamoto, 2004, pp. 412–413.

[26] Takayanagi, 1976, p. 174.

[27] Mitsukuri, 1871. The official, one-volume translation of the French Civil Code was published by the Ministry of Education in 1874. The three-year delay resulted from R. Mitsukuri's appointment to draft a bill on the education system in Japan, which he received from the Ministry of Education in 1871. The translated Civil Code was one of five French codes published in Japan – the Penal Code, the Civil Code, the Commercial Code, the Code of Criminal Instruction and the Code of Civil Procedure. The translation series also included the French Constitution of 1852. Mitsukuri, 1874.

Japanese translation.[28] Yet, the Bureau of Procedural Proceedings published the first draft of the Civil Code in two parts in June 1871, named *Mimpō Ketsugi* – the Civil Law Resolution.[29] There is no evidence that the resolution was intended to be submitted to the legislative procedure as it was not a bill in the present-day meaning. The document probably summarized the current state of work on the Civil Code to initiate further debate on linguistic and legal issues. Still, the Civil Law Resolution was undoubtedly the first important step in drafting the new Civil Code. It made the enthusiasts of the direct adoption of the French Civil Code aware that a seemingly simple translation task was beyond the competence of the Bureau of Procedural Proceedings, soon replaced by the Ministry of Justice.

R. Mitsukuri, even having the support of the Civil Law Council, could not resolve translation issues concerning French legal terminology. In early 1872, the Ministry of Justice, finding the dead end in internal discussions, asked for help from foreign legal specialists who temporarily resided in Japan and were on government contracts. The Ministry of Justice soon chose George H. Bousquet, a French jurist, a graduate of the University of Paris,[30] who arrived in Japan in 1867 as one of the members of the first military mission of the French Empire.[31] In 1870, he became a legal adviser to the Meiji government and participated in translating legal texts into Japanese. In addition to the positive assessment of G. Bousquet's professional skills, the Ministry of Justice decided to employ him after a personal conversation with S. Etō. The Minister of Justice received the assurance that, despite the apparent differences between the two countries, it would be possible to introduce the French Civil Code based on *tenri jindō* – the laws of nature and humanity – and this task could be done without any additional obstacles.[32]

Parallel to the attempts to secure support for improving the French Civil Code translation, the newly established Meihōryō – the Law School at the Ministry of Justice[33] From 12 April to 13 July 1872, parallel to the attempts to secure support for

[28] Imamura, 1890, p. 2.

[29] Mimpō Ketsugi, Dai 1–2. The first part of the Civil Law Resolution was accidentally discovered by R. Ishii, who reprinted its content in 1944. Part two was discovered by N. Toshitani in 1959.

[30] Bousquet, 1877, p. 57.

[31] The idea of hiring foreign advisers was born in the final years of the Tokugawa shogunate. The first Western adviser to the Japanese government was a Dutchman, Guido Verbeck, who came to Japan in 1858 as a lecturer in English, political science, economics and science (in general) at one of the clan schools in Nagasaki. In 1869, after the Meiji Revolution, G. Verbeck moved to Tokyo, where he educated the future Japanese political elites, emphasizing the importance of an efficient legal system for the effective modernization of the state. Umetani, 2007, pp. 73–80.

[32] Hoshino, 1943, p. 20.

[33] The originator of Meihōryō, established on 17 September 1871, was Hideyo Kusuda. His goal was to create an official school of the Ministry of Justice to provide legal education to the future staff of the Japanese judiciary and public administration. Ishii, 1979, p. 188; Tezuka, 1967, pp. 57–100.

improving the French Civil Code translation, the newly established Meihōryō – the Law School at the Ministry of Justice – prepared a second draft of the civil code, based largely on the first edition of R. Mitsukuri's translation. The document entitled *Kōkoku Mimpō Kari Kisoku* – Civil Law Provisional Regulations of the Empire of Japan – was published in October of the same year. It consisted of 2,085 articles (actually 1,184 due to the omission of some numbers) divided into nine titles grouped into three books: Personal Law, Property Law and Contract Law.[34] Some Japanese legal scholars also argued that Meihōryō made the first attempt to present a complete draft of the Civil Code.[35]

There is no evidence of the extent of G. Bousquet's influence on the shape of the draft from October 1872.[36] Despite introducing many amendments to the first version, S. Etō was still not satisfied with the outcome. He expressed concern that the document had many internal discrepancies and unclear passages. The most significant issue, however, was the collision with the norms of *Kosekihō* – the Family Registration Law – adopted a year earlier.[37] In the new population registration system, which replaced the existing clan registers, the *seitai* – household – was indicated as the basic unit of society.[38] This provision derived from the Japanese legal tradition,[39] providing for the legal presumption of *kazoku=ko* – family=household[40] – and granting legal capacity only to *koshuken* – the head of the household. This principle contradicted the concept of the individual legal capacity characteristic of modern civil law.[41]

The draft from October 1872 became the subject of heated discussions, revealing divergent views of the Civil Code Council members on fundamental legal issues. Direct implementation of the French Civil Code proved to be impossible. In particular, the authors of the draft deliberately departed from the French model of intestate inheritance in favour of establishing a principle of the eldest son's exclusive succession, better known in the West as the law of primogeniture. Regardless of the intention of establishing an effective tool for capital accumulation, G. Bousquet

[34] *Kōkoku Mimpō Kari Kisoku*. For more on the systematics of the code and description of each title, see Sakamoto, 2004, p. 330.

[35] Kawashima, Toshitani, 1958, p. 7.

[36] Ishii, 1979, p. 195. The author argues that G. Bousquet's influence on the draft of the Civil Code is noticeable, but at the same time was not significant, because he formally became an adviser to the Ministry of Justice in February, and he joined the Civil Law Council in April.

[37] The Family Registration Law was introduced by *Mimbushō* – the Ministry of Population. The law was enacted on 5 April 1871. Kosekihō o Seitei Su; Kawaguchi, 2014, pp. 86–87, 90–91.

[38] Matsumoto, 1975, pp. 205–206.

[39] Akiyama, 1974, pp. 65–83.

[40] Takatani, Koishikawa, 2018, p. 268.

[41] Hozumi, 1912, p. 24.

perceived the succession law norms as a relic of Japanese feudalism. Despite S. Etō's desire to abolish patriarchal regulations in Japanese private law, he stubbornly supported the traditional law of primogeniture,[42] refusing to agree to G. Bousquet's arguments, yet their exchange of views was cordial.[43] The other members of the Civil Code Council were even more conservative and did not support family and succession law changes. They considered the proposed Western ideas too radical, and the drafting process stalled. S. Etō's initial goal was rapidly adopting a new civil code.[44] Despite transferring work on the project from Meihōryō to the Main Office of the Ministry of Justice in October, he could not compromise with his co-workers and resigned in January 1873.[45] The excessive haste in the civil code drafting was noticed by G. Bousquet, who pointed out the numerous dangers inherent in the premature adoption of a law unsuitable for and unfamiliar to Japanese society.[46]

The pressure that S. Etō exerted on the drafting of a new civil code largely resulted from the parallel work on the Penal Code. The codification of the sister branch of law did not encounter unexpected setbacks. Once R. Mitsukuri's translation was approved in January 1870, the Grand Council of State publicly introduced the first modern Penal Code named *Shinritsu Kōryō* – the New Law Outline – and began distributing copies throughout the country at the end of December.[47] Although the Ministry of Justice soon initiated work on a revised version of the Penal Code, the publication of *Shinritsu Kōryō* was undoubtedly the first crucial step towards codifying criminal law in Japan.[48]

2.1.2. Drafting the Civil Code under T. Ōki's leadership (1873–1879)

S. Etō's resignation initially did not influence the civil code drafting, which the Ministry of Justice continued with the support of G. Bousquet. In the meantime, the Meiji government introduced *Jinshin Koseki* – the new Family Registration Law – breaking with the previous principle of granting legal capacity only to the head

[42] Kawashima, Toshitani, 1958, p. 16.

[43] "The inheritance of property by the eldest son in Japanese [succession] law cannot be revised." – S. Etō's opinion on the law of primogeniture was openly expressed in the correspondence to G. Bousquet. Fukushima, Yoshii, 1993, p. 239.

[44] Tezuka, 1990, pp. 29–30; Ikeda, 2011, p. 78.

[45] In February 1874, S. Etō, dissatisfied with the Meiji government's domestic and foreign policies, withdrew from the Ministry of Justice and actively supported a rebellion in Saga Prefecture. Japanese government forces eventually suppressed the riots within a month and captured S. Etō. He was sentenced to death and his execution was carried out in April. Sakamoto, 2004, pp. 336, 345, 358.

[46] Sakamoto, 2004, pp. 340–342.

[47] Shinritsu Kōryō.

[48] Hōyō, Miyahira, 2009, pp. 13–57.

of the household.[49] By the end of March 1873, G. Bousquet and a group of Japanese jurists prepared another draft of the civil code called *Mimpō Kari Hōsoku* – the Provisional Civil Code. The draft, published as an interim document intended for further deliberation and amendments, comprised a short introduction in the first six articles and a demo part comprising 88 articles.[50] Looking at *Mimpō Kari Hōsoku* systematics and its principles, it was still a faithful copy of the French Civil Code, based on R. Mitsukuri's early translation. The discontented Ministry of Justice rejected the project and temporarily postponed the drafting team's subsequent meetings to find better solutions.[51]

R. Mitsukuri, who in October 1873 bent to the new Minister of Justice, Takatō Ōki, took the lead in a discussion on the shape of the future civil code.[52] In the second half of 1873, *Sain* – the Japanese Legislative Body – returned to the analysis of the October 1872 draft. Despite introducing many amendments, no binding decision was made on submitting it to legislative procedure.[53] Once he had taken the head position in the Ministry of Justice, T. Ōki faced considerable dissatisfaction among the Civil Law Committee members, who criticized S. Etō's authoritarian and patronizing leadership style. The more reserved T. Ōki did not strive to adopt the Civil Code at all costs, focusing on the current tasks outlined by the Grand Council of State. In April 1874, the Meiji government decided to carry out a military intervention against the pirates based in Formosa (present-day Taiwan). The Ministry of Justice started to seek international recognition for the annexation of the island, although some Western powers were equally interested in seizing it. Due to an abrupt shift in Japanese foreign policy that also influenced domestic policy, further work on civil code drafting was suspended for about two years.[54]

Gustave E. Boissonade, a French jurist and an expert on international law, contributed significantly to international recognition of the Japanese right to carry out the military intervention on Formosa.[55] In 1873, he arrived in Japan as a lecturer in

[49] Jinshin Koseki.

[50] Mimpō Kari Hōsoku – zen.

[51] Ishii, 1979, pp. 183–187.

[52] Taniguchi, Ishida, 2002, p. 10.

[53] Japanese legal history scholars named it *Sain no Mimpō Sōan* – the Civil Code Draft of the Legislative Body. Ishii, 1979, pp. 67, 108; Kawashima, Toshitani, 1958, pp. 13–18.

[54] Hoshino, 1943, p. 27.

[55] Gustave E. Boissonade was born in 1825 in Vincennes and was a son of the famous French explorer Jean François Boissonade de Fontarabie. In 1852, he defended his doctoral dissertation in law at the University of Paris and, in 1864, he was appointed as an Associate Professor at the Faculty of Law of the University of Grenoble, where he taught public law for the next three years. After changing his place of employment to the Faculty of Law of the University of Paris, in 1873, he received an offer from Hisanobu Samejima, a Japanese diplomat in France, to go to Tokyo to "modernize and improve the Japanese legal system". Signing a contract with the Japanese government in June of the same year,

cours de droit naturel/shizenhō kōgi – natural law – at Meihōryō.[56] Compared to other foreigners on ministerial contracts, G. Boissonade became known as an outstanding specialist in law who achieved the recognition and trust of the Ministry of Justice in a short time.[57] His favourable position became more apparent at the beginning of 1874 when the Meiji government entrusted him with preparing the drafts of the new Penal Code and the Code of Criminal Procedure.[58] At the same time, G. Boissonade also began teaching Property and Contract Law at Meihōryō, partly replacing G. Bousquet, who remained responsible for teaching family and commercial law.[59]

The need for a constitution and private law codes became an increasingly growing problem for the Meiji government and Japanese society in transitioning from feudal to modern statehood. In June 1875, the Grand Council of State issued Edict No. 103, which regulated *saiban jimu kokoroe* – the organization of the work of courts in legal matters. Pursuant to Article 3, if the Japanese courts found no statutory law while examining civil cases, they had to consider customary law as a ground for passing the verdict. Yet, they were instructed to follow the equity principle if they found no customary law norms.[60] The established procedure was compelling, even though the lack of a civil code and the limited set of recognized private law customs meant that the courts relied heavily on solving cases based on the equity principle. N. Hozumi argued that Article 3 became a gateway to the involuntary and chaotic introduction of foreign legal norms to the Japanese legal system as the understanding of the equity principle depended on an individual judge, who sought analogous solutions adopted in the French Civil Code or Anglo-American common law.[61]

he left France in September and arrived in Yokohama in November. Boissonade was to focus solely on legal advisory works since Article 8 of the contract expressly forbade him to engage directly or indirectly in industrial or commercial activities and to interfere in the political and religious affairs of Japan. Ōkubo, 1991, p. 389; de La Mazelière, 1991, pp. 127–134.

[56] Kawaguchi, 2014, p. 111; Ikeda, 2011, p. 13.

[57] Ōkubo, 1977, p. 88.

[58] Ōkubo, Takahashi, 1999, p. 28.

[59] Ōkubo, 1977, p. 54. Despite having much more experience with teaching and researching Japanese private law, G. Bousquet was more than 20 years younger than G. Boissonade. Since *nenkō jōretsu* – the seniority rule – has always been considered a crucial assessment factor in Japanese work culture, G. Bousquet gradually lost his unique position in the Ministry of Justice. G. Bousquet, marginalized and without significant influence, eventually terminated the government contract and returned to France in 1876.

[60] The full content of Article 3 reads as follows: "Minji no saiban ni seibun no hōritsu naki mono wa, shūkan ni yori, shūkan naki mono wa jōri wo suikō shite saiban subeshi", which can be translated as: "In civil cases, if the statutory law does not exist, the court is to decide on the basis of customary law and, if it does not exist, to conclude on the basis of equity." Own translation based on: Meiji 8-nen Dajōkan Fukoku Dai 103 Gō.

[61] Hozumi, 1912, p. 18.

Observing the increasingly contradictory judicial decisions of the civil courts, T. Ōki eventually returned to the codification of all branches of Japanese law. In August 1876, he established the Fifth Department of the Ministry of Justice responsible for drafting five codes: civil, criminal, commercial, criminal procedure and civil procedure.[62] The legislative activity of the Ministry of Justice during his leadership focused on developing new codes, filling in the most critical gaps in the Japanese legal system and unifying the most significant discrepancies in judicial decisions. For example, in October 1873, the Grand Council of State promulgated a law that unified time limits for legal claims on loan agreements. T. Ōki's positive contribution to the Japanese legal system also included the Act Regulating the Age of Majority promulgated in April 1876, which set the age of 20 years throughout Japan.[63]

Work on the new Criminal Code and the Code of Criminal Procedure was already advanced. In July 1877, G. Boissonade submitted complete drafts of both legal acts in French to the Ministry of Justice. After translating them into Japanese by the end of 1879, the Grand Council of State promulgated them in July 1880.[64] Two years later, both acts came into force as the first modern criminal law acts applied in Japan. Since G. Boissonade used the comparative legal method, particularly adopting the best solutions of the French, Belgian, Italian and German criminal codes, Japanese jurists highly appreciated his bills which maintained harmony between the proven principles of European criminal law and the traditions of Japanese society.[65]

Parallel to legislative initiatives regarding the Criminal Code and the Code of Criminal Procedure, the Ministry of Justice resumed intensive work on developing the civil code. By April 1878, R. Mitsukuri and Michiteru Mutakuchi prepared a new draft, which went down in history as *Meiji 10/11-nen Mimpō Sōan* – the 10/11 years of the Meiji-Era Civil Code Draft – comprising three books.[66] Although the Ministry of Justice wished to complete the civil code drafting process and intended to establish a Review Committee in the summer of 1879, it eventually rejected the project as not meeting expectations.[67] This decision was based on the assessment that R. Mitsukuri's and M. Mutakuchi's draft contained many translation errors and abbreviated articles. More importantly, it was still an inferior copy of the French Civil Code.[68] R. Mitsukuri felt bitterly disappointed and recalled the difficulties during the drafting process, emphasizing the burden he had to carry with M. Mutakuchi. As time passed, however, he admitted that it was a bill that could not

62 Ōkubo, Takahashi, 1999, p. 18.

63 Asako, Itō, Ueda, Jimbo, 2010, pp. 300–301.

64 Keihō Meiji 13-nen Dajōkan Fukoku Dai 36-gō; Chizaihō Meiji 13-nen Dajōkan Fukoku Dai 37-gō.

65 Saeki, Kobayashi, 1958, p. 226.

66 Mimpō Sōan: Dai 1–2 Hen; Mimpō Sōan: Dai 3 Hen.

67 Ishii, 1979, p. 209.

68 Hoshino, 1943, p. 71.

come into force.[69] Looking through the prism of the new Criminal Code and the Code of Criminal Procedure, the Ministry of Justice strongly discouraged Japanese jurists from copying French acts and presenting them as law that could be applied to the Japanese legal system. At that stage, Japanese jurisprudence, including the Ministry of Justice, was increasingly leaning towards drafting a civil code which, apart from being inspired by the French Civil Code, would also consider preserving some customary private law norms.[70] The epochal change of views on researching the hitherto unpopular Japanese customary law happened in May 1877, when the Ministry of Justice published a collection of national *minji kanrei* – civil law customs – edited and portrayed by Keihi Nagamori.[71]

2.2. Drafting the Civil Code under the leadership of G. Boissonade and a team of Japanese jurists (1879–1889)

G. Boissonade's Criminal Code and Code of Criminal Procedure met the expectations of the Ministry of Justice, which decided to employ him as leader of the team responsible for drafting the civil code. According to various sources, the official governmental offer was submitted in February or March 1879, along with the appendix for the existing contract.[72] G. Boissonade accepted this proposal and said that the Japanese civil code should be prepared *zero mama* – from scratch.[73] He divided the drafting process into several stages lasting five years.[74] During the early stages of preparation to begin the project, he also developed an original concept for the code comprising five books in the following order: (1) Personal Law (*Jinjihō*), (2) Property Law (*Zaisanhō*), (3) Contract Law (*Tokutei/Hōkatsu Meigi no Shutokuhō*), (4) Security (*Saiken no Tampo*) and (5) Evidence (*Shōko*).[75]

[69] Ōtsuki, 1907, p. 103; Tezuka, 1990, pp. 8–9.

[70] Hoshino, 1943, p. 71.

[71] Nagamori, 1877.

[72] Japanese legal history researchers are unable to clearly determine the date when Boissonade was entrusted with drafting the civil code, but most sources indicate that it was the winter or spring of 1879. Ōkubo, Takahashi, 1999, pp. 23–25; Hoshino, 1943, p. 71; Ikeda, 2011, p. 80; Taniguchi, 1939, p. 20; Iwata, 1943, p. 10.

[73] Ōkubo, Takahashi, 1999, p. 20.

[74] Boissonade later admitted that he was reckless to consider five years sufficient time to prepare a compelling draft of the Japanese Civil Code. Ōkubo, 1977, p. 134.

[75] Miyakawa, 1962, pp. 109–140. M. Ikeda also claims that the systematics of the Old Civil Code was G. Boissonade's original concept, yet it was inspired by the *Institutes* of Gaius and thus should be considered an improved version of the systematics adopted in the French Civil Code. Ikeda, 2011, p. 67.

The first stage of work focused on preparing the draft Property Law, which was the least historically developed and least described part of Japanese civil law.[76] G. Boissonade intended to adopt the comparative law method, as he did to draft the Criminal Code and the Code of Criminal Procedure. Japanese Property Law was supposed to be based on the Napoleonic Code, modified with improved regulations from other European civil codes. G. Boissonade took a closer look at the Italian Civil Code of 1865, which mostly copied its French counterpart, yet also contained discernible amendments resulting from the natural evolution of private law and the legal practice in the last 40 years.[77] Additionally, his attention was drawn to the innovative mortgage provisions of the Belgian *Loi Sur la Révision du Régime Hypothécaire* – Mortgage Act of 1851 – which amended part of the Napoleonic Code being in force since 1830.[78] As well as omitting the Anglo-American norms of common law, G. Boissonade had no intention to study the provisions of the Prussian Landrecht, which he regarded as an archaic work with no real influence on legal scholarship. The national civil code for unified Germany was still in preparation, so it was excluded from the analysis as a project with an uncertain outcome.[79] Contrary to the Meihōryō proposal of October 1872, G. Boissonade also wished to preserve *yoki yūeki na kyūkan* – favourable old Japanese customs.[80] To identify these customs and apply the most relevant ones to the draft, he needed the assistance of Japanese jurists fluent in searching old customary law and reading traditional Japanese. He was aware that without the helping hand of the Japanese lawyers, he could not complete drafting the most contentious parts of the civil code: Family and Succession Law.[81] Initially, the Ministry of Justice joined the investigation of the "favourable customary law" and, in July 1880, published the monograph entitled *Supplementary Collection of Private Law Customs*.[82] Yet, in October of the following year, government research was suspended due to the death of the leader of the project, Kuwashi Ikuta.[83]

G. Boissonade, an undisputed leader of the drafting team, worked on provisions concerning Property Law in French. At the same time, Japanese jurists were

[76] Ōkubo, 1977, p. 136.

[77] Despite the visible amendments, the Italian Civil Code in some of its parts was also a step back compared to other legislation of the second part of the 19th century. For example, the Italians removed the provisions on divorce and this decision was critically assessed by G. Boissonade and the Japanese jurists. Itō, 1966, p. 198.

[78] Fujiwara, 1995, p. 3.

[79] Seiler, 2005, pp. 315–316.

[80] Takahashi, 1996, pp. 191–196.

[81] Ōkubo, 1977, p. 135.

[82] Ikuta, 1880.

[83] Ōkubo, Takahashi, 1999, p. 48.

responsible for translating them into Japanese and introducing the necessary corrections.[84] In the Japanese historiography, Boissonade's undertaking received the abbreviated name of *Puroje* – the Project. It resulted from the title of the document in French – *Projet de Code Civil pour l'Empire du Japon* – which was updated as it slowly progressed in the following days, months and years.

To give a formal framework to the drafting process, on 30 April 1880, the Ministry of Justice established *Mimpō Hensan Kyaku* – the Civil Law Codification Department – led by the Minister of Justice, T. Ōki.[85] Apart from G. Boissonade, it also comprised R. Mitsukuri and two other Japanese jurists who completed legal education in France: Shirō Isobe and Sei'ichirō Kurogawa.[86] In June, the Civil Law Codification Department was moved from the supervision of the Ministry of Justice to *Genrōin* – the Chamber of Elders[87] – which replaced the legislative body.[88] In parallel to this shift, nine other Japanese jurists who had pursued legal training in France, or had practised civil law, were also assigned to the work.[89] Another essential step towards speeding up the codification of Japanese private law was the establishment in October 1881 of *Sanji'in* – the Legislative Office at the Grand Council of State. It supervised the progress of individual drafting projects, including civil law, providing necessary organizational changes or substantial help.

Between January and July 1882, the Ministry of Foreign Affairs held a series of secret conferences to determine the policy of revising unequal treaties. One of the inevitable conclusions was related to the need to accelerate the work on the remaining codes – the Civil Code, the Code of Civil Procedure and the Commercial Code.[90] When G. Boissonade was asked to submit the complete draft of the Civil Code before the initial deadline, he expressed his concern about the reckless haste. He instructed his Japanese co-workers to re-study the Book on Property Law, which had been drafted to date. Despite the dissatisfaction of the entire team with the Meiji government's instructions, they strove to adjust to the new policy. Volume one

84 Nagumo, 2017, pp. 34–54.

85 Niida, 1943, p. 5. Some Japanese legal historians indicate that the Civil Law Codification Department was inaugurated on 1 June 1880. Kawaguchi, 2014, p. 182.

86 Ōkubo, Takahashi, 1999, p. 46; Kawaguchi, 2014, p. 183.

87 Kokuritsu Kōbunshokan: Ref. 太00707100, Mimpō Hensan Kyoku o Genrōin ni mōku.

88 This shift was mainly related to the change in the position of the Minister of Justice because T. Ōki in February 1880 was appointed Chairman of the Chamber of Elders. In March of the same year, Fujimaro Tanaka assumed the position of the Minister of Justice.

89 The names of the other members of the Civil Law Codification Department are listed by K. Miyakawa, who provided the wrong date of transferring the supervision to the Chamber of Elders. Miyakawa, 1962c, p. 125.

90 According to some unconfirmed sources, German, British and French diplomats in Tokyo admitted that the revision of unequal treaties with Japan was possible upon the Meiji government introducing three missing codes. Takase, 1995, pp. 232–233.

of the *Draft Civil Code for the Empire of Japan*, initially in French, was published at the end of 1882. It contained part of Book Two of the Civil Code – Property Law.[91] As G. Boissonade explained in the introduction, Book One on Personal Law and Book Three on the Acquisition of Property were still under preparation.[92] A year later, volume two of the *Draft Civil Code for the Empire of Japan* was also published in French, which disclosed the remainder of Book Two.[93] Additionally, the Civil Law Codification Department had completed most of Book Three of the Civil Code by mid-1883. Still, the part on succession law was not yet ready, and thus the publication of volume three was postponed.

Parallel to the publication of subsequent parts of the Civil Code draft in French, intensive translation work was carried out by Japanese jurists. In March 1885, they submitted to the Grand Council of State a complete version of Book Two and Book Three, without the provisions on succession law and matrimonial property.[94] Immediately after that, G. Boissonade told them to independently draft Family and Succession Law, which would enable completion of Book One and Book Three. In addition to the experienced and trusted S. Isobe, the drafting team established on 12 April 1885 included Binzō Kumano, Sanatsugu Takano, Takeo Kikuchi, Seiji Komatsu, Nobuyuki Imamura, Mikao Nambu, Shōichi Inoue and Saburō Kōmyōji.[95]

In December 1885, the Grand Council of State was replaced by *naikaku* – the cabinet – which reflected the aspirations of the Meiji government in the last two decades to create a modern state with an efficient executive body similar to Western powers. Hirobumi Itō, the new Prime Minister of Japan, delayed the policy of revising unequal treaties by adopting the so-called *taisei shugi* – the Western doctrine.[96] It presumed that if Japan, following the example of continental European countries, established a judiciary operating under statutory law and introduced five fundamental codes of law, the cabinet could revise the unequal treaties.[97] To comply better with this

[91] Boissonade, 1882. This was the second, revised edition of the first volume. The first edition was published in 1880 for internal use by the Civil Law Codification Department.

[92] Boissonade, 1882, pp. 1–3.

[93] Boissonade, 1883. It was also the second, revised edition of the first volume.

[94] The Japanese version of Book Two was published in 1880 in three editions comprising five, eight and nine volumes, respectively. The Ministry of Justice edited a collective translation of 600 Articles of Book Two. Shihōshō, Boasonaado-shi Kisō Saietsu Mimpō Sōan Seijō Bukken Jinken Zen; The Japanese version of Book Three was initially published as a separate translation, and in a subsequent edition together with the earlier Book Two. Shihōshō, Boasonaado-shi Kikō Mimpō Sōan Shūseibun. Ji 501-jō shi 1502-jō.

[95] T. Hoshino, 1943, pp. 83–84. Hoshino presented the composition of the drafting team after three personal changes from 22 April 1885, 24 April 1886 and 27 September 1886.

[96] Kashimi, 2014, p. 126.

[97] Oka, 2014, pp. 37–48; Suzuki, 2004, pp. 117–119.

policy, the Civil Law Codification Department was abolished in March 1886[98] and replaced by a more complex *Hōritsu Torishirabe I'inkai* – Law Research Committee – supervised by the Ministry of Foreign Affairs and informally supported by the Ministry of Justice.[99] The Minister of Foreign Affairs, Kaoru Inoue, was appointed its chairman, and G. Boissonade, one of three foreign law experts hired by the Japanese government, served as a regular member with an advisory vote.[100]

In December 1886, the Chamber of Elders began to analyse the submitted draft of Book Two and Book Three of the Civil Code. Despite the cabinet's pressure for hasty approval, it was sceptical of giving final consent without an in-depth review. The intervention of the cabinet, justified by carrying out the Western doctrine, led to a heated debate on its legitimacy and principles. Many Japanese politicians refused to accept the notion that Japan had to adjust its legal system based on the demands of foreign powers. The discussion ended up with the resignation of K. Inoue as Minister of Foreign Affairs in September 1887. He was soon replaced by Prime Minister H. Itō, the most prominent advocate of Western doctrine, who was determined to push it through.[101] In October, the Law Research Committee was resubordinated to the Ministry of Justice, and the Minister of Justice, Akiyoshi Yamada, became its chairman.[102] The Committee consisted of ten permanent members, including five foreign law experts.[103] By May of the following year, it was enlarged by appointing two Japanese judges and two members of the Chamber of Elders.

A. Yamada, who insisted on the rapid introduction of the missing codes, instructed G. Boissonade to prepare the missing part of Book Three and the entirety of Book Four and Book Five.[104] Japanese jurists cooperating with G. Boissonade were banned from discussing the content of the regulations. They received an order to translate all articles directly from French to Japanese without additional

98 Summary of the activities of the Civil Law Codification Department concerning drafting Civil Code: Kokuritsu Kōbunshokan: Ref. 類00527100: Mimpō Hensan Kyoku Jōshinan. Other documents regarding the activities of the Civil Law Codification Department during the last six years: Kokuritsu Kōbunshokan: Ref. 太00712100 – Ref. 太00780100; Kokuritsu Kobunshokan: from Ref. 公02926100 to Ref. 公03885100; Kokuritsu Kobunshokan: from Ref. 記00577100 to Ref. 記00641100.

99 Kokuritsu Kōbunshokan: Ref. 類00289100, Hōritsu Torishirabe I'inkai oyobi Shoki o meisu.

100 Ōkubo, Takahashi, 1999, p. 53.

101 Kanhō Newspaper, 19 September 1887.

102 The formal transfer of control over the Law Research Committee to the Ministry of Justice took place on 9 November. The Committee Office was transferred earlier, on 21 October. Kokuritsu Kōbunshokan: Ref. 類00289100, Hōritsu Torishirabe Jimu o Shihō Daijin no Kanri ni Zokusu; Kokuritsu Kōbunshokan: Ref. 類00291100, Hōritsu Torishirabe I'inkai o Shihōshōchū ni Kaisetsu su; Nihon Daigaku, 1963, p. 750.

103 List of the Law Research Committee members without foreign experts, Kokuritsu Kōbunshokan: Ref. 類00289100, Hōritsu Torishirabe I'inkai Ryaksoku o Sadamu.

104 Hoshino, 1943, p. 94.

deliberations. A. Yamada's order, however, was not strictly followed since the Japanese jurists tried to improve G. Boissonade's provisions as part of their translation work. At the end of 1887, the opinion of the Chamber of Elders was submitted to the cabinet. Surprisingly for everyone, it revealed the critical assessment of Books Two and Three of the Civil Code. One of the Chamber members, Saburō Ozaki, emphasized that the regulations were ambiguous, difficult to understand and incompatible with Japanese social conditions. His opinion meant that the entire draft of the Property Law required numerous amendments.[105]

The bitter criticism, however, did not slow down the work of the Law Research Committee, which by October 1888 received a draft of Personal Law (including family law),[106] Succession Law and the rules concerning matrimonial property from the Japanese team led by S. Isobe and B. Kumano.[107] Besides clear influences from the French Civil Code, the Japanese also adopted solutions applied to the Italian Civil Code and the draft of the new Belgian Civil Code.[108] Having submitted the missing provisions of Book Three of the Civil Code, after almost five years of hiatus, volume three of G. Boissonade's *Draft Civil Code for the Empire of Japan* was finally published.[109]

The draft of Personal Law (including family law) and Succession Law, understandably, aroused great interest. Many jurists considered completing the draft of the Civil Code an essential step towards revising unequal treaties. Conversely, a significant number of jurists were also critical of the draft since it adopted radical social patterns peculiar to French realities, ignoring favourable Japanese customary law.[110] The Chamber of Elders established a Special Committee that analysed the articles individually and proposed multiple amendments. Opinions were also divided among the new cabinet ministers led by Kiyotaka Kuroda.[111] The Prime Minister, however, withheld the official declaration until all the provisions were translated from French into Japanese.

On 11 February 1889, Emperor Meiji promulgated the Constitution of Japan, which went down in history as the Meiji Constitution.[112] The first basic law in Japanese history would come into force on 29 November 1890, marking the critical point of over 20 years of intensive modernization of the country, which would transform into a constitutional monarchy with a statutory law system based on five fundamental codes. Once the Constitution was promulgated, and two codes

105 Ōkubo, Takahashi, 1999, pp. 9–14.
106 Tezuka, 1991, p. 108.
107 Mimpō Sōan Jinji Hen; Mimpō Sōan Kakutoku Hen Dai Ni Bu Riyūsho.
108 Ume, 1898, pp. 333–352.
109 Boissonade, 1888. It was the first edition.
110 Hirai, Murakami, 2007, pp. 7–8.
111 Tezuka, 1991, pp. 270–272.
112 Dai Nippon Teikoku Kempō.

were already in force, the cabinet intended to finalize work on the missing three codes, planning to promulgate them before the entry into force of the Constitution. G. Boissonade fulfilled his promise to deliver the comprehensive draft of the Civil Code within ten years and, in 1889, published volumes four and five of the *Draft Civil Code for the Empire of Japan* in French, which respectively corresponded to Book Four and Book Five.[113] When both volumes became available to the public, translating the last two books into Japanese was already in the advanced stage.

The submission of three books and the translation work on the last missing parts from French into Japanese led Kuroda's cabinet to a point in which it had to decide whether to implement the Civil Code or postpone the legislative procedure to reconsider its content. The steadfastness of the cabinet, which manifested in putting pressure on the Law Research Committee to complete the translation as soon as possible, led to the general notion that the new Civil Code would be promulgated before the entry into force of the Constitution without considering critical opinions presented by some Japanese jurists and the members of the Chamber of Elders. Some legal history scholars also claimed that the cabinet's decision to adopt the draft Civil Code in its original shape with no amendments, even if it would require publishing two separate parts at different times, could have been inspired by other circumstances. In April 1888, Montenegro promulgated *Opšti imovinski konnik za Knjaževinu Crnu Goru* – the first Civil Code in the country's history. The achievement of the Montenegrin government intrigued many countries around the world, not only because a tiny mountainous country in the Balkans outperformed Germany and Switzerland in the codification of private law but also because it extracted the Family and Succession Law from the Civil Code, giving it unique systematics and establishing new standards in civil law jurisprudence.[114]

Until October 1888, most of the work on the Civil Code rested on G. Boissonade and the team of Japanese jurists who provided for the remaining translation and ad hoc corrections. Notably, the part of Property Law drafted directly by G. Boissonade before 1885 had much more loyal supporters than harsh critics.[115] By contrast, the draft of the Personal Law (including family law) and Succession Law, supervised by S. Isobe and B. Kumano, suddenly triggered resentment among a conservative part of Japanese jurisprudence. This stir soon evolved into the Civil Code Controversy, which eventually engaged people outside the legal profession and made it one of the most critical matters of domestic policy.

113 Boissonade, 1889a; Boissonade, 1889b. Both volumes were the first editions.

114 Luković, 2008, pp. 175–188.

115 In response to Prime Minister H. Itō's criticism that G. Boissonade's project was taking too long, Minister of Justice A. Yamada, in a letter dated 5 October 1887, suggested only introducing the amendments that would allow better implementation of the Napoleonic Code principles in the specific conditions of the Japanese legal system. Ōkubo, Takahashi, 1999, pp. 138–140.

CHAPTER THREE

SCHOOLS OF LEGAL SCHOLARSHIP IN JAPAN – THE MAIN ACTORS IN THE CIVIL CODE CONTROVERSY

Abstract

This chapter outlines the schools of legal scholarship in Japan during the Meiji era, preserving the chronology of their establishment and the hierarchy of influence in the Ministry of Justice. Along with the general characteristics of the French, English and German Schools of legal scholarship, the chapter covers a short history of their most important academic centres and a description of two factions, the main participants in the Civil Code Controversy.

Keywords: legal scholarship in Japan, Japanese jurisprudence, Japanese law schools, Civil Code Controversy

"And we, Bachelor of Laws, swear to protect the legal principles and the nation's best interest (...)"

—The Tokyo Law School's graduation ceremony oath

This chapter briefly presents the characteristics of schools of legal scholarship in Japan, which formed two opposing factions that became the main actors of the Civil Code Controversy in 1889–1892. The term "schools of legal scholarship" requires an explanation for the Western reader unfamiliar with the details of Japanese jurisprudence in the Meiji era. These schools were the three distinct groups of jurists who were educated to be experts in a particular legal system of one of the foreign countries that the Meiji government considered worth studying for comparative purposes. Since the reformers had not inherited from the Tokugawa shogunate a legal education system which could provide the future staff of state institutions, including the most critical judiciary or administration, the first modern Japanese jurists became experts in foreign law to support the codification efforts in their country and teach the next generations of lawyers. Therefore, Japanese legal scholars distinguish three law schools: *Futsuhōha*, *Eihōha* and *Dokuhōha* – the French, English, and German schools of legal scholarship. The names of each school resulted directly from the legal systems of the countries that were the primary subject of their legal curriculum and research. Some Japanese jurists had degrees in two or more European legal systems. Their affiliation to a particular school was based on independent choice or exercising a public function, which required specific legal knowledge.

Although the Ministry of Justice initiated the research on domestic customary law in the late 1870s, the independent Japanese School did not develop until the end of the Civil Code Controversy. Due to the practical non-existence of legal scholarship in Japan, Japanese jurists in the early years of the Meiji Restoration were mainly educated at European universities (as government scholarship recipients) or at foreign law schools in Japan, which had been established since the late 1860s.[1] In practice, the organization of Japanese legal education led to a peculiar pattern: jurists first learned about the foreign legal system in a foreign language,[2] and only later, at the next stage of their education, did they acquire specialized knowledge in the domestic law of statute, which still was primarily based on the European law. Regardless of the legal education path, Japanese jurists of the Meiji era were aware of the existence and nature of Japanese customary law and its profound influence on society. Their knowledge of the substance of this law, however, was limited to specific regions and fields. Still, particular scholars emphasized or depreciated the importance of customary law during the codification process, depending on their affiliation to one of the three existing law schools or their individual views.

Japanese legal historians distinguish two parties in the Civil Code Controversy: *dankōha* and *enkiha*, which can be translated as the "decisive" and "postponement" factions. The decisive faction derived its name from the Japanese word *dankō*, which means "decisive action" or "resolute enforcement", in this case regarding the Civil Code. The postponement faction's name was based on the word *enki*, meaning "postponement" or "deferment".[3] The decisive faction supported the Western doctrine principle and advocated the immediate publication of the Civil Code drafted by G. Boissonade and his team of Japanese jurists. After the publication of the Code by Kuroda's cabinet in 1890, there was a three-year interregnum before its coming into force. Accordingly, the decisive faction called for its enforcement without delay. They also opposed any amendments, which would have led to additional waiting. The draft Code was leaked, and in response, the postponement faction opposed its publication. When Kuroda's cabinet decided to go ahead in the face of this opposition, the postponement faction said that delaying the coming into force

[1] Government scholarships for legal education in Europe were also granted in the Tokugawa shogunate's late years.

[2] Takatani, Koishikawa, 2018, p. 219.

[3] Iwata, 1943, p. 30.

of the Code was imperative, as it was necessary first to discover the respective positions of the law schools on the formal and substantive issues of the Code.

One should agree with the assessment of N. Hozumi, who associated the decisive faction with the French School and the postponement faction with the English School despite a few exceptions to this visible division.[4] Exceptions included Masaakira Tomii and Hiroji Kinoshita, French School representatives, who belonged to the postponement party,[5] and Saburō Shimada, an English School representative, who supported the decisive faction.[6] The German School did not develop an independent position, and its representatives were divided between the decisive and postponement parties.[7]

Differences in views regarding the introduction of the Civil Code between the decisive and the postponement faction resulted directly from the legal education path of their representatives. The graduates of the French School, trained at French universities, were experts in the French legal system based on Napoleonic codes applying the natural law doctrine principles. On the contrary, the English School representatives, educated at English and American universities, were not only acquainted with Anglo-American statutory law, but some of them also became practitioners in the common law system. Although the Civil Code Controversy generally did not oppose the fundamental issue of reforming Japanese private law by introducing a system of statutory law, the English School emphasized the importance of the historical development of law and its national spirit. N. Hozumi compared the Controversy to the famous dispute between A. Thibaud and K.G. von Savigny. In Japan, however, the English School underlined the importance of Japanese customary law and pressed for the drafting of a code that would follow the latest codification trends and would not require numerous amendments.[8]

Having analysed the postulates of both law schools, it is impossible to attach to them unambiguous conservative or progressive views, as each sought to reform the Japanese legal system, yet in a different way. Japanese legal scholars also disagreed in the past on the nature of the Controversy, even by reducing it to a dispute motivated only by ideological divergences. For example, Tōru Hoshino argued that it was a dispute between liberalism based on foreign patterns and national traditionalism. At the same time, Kikuo Nakamura, Hoshino's main adversary, tried to prove that the conflict was focused on legal aspects.[9]

[4] Hozumi, 1980, p. 329.
[5] Hozumi, 1912, pp. 9–10; Shichinobe, 2009f, pp. 64–65.
[6] Ōkubo, 1977, p. 180.
[7] Hoshino, 1943, p. 125.
[8] Hozumi, 1980, p. 344.
[9] Shigematsu, 2005, pp. 175–189.

Once the Meiji government decided to codify the legal system, the Ministry of Justice became the intellectual centre of Japanese jurists. In the 1870s, legal research in Japan was limited to studying the statutory law of Western European countries, which was very complicated in the eyes of the Japanese jurists. They devoted much time and effort to understanding all legal systems and identifying specific mechanisms that would work perfectly in domestic conditions. As Y. Noda indicated, many prominent Japanese jurists believed that if a particular legal system worked well in its country of origin, it could also be adapted in Japan after minor improvements. Comparative law in that period was only used to speed up the legislation, and the law itself was considered only as statutory law.[10]

In the first years of the Meiji era, jurisprudence in Japan was treated instrumentally as the art of perfecting the law and its mechanisms.[11] Japanese jurists adopted the legal jurisprudence model distinctive to Germany, best suited to solving current legislative problems.[12] Despite this initial assessment, several legal education centres were established in Japan between 1871 and 1889. They had different views on the legal system that the Meiji government should adopt. Kazuhiro Murakami, a distinguished Japanese legal scholar, identified 23 law schools belonging to either French, English or German Schools that participated in the Civil Code Controversy.[13] The establishment and development of individual law schools and their most influential academic centres, which emerged until the conclusion of the Controversy, are presented in the subsequent part of this chapter.

3.1. French School of legal scholarship

The French School was the first school of legal scholarship that emerged in Japan. Interest in French law was born in the declining period of the Tokugawa shogunate when Japanese delegates were sent to European countries to familiarize themselves with the achievements of the French legal system and its importance for the development of legal scholarship in Europe.[14] During the Meiji era, mainly due to the language barrier and a small number of jurists, research on French law was limited to translating French codes into Japanese. A lack of in-depth knowledge of French history and culture made the French law principles more ambiguous to

[10] Noda, 1961, pp. 3–59.

[11] Noda, 1976, pp. 6–7.

[12] Leszczyński, 1995, pp. 180–181.

[13] Murakami, 2008a, p. 268.

[14] M. Itō dates the beginning of Japanese research on French-related matters (initially such as a study of French literature) to 1858. In 1865, the second consul general of the Empire of France in Japan, Léon Roches, became a lecturer in French at the French Language School in Yokohama. Itō, 1966, p. 185.

Japanese jurists. This situation gradually changed with the arrival of French jurists to Japan. Initially, G. Bousquet, and later G. Boissonade, apart from giving lectures on substantive and procedural French law, also shared their knowledge with students on the theory and philosophy of law.[15] After G. Bousquet returned to France, G. Boissonade became an unquestionable leader of the French School, who raised future generations of Japanese jurists, with graduates of various academic centres sharing his knowledge. Therefore, G. Boissonade himself had a massive impact on the shape of the French School. Still, along with the graduation of successive generations of Japanese jurists, the main current of the French School, initially centred around the Law School at the Ministry of Justice, was split into several smaller ones, which carried out independent research. Yasuo Ōkubo claimed that *shizen hōgaku* (the natural law doctrine), thus the French Law School, reached the peak of its dominance in Japanese legislative policy in 1887.[16] Nevertheless, until the publication of the Meiji Civil Code in the second part of the 1890s, the vast influence of the French School representatives on the Ministry of Justice was noticeable for Japanese jurisprudence.[17]

The Civil Code Controversy was inherently tied up in the varying and often seemingly contradictory values of G. Boissonade, the author of Books Two, Three (in part), Four and Five of the Code. Even by European standards (which seemed full of contradictions for Far East researchers),[18] G. Boissonade was unusual. He was religious, to the point that K. Tanaka noted his *croyance en Dieu* (faith in God), suggesting that he viewed this juxtaposition of faith and legal scholarship as anomalous. K. Tanaka viewed him as a representative of the religious branch of lawyers supporting natural law doctrine,[19] which was necessarily tied to Christianity and, therefore, problematic to Japanese people because of its perceived antithetical nature. G. Boissonade, however, held other views which counterbalanced his Christianity. According to Antoine de La Mazelière, he was primarily a rationalist and humanitarian.[20] According to Jean L. Sourioux, he was a great reformist (with the implication that his reforms aligned with secular goals), who developed many innovative solutions to civil law problems.[21]

[15] The exact content of G. Bousquet's lectures remains unknown, but the notes of Japanese students show that G. Bousquet and G. Boissonade were always open to all questions and explained all issues very clearly. Itō, 1966, p. 201.

[16] Ōkubo, 1977, p. 69.

[17] Murakami, 2007, pp. 131–132.

[18] Ikeda, 2011, pp. 11–12.

[19] Tanaka, 1952, pp. 109–155.

[20] de La Mazelière, 1991, p. 129.

[21] Sourioux, 1991, pp. 357–366.

It is known from Japanese testimonies and lecture notes that G. Boissonade often quoted the philosophy of Aristotle and Thomas Aquinas.[22] He also often spoke positively about the importance of the traditional values promoted by the Catholic Church. At the same time, he recognized civil divorce introduced by the Napoleonic Code and supported the abolition of torture and the death penalty.[23] G. Boissonade also believed that human nature is generally good,[24] so he was a great enthusiast of Adam Smith's economic theories.[25] Additionally, his views were far from J. Rousseau's concept of natural upbringing and social contract theory, which had become the hallmarks of mainstream French natural law doctrine thinkers.[26] Notwithstanding this eclecticism, some Japanese jurists were suspicious that G. Boissonade's Christianity would deform the Code. G. Boissonade tried to convince them that his work was based on ideas derived from the teaching of the Catholic Church and Montesquieu's thoughts, which he claimed were not contradictory to Confucian and Buddhist philosophy, but his opponents remained unconvinced.[27]

For almost two decades, functioning academic centres belonging to the French School educated the largest and most influential group of Japanese jurists who established the Japanese legal system and the first modern codes. The development of research on the legal systems of other countries, especially the United Kingdom and Germany, led to the loss of the dominant position of the French School in Japanese jurisprudence. It should be noted, however, that the French School representatives contributed the most to drafting the Old Civil Code and Meiji Civil Code. The establishment and development of the six most influential academic centres belonging to the French School are presented below.

3.1.1. Law School at the Ministry of Justice

One of the reasons why the Meiji government established the Law School at the Ministry of Justice, known as the Meihōryō, in September 1871 was that R. Mitsukuri had issues with the translation of the French Civil Code.[28] The school's primary goal was to educate future generations of Japanese legal professionals (particularly for the Ministry of Justice) by teaching the French legal system with an emphasis on practice.[29] Meihōryō alluded to the best traditions of Western scholarship education

22 Ōkubo, 1977, pp. 61–62.
23 de La Mazelière, 1991, pp. 129–130.
24 Boissonade, 1892, pp. 65–73.
25 Ikeda, 2011, p. 48.
26 Kishigami, 1996, pp. 7–37.
27 Tanaka, 1952, p. 145.
28 Tezuka, 1988, pp. 6–7; Miyahara, 2010, p. 4.
29 Mukai, 1982, pp. 41–62.

in Japan during the Tokugawa shogunate. To attract the best talent from all over the country, despite their social background, the entrance and tuition fees were deliberately waived, and a scholarship covering the basic costs of living was introduced. The criteria for admission to Meihōryō included passing the entrance exam in *kango* – traditional Japanese – and French. In July 1872, twenty students, mostly graduates of the prestigious Daigakuminami School, formed the first Meihōryō class. In the latter part of 1872, G. Bousquet became the first foreign lecturer. He was also the first person to promote independent Japanese jurisprudence creation. When G. Boissonade arrived in Japan at the end of 1873, Meihōryō already had four professional lecturers.[30] Since most of the lectures were provided in French by native speakers, the school developed into an elitist university. Based on M. Inoue's notes written in French, it can be assessed that G. Bousquet and G. Boissonade taught criminal law, civil law, commercial law, administrative law, and the theory of natural law.[31]

The Ministry of Justice initially estimated that Meihōryō would be able to educate 100 lawyers at a time. Due to staff and financial shortages, however, the number of students in the first cohort was limited to only 20. This setback did not discourage the Japanese from increasing the number to 100 in the subsequent admissions. Meihōryō's students were a small group, yet the school already had significant influence in the codification of civil law, as it independently prepared one of the drafts in just a few months. Although the Ministry of Justice rejected it in 1872, the students demonstrated their dedication to contributing to legislative matters.

In May 1875, Meihōryō was transformed into Shihōshō Hōgakkō – the Law School at the Ministry of Justice.[32] In July 1876, the first group of 20 lawyers graduated from the school and received the degree of *hōritsu gakushi* – Bachelor of Laws. The same degree was also awarded to five scholarship recipients who returned the same year to Japan from their legal education in France.

For the second cohort, the education path was significantly extended – the students had to attend a four-year preparatory course in French first. Later, they studied French law for the following four years.[33] In January 1879, the Law School hired a new lecturer, Georges V. Appert, an attorney and PhD in law at the University of Paris.[34] The beginning of the 1880s also marked the peak of the influence of the Law School at the Ministry of Justice in Japan, mainly due to the successful codification of criminal law and entrusting the drafting of the Civil Code to G. Boissonade.

[30] The other two lecturers, responsible for the teaching of French, were Henri de Riberolles and Gaston Garie. Tezuka, 1988, pp. 13–15.

[31] Takami, 2001, pp. 803–840.

[32] Tezuka, 1967, p. 53.

[33] Takatani, Koishikawa, 2018, p. 224.

[34] Tezuka, 1988, p. 20.

When the second cohort completed the French preparatory course in 1880, the Law School announced the third admission round. The second-cohort graduates left the university in July 1884. Thirty-three students and four scholarship recipients in France received the Bachelor of Laws degree from the Ministry of Justice. The fourth and final admission round was carried out in October of the same year. For the first time, however, the principle of government funding for students was abandoned, requiring candidates to secure a self-funding.

In December 1884, Shihōshō Hōgakkō came under the supervision of the Ministry of Education and changed its name to Tōkyō Hōgakkō – the Tokyo Law School. As a result of a thorough reform of the legal education system in Japan, Tōkyō Hōgakkō became part of the Old University of Tokyo as the Department of French Law within the Faculty of Law in September 1885. All students were automatically transferred to the Old University of Tokyo. The last group of students, who were recruited by the Law School at the Ministry of Justice and completed their legal education, included 72 graduates from the third and fourth admission rounds.[35] At that time, the university was already known as an academic centre that educated the first Japanese judges, prosecutors and staff of the Ministry of Justice.[36]

Among the most famous graduates of the Law School at the Ministry of Justice who took part in the Civil Code Controversy were S. Isobe, M. Inoue, S. Inoue, H. Kinoshita, T. Kishimoto, B. Kumano, Toyozō Takagi, K. Ume, Y. Kawamura and T. Terao.

3.1.2. Tokyo Law School

Tōkyō Hōgakkō (the Tokyo Law School), mistakenly described as the formal successor of the Law School at the Ministry of Justice in 1884–1885, was in fact a separate law school that focused on French-related subjects. From April 1880, it functioned as Tōkyō Hōgakusha – the Tokyo Jurisprudence Association – founded by seven lawyers and employees of the Ministry of Justice.[37]

Initially, the Association consisted of Kōhōkyaku and Daigenkyaku – the Lecture Department and the Attorney Department. The Lecture Department invited Japanese and French jurists to lecture on domestic statute and French law. The Attorney Department prepared future lawyers for the profession and organized mock trial court hearings managed by practising lawyers and sessions for joint preparation of *kōso* and *jōkoku* – appeals and final appeals. The Association also established the Legal Clinic, which educated future lawyers without practical experience on providing professional legal opinions on various matters through the patronage

[35] Asakuro, 1969, pp. 289–292.
[36] Tezuka, 1988, p. 185.
[37] Yoshii, 1992, p. 46.

system. Despite the low legal consciousness among ordinary Japanese people, the first Legal Clinic in the history of Japanese jurisprudence enjoyed great popularity.

In May 1881, after the separation of the Lecture Department, it was renamed the Tokyo Law School. It soon received financial and personnel support from the Ministry of Justice. In May 1884, the school came under the control of the Ministry of Education, which in September of the following year merged it with the Faculty of Law of the Old University of Tokyo. As a result of unification, however, the Tokyo Law School did not formally cease to exist and, in reality, absorbed the academic staff of the Faculty of Law of the Old University of Tokyo.

In 1885, Chūō Hōgakukai – the Capital Law Society – was established at the Tokyo Law School, which issued three times a month *Chūō Hōgakukai Zasshi* – the Capital Law Society Journal. Its content focused on reprinting law lectures and providing legal opinions in response to readers' letters.

Based on the Special Ministerial Regulation on the Supervision of Private Law Schools Law of November 1886, the Tokyo Law School was included in *Godai Hōritsu Gakkō* – the so-called "Big Five" of Law Schools – which a year later received a special licence from the Ministry of Justice to grant professional and academic titles.[38] In May 1888, the Ministry of Education merged the Tokyo Law School with the Tokyo French School, creating a joint Wafutsu Hōritsu Gakkō – the Japanese-French Law School.

The Tokyo Law School has gone down in the history of Japanese legal education as an academic centre opposing liberal movements and broad civil rights, the ideas supported by the rival Meiji Law School. Today, its mission is continued by Hosei University.

3.1.3. Tokyo French School

Tōkyō Futsugakkō – the Tokyo French School – was founded in April 1886 by seven political activists of the Meiji era who planned to create an academic centre in Tokyo to study various aspects of *Furansugaku* – French studies. According to the policy statement, presented on 6 November 1886 in the Tokyo edition of the *Asahi Shimbun* newspaper, the most important goal of the establishment of the Tokyo French School was to diversify research on broadly understood French-related subjects.[39]

The school began its educational activities by teaching French (emphasizing theoretical and practical skills), traditional Japanese literature in French, history, mathematics, chemistry, physics and geography. Profiting from the financial support of the Ministry of Justice, Tōkyō Futsugakkō employed G. Boissonade in

[38] Shiritsu Hōritsu Gakkō Tokubetsu Kantoku Jōki.

[39] *Tokyo Asahi Shimbun* from 6 November 1886.

September 1887 and then also offered lectures on French law. In August of the following year, the Ministry of Education granted the school a special licence which meant that graduates could take the state examination to become civil servants, judges and prosecutors.

In September 1888, after employing several graduates of the former Law School at the Ministry of Justice who received the Bachelor of Laws degree, Tōkyō Futsugakkō established a separate law institute. Soon after, it merged with the Tokyo Law School. When the Ministry of Education approved its new statute in May 1889, the school changed its name to the Japanese-French Law School, comprising three institutes: French Language Studies, Legal Studies in French and Legal Studies in Japanese.[40]

The Tokyo French School soon became an important academic centre of research on French law because it not only employed some of the most eminent French jurists residing in Japan at that time (G. Boissonade and G. Appert) but also because it entrusted the teaching of law to young Japanese Bachelor of Laws graduates. Among those associated with the Tokyo French School who then participated in the Civil Code Controversy were M. Tomii, S. Inoue, B. Kumano, K. Kinoshita, S. Kameyama, T. Kishimoto, K. Miyagi and S. Kōmyōji.

3.1.4. Meiji Law School

Meiji Hōritsu Gakkō – the Meiji Law School – was founded in January 1881 by three graduates of the first cohort of the Law School at the Ministry of Justice: T. Kishimoto, K. Miyagi and M. Yashiro.[41] According to the programme declaration, they intended to thoroughly "research the law and teach about its true essence". Another equally important goal of the Meiji Law School was to spread knowledge about civil rights and promote liberal movements.[42] Greatly impressed by the impact of the French Revolution on the history of France and Europe, the school's founders intended to convince the Meiji government that a strong civil society had its roots in civil liberties guaranteed by statutory law. In the initial period, the school functioned mainly thanks to the financial support of two former clan leaders: T. Ikeda from Tottori and T. Matsudaira from Shimabara.

Using personal connections with the Ministry of Justice, the Meiji Law School employed G. Appert as lecturer in January 1882. Apart from him, lectures were also given by S. Inoue (administrative law), T. Kishimoto (commercial law), K. Miyagi

[40] The modern successor of the Tokyo French School and the Tokyo Law School (and thus the Japanese-French School of Law) is Hōsei University. Hōsei Daigaku, Hōsei Daigaku 80-nen shi.

[41] Meiji Daigaku, 1940, p. 3.

[42] Meiji Hōritsu Gakkō Setsuritsu no Shushi.

(Japanese criminal law), M. Yashiro (French civil contracts with intermediaries) and Y. Ichinose (French lease contracts). The school also had a weekly discussion club moderated by Prince Saionji Kim'mochi. In 1886, Meiji Hōritsu Gakkō was divided into the Faculty of Law and the Faculty of Administration. Until then, additional lecturers were employed at the school, primarily recruited from among the graduates of the Law School at the Ministry of Justice. Apart from G. Boissonade, Alessandro Paternostro, an Italian jurist and graduate of the University of Rome, was also hired by the Meiji Law School.

Based on the Special Ministerial Regulation on the Supervision of Private Law Schools of November 1886, the Meiji Law School was included in the "Big Five" of Law Schools, and a year later, it received a special licence from the Ministry of Justice to grant professional and academic titles in law.[43] Although the views on civil rights expressed by the Meiji Law School were unusual for the French School (they were conservative), during the Civil Code Controversy, its representatives formed a joint position with the Japanese-French Law School. They soon became a strong voice in the decisive faction, which criticized the postulates of delaying the date of entry into force of the Code.[44] Today, Meiji University is a continuator of the Meiji Law School.

3.1.5. Kansai Law School

Kansai Hōritsu Gakkō – the Kansai Law School – was founded in Osaka at the end of 1886 to promote legal scholarship and educate future generations of Japanese lawyers outside the capital city of Tokyo, also among ordinary citizens.[45] The immediate reason for the creation of the school was the establishment of a temporary court of appeals in Osaka to conduct public hearings on the Osaka incident, which took place in December 1885 and was associated with the left wing of the Liberal Party. The Ministry of Justice dispatched two judges (M. Tsurumi and S. Inoue) and two prosecutors (M. Hotta and H. Ogura) to the Kansai region. While examining the case details, the four jurists discussed their legal doubts with their superiors in the capital. They soon noticed that the "Big Five" law schools were in Tokyo. Thus, the provincial justice system depended on cadres from the distant and culturally different capital region of Kantō.

After obtaining a licence from the Ministry of Justice to train law students, the Kansai Law School, despite financial difficulties, began lecturing in December 1886

[43] Shiritsu Hōritsu Gakkō Tokubetsu Kantoku Jōki.

[44] Meiji Daigaku, 1940, p. 16.

[45] For the full text of the original declaration on the importance of establishing the Kansai Law School, see Yamano, 2020.

with a three-year evening school programme. Hisashi Ogura, a first-cohort graduate of the Law School at the Ministry of Justice, became its first director. The rest of the university staff members were also recruited from graduates of the Law School at the Ministry of Justice.[46] For this reason, classes focused on French law, which was taught only in Japanese, unlike most law schools in Tokyo. In November 1887, the Kansai School of Law published the first transcripts of its lectures, and in April of the following year, it was visited by Boissonade, who gave a series of guest lectures. In May 1889, Chojirō Mizukami, a second-cohort graduate of the Law School at the Ministry of Justice, became the school's new headmaster.

The Kansai Law School significantly influenced the development of legal education in western Japan, particularly the expansion of the French Law School beyond Tokyo and the Kantō region. Although the academic staff employed at the school were not officially involved in the Civil Code Controversy, they supported the decisive faction and the Code as former students of G. Boissonade,[47] thus jurists raised on natural law doctrine.[48]

3.1.6. Kyoto Law School

Kyōto-to Hō Gakkō – the Kyoto Law School – was the last of the academic centres belonging to the French School, which was established in Japan before the beginning of the Civil Code Controversy. According to the programme declaration of January 1888, its goal was to educate future generations of lawyers and promote knowledge about French law and Japanese statute law. The private school specialized in French private law, offering additional economics courses.

Keijun Yamazaki, a graduate of the second cohort of the School of Law at the Ministry of Justice, became the school's first director. In addition, Kyōto-to Hō Gakkō employed Y. Kawamura, K. Shikata and I. Shimizu as lecturers, graduates of the same cohort of the Law School at the Ministry of Justice. Similar to the Kansai Law School in nearby Osaka, the Kyoto Law School supported the decisive faction in the Civil Code Controversy. Eventually, Kyōto-to Hō Gakkō was absorbed by Kyōto Hōsei Gakkō – the Kyoto School of Law and Politics.[49]

[46] Yamano, 2020, p. 18.

[47] Among G. Boissonade's former students (from the Law School at the Ministry of Justice) employed at the Kansai Law School were M. Inoue, Y. Ichinose, H. Oguro, K. Kabuto, C. Mizukami, Y. Oda and M. Tsurumi. For more about G. Boissonade and his lecturers at the Kansai Law School, see Haruhara, 1965, pp. 10–13.

[48] Takeshita, 2015.

[49] Ritsumeikan 100-nen Shi: tsūshi dai ikkan.

3.2. English School of legal scholarship

The English School originates from Japanese students sent as government scholarship recipients to the United States or the United Kingdom in the early 1870s to study American and British (English) politics and law. N. Hozumi dates the establishment of the English School to 1874 by identifying the teaching of Anglo-American Law at the Tokyo Kaisei School from this date.[50] There was a swift increase in English School jurists and practitioners as scholars graduated rapidly from the Tokyo Kaisei School. The English School's history cannot be understood in isolation from its rivalry with the French School, which also had a political and ideological dimension apart from the legal aspect. The Japanese attitude towards the United Kingdom/the United States and France, and therefore their legal systems, was shaped during the last years of the bakumatsu period. Unlike France, which initially established close economic and military relations with the Tokugawa shogunate,[51] the United Kingdom and the United States actively supported the reformist forces opposing the old order. For this reason, apart from the unequal treaties, after the Meiji Restoration, relations between Tokyo, London and Washington were generally positive and fostered knowledge exchange.

The English School based its teaching on *bunseki hōgaku* – the analytical jurisprudence of John Austin – and *rekishi hōgaku* – the English legal evolution doctrine of William Blackstone, Frederic Maitland and Henry Maine.[52] Compared to the French School, the English School representatives were fluent not only in the historical works of thinkers and philosophers of their field but also in the current debates in American and English jurisprudence, in which they actively participated. Although the Meiji government wished to focus on the codification of the Japanese legal system, the English School representatives mainly emphasized the need to study the American and English common law systems and the most significant statute law that had influenced the shape of the legal system of both countries. In addition to historical precedents and the role of customary law, they were especially interested in researching Magna Carta, the Habeas Corpus Act and the Declaration of Rights of 1689, which were the foundation of the rights of what was then the largest colonial empire in the world.[53]

The logical consequence of supporting Blackstone's legal evolution doctrine was that the English School representatives opposed natural law doctrine as

[50] Hozumi, 1980, p. 331.

[51] Itō, 1966, p. 184.

[52] Hoshino, 1943, p. 145; Itō, 1966, pp. 264–265.

[53] Iwamura, 1996, p. 113.

revolutionary, disturbing the gradually changing social order.[54] There were also some fundamental discrepancies between English and Japanese versions of the legal evolution doctrine derived from historical experiences and cultural differences between both countries. Having observed the events in revolutionary and Napoleonic France, domestic English jurists opposed instrumental legislation driven by natural law doctrine. Yet, they also saw its positive aspects, such as establishing a secular state of law and equal rights for men and women.[55] In contrast, the Japanese jurists resisted the idea of the equality of both sexes. As Masao Fukushima emphasized, this idea was too advanced for Japanese society and its elites at that time, which raised the question of reforming the entire legal system within the lives of one generation.[56]

Leaving aside the issues characteristic of the European political and sociology discourse, the English School representatives shared J. Bentham's and J. Austin's beliefs of codifying the law considering its national and historical spirit.[57] They understood that Japan, which did not have its codes and was trying to establish a modern legal system, could not develop nor adopt a common law system similar to the United Kingdom. At the same time, they argued that the Japanese legal system should not be codified by merely translating or copying French codes, which would be detached from their primary environment, thus becoming a foreign body in the state. Since the Meiji government had decided to codify the law, the English School encouraged the Japanese legislator to apply the rule of *kanshūhō no kokusuiron* – the presumption that domestic customary law was a specific type of existing Japanese law in non-organized form for centuries, which now had to be transformed into legal norms expressed in statute law.[58]

As a part of the analysis of the English School postulates and the legal evolution doctrine, it is worth mentioning the American influences. Its leading representative was Henry T. Terry, a graduate of Yale University (Bachelor of Arts), who acquired his professional title of an advocate in 1872 after completing the regular legal

[54] Itō, 1966, pp. 265–266.

[55] Regardless of the postulates of natural law doctrine, the Napoleonic Code promoted the dominance of men in civil law. Only the Married Women's Property Act 1870, introduced by the British Parliament, drastically changed the position of women in marriage, recognizing their right to property, to have their own income and to inherit property, and granting legal capacity to sue the spouse. According to William Gladstone, the British Prime Minister of the Liberal Party, these changes shocked even the most liberal activists across Europe. The Japanese perspective on changes in Great Britain is described in Kuryū, 1928, p. 40.

[56] For more about the English School representatives' views on the issue of legal equality between men and women in marriage, see Fukushima, Yoshii, 1993, pp. 277–280.

[57] Hozumi, 1890, pp. 6–8; Koyanagi, 1981, pp. 108–109.

[58] Iwata, 1928, p. 191.

traineeship in Connecticut. Although he resided outside of Japan during the Civil Code Controversy (he returned to Tokyo to become a lecturer at the Tokyo Imperial University in 1894), he gave lectures on common law to Japanese law students at the Kaisei School in the second half of the 1870s,[59] openly criticizing the natural law doctrine and G. Boissonade's teaching and thus the entire French School.[60]

The most famous of the English School representatives who took part in the Civil Code Controversy were Kenzō Takahashi, Rokuichirō Matsushima, Hajime Motoda, Katsunan Kuga, Teruhiko Okamura, Junjirō Hosokawa, Chū Egi, Kamenosuke Misaki, Kenchō Suematsu,[61] Ikuzō Ōoka, Tomotsune Komura and Kinosuke Yamada.

Although the English School opposed the much more prominent French School, the determination of the postponement faction made it victorious in the Civil Code Controversy. This success significantly elevated the English School's position in the eyes of Japanese jurisprudence. It also made Japanese jurists more aware of the role of domestic customary law, especially Family and Succession Law, which eventually was not replaced by French norms of the Napoleonic Code. Over the next decade, mainly due to the introduction of the revised Civil Code, interest in researching common law became noticeably weaker. The English School representatives possessed extensive knowledge of the Anglo-American case and statute law. Yet, they did not study Japanese customary law in depth and thus could not offer anything more than an objection to natural law doctrine.[62] The critical attitude towards the changes in the Civil Code advocated by the French School can be deducted by reading the numerous works by N. Hozumi, published in Japanese and English from 1890 to 1936.[63]

The establishment and development of the four most important academic centres of the English School are presented below.

3.2.1. Old University of Tokyo/Imperial University

Kyū Tōkyō Daigaku – the Old University of Tokyo – has its roots in the public Kaisei School, which the Meiji government established in September 1868 to promote knowledge about the Western world, particularly the United Kingdom, Germany and France. The school employed foreign lecturers and followed restrictive

[59] Tezuka, 1988, p. 208.

[60] Itō, 1966, p. 266; Shiraha, 1995, p. 131.

[61] Shichinobe, 2009d, pp. 86–88.

[62] Takayanagi, 1955, pp. 60–69.

[63] N. Hozumi's works were also published after his death (1926), mainly by editing handwritten notes and records of speeches. His most recognized works include *The Theory of Codes* (1890), *The System of Collective Responsibility of Five Farms* (1902), *The New Japanese Civil Code: Material for the Study of Comparative Jurisprudence* (1904) and *Custom and Law* (1929).

traditional teaching methods from the Edo period.[64] It soon received a reputation as a place that provides ideal conditions for the upbringing of exceptional talent. In December 1869, the Kaisei School was renamed the Daigakuminami School, receiving the status of *daigakkō* – the supreme school.[65] Based on this name, the modern Japanese term for university (*daigaku*) was created. At that time, the Daigakuminami School had two factions that advocated either focusing on Sino-Japanese or Western studies.[66] Although neither side gained an advantage, the dispute led to numerous organizational changes in the school and it changing its name twice. In August 1873, the curriculum was expanded with five new subjects, including law taught in English.[67] After separating strictly linguistic departments, which formed Tōkyō Gaikokugo Gakkō – the Tokyo School of Foreign Languages – in May 1874, the specialized departments created the Tōkyō Kaisei Gakkō – the Tokyo Kaisei School. N. Hozumi highlights this moment as the beginning of the English School because in addition to teaching law in English, legal education was focused on analysing the common law system.

In 1875, the Tokyo Kaisei School management board recommended 11 regular and preparatory students to the Ministry of Justice, who were sent to the United States for legal education. This group also included four law graduates with the highest final-year results: Kazuo Hatoyama, Jutarō Komura, Takeo Kikuchi and Jūichirō Saitō. T. Kikuchi and J. Saitō were accepted by Boston University,[68] while K. Hatoyama studied at Columbia University and J. Komura at Harvard University.[69] They all received a unique opportunity to obtain a professional title in the United States, becoming the first licensed attorneys in the history of Japan. The following year, another three law students were sent to the United Kingdom.[70] N. Hozumi was one of them, yet he had to secure financial support from his adoptive family before he started his education at the University of London.[71]

In the early period of the school's educational activity, it struggled with a shortage of foreign teachers. Anglo-American Law was taught by only two jurists: Charles Tarring from the United Kingdom and, previously mentioned, H. Terry from the United States.[72]

64 Amano, 2004, p. 20.

65 Takatani, Koishikawa, 2018, p. 220.

66 Tōkyō Kaisei Gakkō Ichiran, Meiji 8-nen 2-gatsu

67 Initially, most of the English language lectures concerned the analysis of English law, but soon law became a separate subject. Itō, 1966, p. 261.

68 Shichinobe, 2009h, pp. 81–83.

69 Katayama, 2011, pp. 14–15.

70 Amano, 2004, p. 39.

71 Shichinobe, 2009c, pp. 64–66.

72 Itō, 1966, p. 262; Takayanagi, 1955, p. 60.

In February 1877, Hiroyuki Katō, a distinguished political and educational activist closely associated with the imperial court, who supported the westernization of Japan and the introduction of a constitutional monarchy, became the new director of the Tokyo Kaisei School. After the incorporation of the medical department in April, the school changed its name to Tōkyō Daigaku – the University of Tokyo. The university consisted of four faculties – Medicine, Law, Humanities and Science – which alluded directly to the European model of higher education.[73]

In 1880, the Old University of Tokyo established the first graduate school to educate the first independent Japanese academics, including people holding a Doctor of Laws degree.[74] A specialist legal course was also created for future judges, attorneys and prosecutors. In June 1881, after the reform of the higher and specialized education system, the Old University of Tokyo gained the status of the leading university in Japan. To unify the public law schools within one academic centre, the Ministry of Education secured the consent of the Ministry of Justice to incorporate the Law School at the Ministry of Justice into the Old University of Tokyo in 1885. Although the Meiji government merged the rival French and English Schools, each retained its autonomy within separate departments of the Faculty of Law. Despite this formal division, English was still the dominant language at the Old University of Tokyo, with Japanese the primary spoken language during the lectures and workshops.

In December 1885, following the American trends, lectures on politics were transferred to the Faculty of Law, which enabled the establishment of Hōsei Gakubu – the Faculty of Law and Politics. In March of the following year, pursuant to the imperial rescript, the Old University of Tokyo was renamed Teikoku Daigaku – the Imperial University. It also became Japan's first national academic centre which had the right to grant academic and professional titles.[75] Teikoku Daigaku, however, was not subject to the Special Ministerial Regulation on the Supervision of Private Law Schools of November 1886 and thus was not included in the so-called "Big Five" as the model university in Japan. During that period, the Faculty of Law and Politics comprised two institutes employing 11 lecturers – three foreign and seven Japanese Professors and one Japanese Assistant Professor.[76] In the first 11 years of its educational activity, 52 lawyers graduated from the university.[77]

During the Civil Code Controversy, jurists employed by the Imperial University mostly supported the factions depending on their affiliation with the English or

[73] Amano, 2004, p. 27.

[74] Terasaki, 2007, pp. 70–71.

[75] Amano, 2004, pp. 89–90, 230.

[76] Within the Institute of Law there were Departments of English, French and German Law.

[77] Amano, 2004, p. 98.

French Schools. Although N. Hozumi did not assign the Imperial University to any of the parties to the dispute,[78] the Faculty of Law and Politics was the first academic centre of the English School, which educated not only the first generation of Japanese jurists studying Anglo-American Law but also the first licensed attorneys in Japan, experts in case and statute law.

3.2.2. Senshū School

Senshū Gakkō – the Senshū School – was founded in September 1880 in Tokyo by four Japanese lawyers and economists (Nagatame Sōme, Inajirō Tajiri, Tanetarō Megata and Shigeta Koma) who in the second half of the 1870s completed their scholarships abroad at prestigious universities in the United States.[79] It was a private night school, and its course lasted two years. The Senshū School was created in response to the Ministry of Justice Resolution of 1876 concerning the establishment of state examinations for licensed lawyers. The high requirements and great interest in obtaining a professional title among law students were noticed by the founders of the Senshū School, who had extensive experience in working with American and Japanese courts and belonged to an organized group of attorneys, established in December 1875 in New York, known as Nihon Hōritsu Gaisha – the Japanese Law Firm. Since they intended to focus on turning the theoretical skills through legal practice, their academic centre was named *senshū* – specialization.

The Senshū School consisted of two institutes: Law and Economics. Anglo-American Law, understood as common law and statute law, was taught in English and Japanese. Compared to the Law School at the Ministry of Justice and the Old University of Tokyo, perfect English language skills were not required from candidates, which was also an opportunity for candidates who had not previously attended specialized language courses or had not completed scholarships abroad. For this reason, most lectures were held in Japanese; as an exception, the specialist exam in the last semester was carried out in English. To meet the formal requirements of the Ministry of Education regarding the education of lawyers, the course was extended to three years starting from July 1883.

In July 1886, the school came under the supervision of the Imperial University but remained a private university specializing in courses for legal practitioners.[80] Based on the Special Ministerial Regulation for the Supervision of Private Law Schools of November 1886, the Senshū School was included in the "Big Five" of

[78] Hozumi, 1980, p. 331.

[79] Hozumi, 1980, p. 331.

[80] Amano, 2004, pp. 151–152.

Law Schools in Japan.[81] Two years later, in August, it received from the Ministry of Justice a special licence to grant professional titles.[82] By then, it also started to publish transcripts of lectures on law and economics regularly, which became a subject of debate for attorneys from the English School and French School practitioners.[83]

By the time the Civil Code Controversy broke out, seven cohorts of Japanese lawyers had left the walls of the Senshū School. Its graduates, the English School representatives, supported the postulates of the postponement faction.

3.2.3. Tokyo Vocational School

Tōkyō Senmon Gakkō – the Tokyo Vocational School – was founded in October 1882 in Tokyo by one of the leading politicians of the Meiji era, Shigenobu Ōkuma. Observing the interest in English-related subjects, he decided to promote knowledge about politics, economics and law.[84] Contrary to the classical organization of the departments at the Old University of Tokyo, he merged the Institute of Politics with the Institute of Economics, thus creating the Seiji-Keizai Gakka unit (The Institute of Politics and Economy). Law as a separate discipline had its own institute within the general Faculty of Humanities. In addition to carrying out educational activities, S. Ōkuma's goal was to "improve the quality of political life in the country, as well as to promote legal research".[85] From 1868 to 1881, Japan witnessed several violent political crises. By "improving the quality of political life", he meant the peaceful development of the domestic party system, which would open political discourse and encourage the citizens (as individuals forming the nation) to express their views.[86] According to S. Ōkuma, the law was an essential factor of political stabilization, which had to protect the internal order and harmonize Japanese society. The role model for S. Ōkuma was the Anglo-American legal system with its well-educated and mindful lawyers. He did not hide the fact that his goal was to educate a group of legal practitioners rather than theoreticians. Therefore, he tried to influence the Meiji government to introduce legal profession regulations based on the British or American model.[87]

In the first cohort, the Tokyo Vocational School recruited 78 candidates, but it admitted an additional group of 74 students during the academic year.[88] In accord-

81 Shiritsu Hōritsu Gakkō Tokubetsu Kantoku Jōki.
82 Senshū Daigaku no Enkaku.
83 Senshū Gakkō Hōritsu Kōgi Hikki.
84 Waseda Daigaku, 1932, pp. 16–18.
85 Yoshii, 1992, p. 43.
86 Nakamura, 1972, p. 177.
87 Piegzik, 2016, pp. 69–84.
88 Waseda Daigaku, 1932, p. 46.

ance with the Ministry of Education guidelines on higher education standards, the legal course lasted three years. In September 1883, year-long preparatory courses were also launched to even out the level of school candidates. In a short time, it gained a good reputation. The school's fame was reflected in the fact that many influential Japanese politicians and educational activists appeared at the graduation ceremony of the first cohort in July 1884. In May 1885, each of the institutes began publishing transcripts of lectures, and the student organizations (including the law section) announced the call for texts for specialized journals. In September of the same year, the institutes were renamed faculties.

Under the Special Ministerial Regulation for the Supervision of Private Law Schools of November 1886, the Tokyo Vocational School was included in the "Big Five" of Law Schools, receiving a special licence from the Ministry of Justice to grant legal professional titles. Like the Senshū School, it also came under the supervision of the Imperial University, and the legal course was extended to four years. With the reorganization of the faculties in November 1887, the curriculum provided two legal programmes in Japanese or English. The most significant innovation compared to other centres was the fact that students could attend both programmes at the same time.

Although in the early 1890s, the Tokyo Vocational School also employed lecturers who were French School graduates, it remained an academic centre strongly bonded with the English School. During the Civil Code Controversy, the graduates and the staff mostly supported the postponement faction.

Today, Waseda University is a continuator of the Tokyo Vocational School.

3.2.4. School of English Law

Igirisu Hōritsu Gakkō – the School of English Law – was established in July 1885 in Tokyo by three Japanese jurists and English School representatives: R. Masujima, N. Hozumi and T. Kikuchi.[89] According to the programme declaration, the founders' main goal was to promote knowledge about Anglo-American Law and create a substantial legal library for lawyers studying common law "in the spirit of the English School".[90] It should also be noted that, apart from the motives indicated in the solemn declaration, the school was established in response to the superior influence of the French School in the Ministry of Justice. From the beginning, the School of English Law employed 18 jurists, graduates or people professionally connected with the Old University of Tokyo, who supported a greater emphasis on legal practice

[89] The school received formal permission to conduct educational activities from the Ministry of Education in July 1885, but the inauguration ceremony took place two months later.

[90] Yoshii, 1992, p. 347.

and promoting liberal thoughts. Despite financial difficulties in the initial period, the school functioned thanks to the annual subsidy from the Ministry of Justice.

Pursuant to the Special Ministerial Regulation for the Supervision of Private Law Schools of November 1886, the School of English Law was included in the "Big Five" of Schools of Law and received a special licence from the Ministry of Justice to grant professional titles.[91] In October 1889, it changed its name to the Tōkyō Hōgakuin – the Tokyo Graduate School of Law.

During the Civil Code Controversy, the School of English Law and the Imperial University formed a joint position in the postponement faction, becoming the greatest opponents of the Code.

3.3. German School of legal scholarship

The German School was the youngest of the three schools of legal jurisprudence in Japan. Its late establishment compared to the French and English Schools resulted mainly from political factors, particularly the turbulent unification process, which influenced the shape of the German legal system in the second half of the 19th century. Although Bismarcksche Reichsverfassung – the Constitution of the German Empire – entered into force in May 1871, the Second Reich was still a country with a non-unified legal system. Like Japan, it decided to introduce new national codes, yet the drafting process and the motives for codification were different.

It should be noted that the development of the German School and education about German law in Japan were not identical to the influence of German law on changes in the Japanese political and legal system.[92] Most Japanese and Western researchers emphasize that the constitutional monarchy introduced in Japan in 1889 directly derived from the Prussian-German model.[93] The Meiji government consulted the draft of the Constitution with four German advisers: Rudolf von Gneist, Lorentz von Stein, Albert Mosse and Hermann Roesler.[94] Despite the federal structure of the Second Reich, the German theory of state supremacy, governed by the rule of law principle, appealed more to Japanese political elites than the unstable

[91] Shiritsu Hōritsu Gakkō Tokubetsu Kantoku Jōki.

[92] Itō, 1966, p. 218.

[93] Karaś, Suzuki, 2008, pp. 65–66; Martin, Wetzler, 1990, pp. 77– 88; Górski, 2003, pp. 43–52. Some researchers also see British influence, such as the Westminster system in parliament, on the Meiji Constitution; Hein, 2009, p. 72.

[94] R. von Gneist and L. von Stein provided advice to the Japanese diplomatic mission that came to Europe (Berlin and Vienna) in 1882 at the behest of H. Itō, while A. Mosse and H. Roesler went to Japan, where they were employed on government contracts.

representative government strictly controlled by parliament.[95] M. Itō expressed that German law, apart from the Constitution and codes, had also considerably affected the organization of Japanese courts and the public administration system.[96]

Japanese jurists of the Meiji era knew that Germany (or German states before unification) had an independent legal tradition based mainly on old Roman law with elements of Germanic law.[97] Additionally, N. Hozumi explained that Japanese jurisprudence was well acquainted with the details of the dispute between the historical school of law represented by F. von Savigny and the positivist school of A. Thibaut, although the Japanese jurists analysed it from a historical perspective.[98]

The Japanese assessment of the German legal system, especially private law, was ambiguous. Apart from the positively evaluated Allgemeines Deutsches Handelsgesetzbuch – the Commercial Code of 1861 for the German Confederation – the Prussian Landrecht was criticized, particularly by the French School representatives, whose legal education was based on postulates of the French Revolution and theory and philosophy of law promoted by the great Enlightenment thinkers.[99] Japanese jurists also perceived Germany as striving to unify and modernize its statutory law system. Yet, after the first negative experiences of the Meiji government from the 1870s regarding the drafting of the Civil Code, they understood the German difficulties concerning adopting customary law into the Code. The establishment of the German Civil Law Codification Commission in 1874 was perceived internationally as an announcement of a thorough reform of the outdated Prussian Landrecht. Still, the first measurable effects of the draft were not published until February 1888.[100] Even then, the new German civil law was not introduced as the first draft of the national civil code and met with disapproval from part of the German jurisprudence.[101]

H. Roesler was undoubtedly the most influential German jurist in Japan during the Meiji era. He was initially employed as an adviser to the Meiji government; the Ministry of Justice asked him to draft a Commercial Code and actively advise the Japanese committee which drafted the Constitution. H. Roesler's contribution to

[95] Beckmann, 1957, p. 7.

[96] Itō, 1966, p. 227.

[97] Köbler, Satō, 1999, pp. 224–225; Iwamura, 1996, p. 115.

[98] Hozumi, 1980, pp. 344–348.

[99] K. Ume criticized the vague content, excessive size and archaic systematics of the Prussian Landrecht; Murakami, 2011b, pp. 217–220.

[100] Some French legal historians mention about 20 years of drafting the new German Civil Code; de La Mazelière, 1991, p. 128.

[101] In February 1888, the first draft of the German Civil Code was described by the Japanese jurists, who noted that there was still a long time before the draft would be published due to the different views among German jurisprudence. See Nihon no Hōritsu, 2008, pp. 273–274; for more about the German jurists' opinions on the draft of the Civil Code, see Iwamura, 1996, p. 172.

reforming the Japanese legal system has often been compared to G. Boissonade, although he was not as famous as his French colleague among Japanese jurisprudence.[102] Still, the Japanese cabinet had great confidence in H. Roesler's skills and ability to assess European legislation. In 1887, Prime Minister H. Itō asked him to present a written opinion on the French Civil Code. Despite being in the final stages of work on the draft of the Civil Code, H. Itō feared that French law might promote a too-individualistic approach to private law and thus provoke chaos in Japanese society. In the late 1880s, Japanese political elites became more interested in German civil law (though not yet codified) and noticed that it protected traditional family ties and conservative values. When H. Roesler presented his opinion on the Napoleonic Code, the Meiji government started to doubt whether it had chosen the proper civil law as the basis for drafting the Japanese Civil Code. He strongly criticized the French Civil Code, as it promoted egalitarianism, weakened family relations, rejected the idea of the head of the family, and advocated democratic solutions in law. In short, he described French private law principles characteristic to revolutionary ideas. In addition, after the publication of the draft of the first book of the German Civil Code in 1888, the Meiji cabinet recognized that German private law was based on Roman law like the French counterpart, but it considered the smallest agricultural household, not a natural person, as the basis of society, which perfectly reflected the Japanese traditional social structure.[103]

The German School advocated *dantaishugi* – collectivism – which contradicted *kojinshugi* – individualism – promoted by the French and English Schools. The German School also rejected formal gender equality, focusing on preserving traditional family ties and gender functions in the household. Like the English School, it emphasized the need to research Japanese customary law, but it was neutral towards it, treating the issue of its inclusion in the Civil Code as a secondary matter. From the economic perspective, the German School encouraged protecting property rights and the freedom to enter civil law contracts.

At the beginning of the Civil Code Controversy, there was only one independent academic centre of the German School in Japan. Although the Old University of Tokyo had a separate Department of German Law within the Faculty of Law and Politics, it had significantly fewer students than the thriving Departments of English and French Law. In 1890–1893, which marked a turning point in the history of Japanese legal education, only 33 students graduated.[104] According to Masutarō Niida, Japanese jurisprudence even denied the existence of a separate German School for a long time. Nevertheless, it should be noted that by the time the Civil

[102] Suzuki, Siemes, 1941, p. 66.

[103] Arichi, 1971, pp. 95–123.

[104] Itō, 1966, p. 227.

Code Controversy was resolved, 69 graduates had completed a legal course at the German School.[105]

The German School took a neutral position in the Civil Code Controversy, and its representatives were divided between the decisive and postponement factions. The decisive faction was supported by Kuniomi Yokota,[106] Keizaburō Motō and Shūichi Kinoshita. The postponement party was supported by Atsushi Kawashima, Yatsuka Hozumi,[107] Keijirō Okano and Miyoji Itō. Keiroki Tsuzumi and Junrokurō Shiba, two other influential German School representatives, did not present a clear position and thus did not belong to any faction. Although the German School was the youngest and least numerous law school in Japan, it soon gained significant influence in drafting the Meiji Civil Code due to the victory of the postponement faction in the Controversy. For example, the Drafting Committee eventually rejected the systematics proposed by G. Boissonade and the French School and adopted the pandectic systematics advocated by the German School.[108] According to M. Itō, the peak of its popularity was on the date of entry into force of the Meiji Civil Code.

The following subsection presents the emergence and development of the only independent academic centre of the German School, which was established in Japan before the beginning of the Civil Code Controversy.

3.3.1. German Academic Association School

Doitsu Gakkyōkai Gakkō – the German Academic Association School – was established as a successor to Doitsu Gakkyōkai – the German Academic Association – and founded in September 1881 in Tokyo with the aim to promote German/Prussian cultural patterns in Japan. Its founders were two meritorious educational activists of the Meiji era: Amane Nishi and H. Katō.[109] The latter was one of the first Japanese jurists who travelled to Germany, in 1860–1868, to learn about local law and customs. His German language skills and extensive contacts in Berlin enabled him in October 1883 to transform the Association into a private school of German politics and law, known as being at the second degree: a secondary school according to the old Japanese education system.[110] Its curriculum was based on the thoughts of the

[105] Niida, 1943, p. 18.

[106] Shichinobe, 2009g, pp. 67–69.

[107] Shichinobe, 2010f, pp. 56–58.

[108] In addition to pandectic systematics, Western and Japanese legal historians also emphasize the general influence of the German Law School on the development of the Meiji Civil Code, especially concerning the theory of law and dogmatic issues; Röhl, 2005, p. 27; Itō, 1966, p. 224.

[109] Kawahara, 2000, pp. 33–45.

[110] Shingū, Doitsu Gakkyōkai Gakkō no Tankan.

German Enlightenment, and it rejected the arguments of the Historical School of Jurisprudence opposed to any codification.[111]

Notwithstanding the founders' intentions to educate about German cultural patterns, the school aspired to focus on teaching about German law and politics. In July 1885, after hiring additional lecturers from Japanese law and politics graduates, Doitsu Gakkyōkai Gakkō established a five-year general course and a two-year specialist course for lawyers. Candidates who turned 14 could be admitted to the school and then proceed through a three-year preparatory course in the German language, the history of Western countries and Japan, and traditional kanji characters. In the following years, students learned about criminal, international, civil and administrative law and the theory and philosophy of law.[112] The course was not limited to legal subjects, as the study of kanji characters and historiography was also continued, introducing the basics of economics. This project would not have been possible without the financial support of the Ministry of Justice,[113] the Ministry of Education and private donors, including the Faculty of Law of Kyushu University.

In 1885, the first German Doctor of Laws, Georg Michaelis, was employed at the German Academic Association School. He was soon joined by other lecturers of German nationality: H. Roesler, Felix Delbrück, Ernst Delbrück, Ludwig Löhnholm, Johannes Wernicke, Otto Herring, Karl Rathgen and Otfreid Nippold.[114] Due to the recent transformation, the school was not included in the Special Ministerial Regulation on the Supervision of Private Law Schools of November 1886. It thus was not mentioned among the "Big Five" of Law Schools. Despite this, in 1887, the school received a licence from the Ministry of Justice to grant academic and professional titles in law.

During the Civil Code Controversy, the school did not side with the decisive or the postponement factions, and its few representatives presented their own opinions in the debate, depending on their views on the Code. Due to the lack of financial resources and problems with the academic staff, in 1895, the German Academic Association School was subordinated to the Department of German Law at the Imperial University.

111 Piegzik, 2015, p. 79.

112 Katada, 1995, pp. 35–38.

113 The Ministry of Justice supported private initiatives to establish law schools because it wanted to educate a group of lawyers in a short time.

114 Katada, 1995, pp. 48–55.

3.4. The birth of the Japanese School of legal scholarship

The upbringing of subsequent generations of Japanese jurists, who gradually assumed posts in various state offices or decided to run their own businesses, forced the Japanese jurisprudence to change the approach towards long-term legal education and professional training policies. At the end of the 1880s, the Ministry of Justice expressed the need to establish the first independent academic centre of Japanese law. Moving away from teaching foreign law, the centre intended to focus on studying the domestic legal system, which expanded yearly with new legal acts and judicial decisions.[115] In addition to the statute law, the Ministry of Justice emphasized the understanding of customary law, looking at it through the prism of Japan's general social conditions and culture, including the lower and upper classes.

The direct motive for establishing the first Japanese School was promulgating the Constitution of the Empire of Japan in February 1889. As the Ministry of Justice foresaw, the new basic law required professional teaching and binding interpretation provided by an independent academic centre, formally separated from each of the three foreign law schools. In just two months, it prepared a programme declaration and, in September, obtained the consent of the Ministry of Education to establish a new school. In October 1889, the official inauguration of Nihon Hōritsu Gakkō – the Japanese Law School – took place in Tokyo.[116] Its founders were 11 jurists gathered around the Ministry of Justice. Three of them were rewarded during the ceremony: a leading representative, Michisaburō Miyagi; the Minister of Justice, A. Yamada; and one of the authors of the Constitution of the Empire of Japan, Kintarō Kaneko, who was also appointed as the first director of the Japanese Law School.

The Japanese School quickly secured financial support from the Ministry of Justice. According to the programme announcement, its curriculum included Japanese statutory law, understood as constitutional law, civil law, criminal law, criminal procedure law, civil procedure law, administrative law and regulations concerning the organization of court work. Graduates of secondary schools could apply for the school. In January 1890, the legal education path was reorganized into a two-year optional preparatory course and a compulsory three-year law course finishing with obtaining the Bachelor of Laws degree.

The first cohort, comprising 46 graduates, left the walls of the Japanese School in July 1893. Although the school did not officially participate in the Civil Code Controversy, its lecturers included French and English School representatives, who privately expressed their opinions on the Code.

[115] Kokugakuin Daigaku, 1970–1979, pp. 100–102.

[116] Fujiwara, 1987, pp. 14–22.

Establishing the first independent Japanese School marked the epochal change in the history of Japanese legal education, becoming the symbolic end of the dominance of foreign law in university curriculums. Notably, the Ministry of Justice not only founded a new school focusing on teaching and researching domestic statute law but also reconciled the French and English School representatives in one academic centre, which allowed for the development of more professional and complex comparative law studies in Japan.

3.5. Summary of legal scholarship schools in Japan from the Civil Code Controversy perspective

The Civil Code Controversy in 1889–1892 was a public debate between French and English School representatives, with little participation from the German School. Differences in the views of Japanese jurists on the Civil Code resulted from a different path in their legal education. The French School representatives belonged in the vast majority to the decisive faction and the English School representatives to the postponement faction. There were some notable exceptions to this rule, as mentioned in this chapter; however, the French and English Schools often underlined their unity and common goals. The views of the German School representatives were not uniform, and they were divided between two existing factions with no visible majority on one of the sides.

Representatives of all schools acquired their law degrees in Japan and became the first members of Japanese jurisprudence. As well as holding a degree in one of the systems of positive law (French, English or German), they were well acquainted with the theory and philosophy of law and had a practical knowledge of at least one foreign language.

Table 1 presents essential information about all three schools of legal scholarship participating in the Civil Code Controversy and their attitude towards the Code.

Table 1: General characteristics of the three law schools in Meiji-era Japan and their views on the Code.

	French School	English School	German School
Date of establishment of the first independent academic centre	1871	1874	1885
Largest academic centre	The Law School at the Ministry of Justice	The Old University of Tokyo/Imperial University	The German Academic Association School
Faction affiliation	Decisive	Postponement	No clear affiliation
Affiliation to a doctrine or movement in the legal scholarship	Natural law doctrine; "firm" legal positivism	Legal evolution doctrine; analytical jurisprudence; "soft" legal positivism	Legal dogmatics principle; pandectic systematics; "firm" legal positivism
Dominant worldview	Individualism; economic liberalism; social progressivism; egalitarianism; internationalism; free market capitalism	Individualism; economic liberalism; social conservatism; exclusivity; nationalism; free market capitalism	Collectivism; economic liberalism; social conservatism; bureaucratism; nationalism; state capitalism
Postulated shape of the Civil Code	Reception of the French Civil Code and parts of domestic customary law (Family and Succession Law)	Drafting of the Civil Code by using the comparative law method with the dominant role of domestic customary law	Drafting of the Civil Code by using the comparative law method while considering Japanese customary law and adopting pandectic systematics
Attitude towards domestic customary law	Extremely negative or indifferent	Positive	Mostly neutral or moderately positive

CHAPTER FOUR

THE FIRST STAGE OF THE CIVIL CODE CONTROVERSY – THE DISPUTE UNTIL THE PUBLICATION OF THE CODES

Abstract

This chapter presents the first stage of the Controversy between April 1889 and April 1890. The time limits of the first stage are marked by the critical opinion of the Association of Jurists on the draft Civil Code, publicly announced and presented to Prime Minister Kiyotake Kuroda, and the publication part of the Civil Code regarding Property Law, Security and Evidence by A. Yamagata's cabinet.

Keywords: Civil Code Controversy, Japanese Civil Code, Codification in Japan

"Drafting codes is not the same as publishing legal papers based on independent research, as it also requires more extended observation of established domestic customs. Despite their beautiful form, logical structure and novelty, codes will not become flawless works if they are contrary to local customs."

—Association of Jurists, A written opinion to the Prime Minister Kuroda, May 22nd year of the Meiji era [1889]

4.1. The beginning of the Civil Code Controversy

4.1.1. The Association of Jurists' opinion (English School, postponement faction)

Japanese legal scholars unanimously identify the beginning of the Civil Code Controversy as being 27 April 1889. At that time, during the general assembly of Hōgakushi Kai – the Association of Jurists – six English School representatives, graduates of the Old University of Tokyo/Imperial University,[1] Kinosuke Yamada, Teruhiko Okamura, Hajime Genda, Takeo Kikuchi, Masamichi Aikawa and Rokuichirō Masujima,[2] passed unequivocally a resolution to submit an official

[1] Hoshino, 1943, p. 119.

[2] Nakagawa, 2016, pp. 35–60.

proposal to postpone the promulgation of the Civil Code and the Commercial Code.[3] The resolution, supplemented with a written opinion, was of fundamental importance for the public debate on the draft Civil Code. It was not only officially handed to Prime Minister K. Kuroda and Chairman of the Privy Council of Japan (*Sūmitsuin*),[4] H. Itō, but also published on 16 May as an official statement from part of Japanese jurisprudence, particularly the English School. Since this opinion initiated a Controversy that lasted over three years, its whole content is presented below:

> The Association of Jurists' opinion on the drafting of the Codes
> 法典編纂ニ関スル法学士会ノ意見
> Hōten Hensan ni kansuru Hōgakushi Kai no Iken
>
> From the beginning, the codification process lacked a substantial and broader discussion, although similar projects are being carried out in European countries such as Germany or the United Kingdom. Many legal scholars have been involved in the project, and many years of hard work have been devoted to submitting several drafts. Eventually, we have reached the point where official promulgation is expected. It is known that such a demanding project requires caution, but we can hear rumours that the government is not only actively supporting the effort to codify the law but also plans to announce [the missing codes] soon. We are concerned that introducing this law in our country is a great mistake and the wrong way to complete this undoubtedly most challenging project. We still hope that it will not happen. Considering that Japanese legal scholarship and legal education system are still developing, and both are far behind the United Kingdom and Germany, which also encountered issues with drafting codes, we want to express admiration for the codification process in our country. Whether the law should be codified is ambiguous and is still a matter of debate for Western jurisprudence. The law should follow social development. However, once a code is in force, as more loopholes and flaws are discovered, changes cannot be made smoothly, despite the awareness of defective norms. If there are loopholes in the law, they must be filled; if there are any bad habits, they must be discussed and changed by a code, making it easy for citizens to act in accordance with the law understandable for them. The law should also be created by observing the needs of the people who are ultimately supposed to be bound by it. When drafting codes, we should avoid introducing numerous amendments, trying to anticipate the direction of social changes. Before enacting any law, we must be sure that people will not suffer because of it. This is the reason why scholars cannot draft codes of law.

[3] Hozumi, 1980, p. 333.

[4] The Privy Council was an advisory body to the emperor of Japan, with certain judiciary and executive powers. It was established on 30 April 1888 as a body modelled on the British Privy Council, but in practice, it served as an office that in the future could limit the influence of the Japanese parliament, especially the lower house.

In European countries, those who draft the codes only modify existing laws and regulations. Even if they introduce new laws in some areas, they do it to adapt customary law to present-day challenges. The codification process in our country looks entirely different. The law will be primarily based on European law, and the promise to protect good old customs is only a game of appearances, especially since there has never been a debate on the shape of the new law. Additionally, the draft of the Commercial Code was prepared by a German and the draft of the Civil Code by a Frenchman. We have no choice but to review these drafts thoroughly, not because we wish to quarrel or oppose the introduction of any codes, but because we see significant differences in views between our law schools.

We do not argue with the fact that the government has set up a committee for the codification of law, but we hope that the codes will not be promulgated in a hurry. Despite the official abolition of feudalism and the implementation of thorough reforms, Japanese society had not changed radically. We cannot follow the path of the old feudal system, but neither should we copy the Western patterns, especially considering our old customs, which should be included in the codes. Nor can codification difficulties be overcome by force because people will suffer from the complex and contradictory nature of the law.

In the present-day world, statutory law describes only things necessary to regulate. Drafting codes is not the same as publishing legal papers based on independent research, as it also requires more extended observation of established domestic customs. Despite their beautiful form, logical structure and novelty, codes will not become flawless works if they are contrary to local customs. If the codes are to bind people efficiently, the government should make the drafts publicly available and give more time to collect critical opinions so that after the amendments are discussed, the whole project can be completed.

Association of Jurists
May 22nd year of the Meiji era [1889][5]

The opinion of the Association of Jurists raised five fundamental issues regarding the publication of new codes. One of these was the criticism of the cabinet's hasty legislative policy. According to the English School representatives, the draft of the Civil Code prepared by G. Boissonade and his team of Japanese jurists not only excessively copied the French Civil Code but also did not adopt the proven and beneficial domestic customary law despite official statements. While the Association of Jurists was not against codifying private law, it believed that the methodology of drafting regulations adopted by the Law Research Committee could have negative social consequences. In particular, as a centre supporting the conservative views

[5] The author's translation of the letter. The translation was modified in some parts to understand better the context of comparisons or metaphors in old Japanese. For a full opinion of the Association of Jurists in Japanese, see Hoshino, 2014, pp. 14–15.

on law, they feared that an overly hasty and radical reform of private law would disrupt the Japanese transformation from feudalism to capitalism due to the drastic contradictions between statutory and customary law practised by people for centuries.[6] Besides the project itself, the Association of Jurists criticized the attitude of the cabinet, which did not hold a public debate on Codes and trusted foreign law experts more than Japanese jurists. The postponement faction did not deny the efforts and professional skills of the authors of the Codes. Yet, it unequivocally called the cabinet to refrain from publishing the Commercial Code and Civil Code until a joint position of jurisprudence was established. If they agreed on norms fitting into Japanese social conditions, they believed that Codes would not have to be amended in the following years.

4.1.2. R. Masujima's opinion (English School, postponement faction)

The opinion of the Association of Jurists was clarified by one of its authors, attorney R. Masujima. On 1 June 1889, he published an article entitled "Discussing the Opinion of the Association of Jurists" in the legal journal *Hōri Seika – The Quintessence of Jurisprudence* (Volume 2, Issue 12), founded at the beginning of 1889 as the journal promoting the English School's worldview.[7]

Referring to the authority of the members of the Association of Jurists, graduates of the prestigious Old University of Tokyo/Imperial University, who held various positions in the judiciary and worked as professional attorneys or government officials, R. Masujima expressed his full support for the critical opinion concerning the Civil Code and the Commercial Code. He wrote that all domestic political issues should be analysed through public debate. The Association of Jurists, conscious of the inevitable changes directly affecting Japan, felt responsible for protecting the social order. He argued that the submission of the written opinion on the Codes was supposed to initiate an exchange of ideas between Japanese jurists and thus positively impact the shape of both Codes.

After quoting the full text of the Association of Jurists' opinion, in the latter part of the article R. Masujima commented on its most important message to the cabinet and jurists. First, he emphasized that the nation's history must not be wholly disregarded in any codification process. He expressed his concern that adopting foreign law without first ensuring it could be applied to Japanese social and political conditions would become a grand experiment of the Drafting Committee. R. Masujima also admitted that regardless of the sympathy or antipathy towards the codification of law, Japan needed the Codes. According to him, the law was not only

[6] Nakagawa, 2015, pp. 349–380.

[7] Masujima, 1889, pp. 28–38.

a tool to protect the country and its people but also a fascinating phenomenon: it could promote progressive values, but at the same time, it could be artificial and imperfect. He stated that English, French and German law had advantages and disadvantages. However, as R. Masujima explained, foreigners should not be responsible for correcting these defects as a part of the law codification in Japan. He referred to the failed codification projects in the first decade of the Meiji era to prove that no one could complete the whole undertaking despite the urgent need to develop all the codes.

Opposing the natural law doctrine, R. Masujima argued that the law did not exist before human civilization, and its evolution was related to social changes and people's expectations. Thus, he claimed that legal theories described in research papers differed from the actual law. He emphasized that even if the jurists had theoretical knowledge and legal education, they could not create the law solving all "substantive and spiritual issues" without having experience in legal practice. He believed that employing theoreticians was the biggest mistake that could be made during the drafting process. The purpose of the law was primarily to protect the parties and create a framework for the judiciary to solve disputes. According to R. Masujima, separating the "substantive" and "spiritual" layers of law must lead to a conflict between the supporters of natural law and legal evolution doctrines. He wrote that the first one was senseless, especially considering the differences between people in Western countries and Japan. Even if the Drafting Committee adopted the natural law doctrine not directly but through various references to the French Civil Code, the outcome would still be disastrous, and ordinary people would bear the high costs of this experiment. Additionally, he wrote that law could not be called law until it was a genuine product of society.

Moving to the following contradiction, R. Masujima argued that Japanese society traditionally considered their country the most perfect globally. The indiscriminate adoption of any European legal system would only emphasize the civilizational superiority of the West. Having compared the failed implementation of foreign law to "a rotten fish that should be thrown into the water", he expressed the opinion that Japan should only imitate favourable and appropriate Western ideas and not focus on copying a distant civilization. He feared that the state would continue to develop contrary to its traditions after adopting foreign law. The role of the legislator was to listen to society's expectations and adapt the law to the most significant changes. R. Masujima believed all legal theories should be discussed if the legislation was to be carried out harmoniously. The final choice must be based on the consistency of national characteristics with the suggested law. He also persuaded the reader that people who knew history should criticize creating the temporary law with "a sword or a pen". Although the English School representative repeated his conviction that legislation must support the natural development of law, he stated that codification and rearranging the legal system is generally a good concept. For him, the legislator should always look after the interests of the citizens, treating the law as an effective tool and knowing that in the case of abstract law, the people could misinterpret it. He claimed that theories imported from Europe would remain European despite being in force in Japan and being ineptly translated into Japanese. He added that European law in Japan would become the same as the old Chinese Codes from the eighth century, which could not be interpreted without comprehensive knowledge in many fields.

R. Masujima did not undermine the competence of the people the Ministry of Justice hired. Yet, he regretted that the Japanese jurists who drafted the Civil Code could not accurately implement Western legal theories in Japan. To adopt a completely alien code, the Drafting Committee must not translate it section by section but find someone who has mastered its content and principles and has the skills necessary to introduce them to the Japanese legal system. He also argued that in addition to creating statutory law, the country needs to develop its legal scholarship and theories, which legal experts should research and analyse. Having shown that in the Tokyo metropolitan area, about 5,000 to 6,000 jurists have graduated from the various law schools, and this number would increase by one-fifth each year, R. Masujima was convinced that lawyers of the younger generation, despite holding a law degree, still had to focus on studying French and English law. He did not doubt that law codification in Japan was an experiment, but it would be useless work until the people started to use the law in practice. In addition, he criticized the politicians pushing Japan to catch up with foreign countries, as they did not develop any plan to preserve national sovereignty. In his opinion, only the solidarity of Japanese society could protect the country from harmful foreign influences. If Japanese men understood the legal ideas introduced by the government, the country had a chance to prevail in the battle to protect the national spirit. R. Masujima believed there was a solution to create a perfect law, but only ordinary people would suffer if the legal system were constantly revised by jurists lacking adequate skills. In such circumstances, the development of codes would not only be unnecessary but also pointless.

In the last paragraph, R. Masujima assured that the Association of Jurists' opinion was not a protest against global trends in jurisprudence. It was also not intended to obstruct the idea of establishing a Japanese parliament and the policy of revising unequal treaties. Its goal was to initiate a discussion on the substance of the law, its development, and legal traditions in Japan since the cabinet must not introduce the law, which would ridicule the citizens. The opinion was not intended to provoke a political crisis but to publicly raise allegations against the Codes by the English School representatives. He tried to persuade the readers that it was not an agitation to all citizens but an encouragement to seek unanimous views among people who supported and opposed the Codes. R. Masujima argued that the

Association of Jurists did not want to stand in the way of drafting codes because they cared about the interests of their state and the legal system. Fearing a misinterpretation of their motives, he explained that the English School representatives only presented their views on legal matters. Even if politicians eventually ignored them, he felt that the English School was obliged to present the criticism of new Japanese codes, which should not mislead society about their real nature.[8]

A vital aspect mentioned by R. Masujima, which was not expressed in the original opinion of the Association of Jurists, was the concern about protecting Japanese political and legal interests. He defended the country and Japanese people from international pressure, criticizing the careless copying of Western ideas. Despite noting that Japanese society and the legal system were behind the times, he also saw native elements that had to be retained by legislators to preserve national identity. R. Masujima also openly criticized the participation of foreign law experts in the codification project, doubting their competence to adapt the foreign legal system to Japanese social conditions. Calling for the unity of the Japanese during the reform of the state based on Western ideas, as well as supporting the widespread belief in Japanese society that their country was still the most developed state in the world despite many visible shortcomings, could also be perceived as promoting nationalistic and chauvinistic views. However, R. Masujima dissociated himself from any political and ideological motives and repeated the call of the Association of Jurists for a public debate on the Codes.

4.1.3. Zenjirō Tsuboya's opinion (English School, postponement faction)

Critical opinions on the Codes were not just published in *Hōri Seika*, which undoubtedly was the most influential legal journal gathering the majority of the postponement faction representatives. In June 1889, Z. Tsuboya, a graduate from the Department of Politics of the Senshū School, wrote the piece entitled "The Association of Jurists and Criticism of Drafting the Codes",[9] released in the academic journal *Nihon no Hōritsu – Japanese Law* (Volume 1, Issue 17).[10]

Z. Tsuboya described his impressions of the codification process in Japan by using the allegory of transplanting trees and flowers peculiar to Europe and Japan to a harsh climate to achieve the artificial effect of beauty. Having identified the

[8] For the full opinion text, see Hoshino, 2014, pp. 16–21.

[9] Tsuboya, 1889, (original pages are unknown).

[10] *Japanese Law* (*Nihon no Hōritsu*) was a journal, which has been published since 1888, formally unrelated to any school of legal scholarship. Its content focused on unbiased presentation of the positions of both sides of the Civil Code and the Commercial Code controversy, yet the editorial team expressed moderate support for the decisive faction. Murakami, 2008a, p. 269.

specific actions of the Meiji government regarding the reform of the legal system and support for the development of Japanese jurisprudence, he expressed concern that during the drafting of the Codes, foreign solutions were excessively copied, and domestic customary law was not sufficiently considered. He claimed that although the Code of Criminal Procedure and the draft of the Civil Code and Commercial Code looked flawless at first glance, they were nothing more than imitations of French and German law. Z. Tsuboya wrote that he was aware of the effort necessary to draft the Codes, but at the same time, he tried to explain the role of the Codes for the domestic legal system, which, apart from the beauty of the form, should function adequately in society. According to him, the Codes showed only the adoption of French and German customary law, which could not resemble old Japanese customs due to geographical and social differences. He argued that German and French laws were effective only in Germany and France. Referring to the ongoing process of civil law codification in Germany, the English School representative mentioned that German jurisprudence had confirmed the importance of old customs and discussed their direct implementation in the new code. He felt disappointed by the rejection of domestic customary law during the codification process in Japan, using colloquial comparisons in his considerations. For example, he compared the straightforward translation of foreign law and introducing it on one's soil to "borrowing someone else's clothes, which at first glance are the wrong size". Z. Tsuboya did not consider himself a national traditionalist who uncritically trusted his beliefs, but on the other hand, he was convinced that "borrowing a foreign law", again compared to someone else's clothes, could not have a positive outcome.

Notably, Z. Tsuboya sympathized with the Association of Jurists' opinion, which was intended to raise the critical issue of thorough examination and adoption of domestic customary law in such essential works as the Codes. For him, translating French and German law and enacting it in Japan as Japanese law was arduous. He agreed with the statement that the revision of unequal treaties should not lead to the rapid adoption of Codes, which envisaged radical social changes designed by a group of jurists just opposed to domestic customary law. Z. Tsuboya argued that some of them were beneficial for Japanese society and, after careful incorporation into the statutory law, would constitute the real strength of the new Codes. He also highlighted that the discussion on the Codes should not be treated as denying the codification principle. Still, it was necessary to reassess the adopted drafting methodology and the speed at which the legislative procedure was carried out.[11]

[11] For the full opinion text, see Murakami, 2008a, pp. 296–299.

4.1.4. Keijirō Okano's opinion (English School, postponement faction)

On 5 July 1889, another opinion of the postponement faction regarding the Codes was published in *Hōri Seika* (Volume 3, Issue 14). It was entitled "Defending in the Name of the English Law".[12] Its author was K. Okano, a Faculty of Law and Politics of the Old University of Tokyo graduate.

K. Okano was the first English School representative not belonging to the Association of Jurists who commented on their opinion. In his article, he emphasized that there had been no serious legal discussion on the Codes in the Japanese press or academic journals. He admitted that the idea of codification was right and in line with the spirit of the times and expressed admiration for the great effort the legislators had to face. By contrast, he wrote negatively about the unnecessary haste in drafting the Codes and the cabinet's intention to publish them as soon as possible. In addition to the excessive speed of the legislative procedure, K. Okano noticed that the Codes did not implement Japanese customary law and elevated foreign legal systems to the pedestal. As a person concerned with protecting national interests, he supported the arguments of the Association of Jurists. He was scared that without prior agreement on a common position of Japanese jurisprudence, the codification of private law in Japan would result in disastrous failure.

Additionally, K. Okano wished to revise the common perception of English law as a legal system without any particular shape. Referring to a large group of Japanese jurists educated in the spirit of English law, he presented the most critical differences between the English, French and German School representatives. The English School representatives were to proudly study judicial decisions and customary law, while the French and German School representatives were to master their knowledge of the legal acts. K. Okano argued that the goal of the English School in the debate on the Codes was the identification of existing norms of Japanese customary law. He criticized the belief among Japanese jurisprudence that only the French and German School representatives should comment on the Codes. By giving examples of academic centres, he proved that the English School is one of Japan's two dominant schools of legal scholarship. He added that although English law had a non-statutory nature, unlike French and German law, its analysis was based on the interpretation of numerous court written decisions. The English School jurists were to be fully aware of the foundations and nuances of statutory law, and their comments on the Codes should not be regarded as less reliable. K. Okano generally opposed the depreciation of the English School since he believed it was a group of outstanding lawyers with theoretical and practical skills.[13]

[12] Okano, 1889, pp. 24–27.

[13] For the full opinion text, see Hoshino, 2014, pp. 21–22.

4.1.5. Yoshito Okuda's opinion (English School, postponement faction)

Y. Okuda, a distinguished graduate of the Old University of Tokyo from the class of 1884, presented another independent voice on behalf of the postponement faction. On 1 August 1889, *Hōri Seika* (Volume 3, Issue 15) published his article entitled "Let's Analyse Deputy Minister of Justice Mitsukuri's Speech".[14]

Y. Okuda's polemic referred to the speech by Deputy Minister R. Mitsukuri, who made an address at the graduation ceremony at the Senshū School on 15 July 1889. In addition to young lawyers, numerous personalities also attended the ceremony and had the opportunity to listen to the congratulatory speech. Observing all the participants, Y. Okuda noticed that some "yawned from boredom" or stared at Deputy Minister R. Mitsukuri with a complete lack of understanding. As the author emphasized, he wanted to learn more about these attitudes and listened carefully to various opinions after the ceremony. Having seen the general confusion among the audience, Y. Okuda found it necessary to clarify the entire speech, especially for the English School representatives.

By comparing the statistics on the number of attorneys and judges to the number of court cases in Japan, R. Mitsukuri referred to his experience related to working with Japanese jurists. He considered lawyers from the English School to be more rigorous than their French School colleagues in contentious matters. Despite this, the English School representatives were not involved in drafting the codes because the United Kingdom was famous for the common law system with no codes. R. Mitsukuri knew that case law was complicated to study. Still, after crossing a specific level of erudition, the English School jurists who worked as judges not only had much theoretical knowledge but also could apply it in practice. For him, French School students had a much easier task since reading a code was compared to reading a letter with many points and annotations. Nevertheless, the most significant difficulty for representatives of both schools of legal jurisprudence, which each had stronger and weaker points, was the correct application of legal norms.

In his speech, R. Mitsukuri explained the differences between the English and French Schools based on the attitude towards the codes. Yet, he stated that the cabinet must publish them soon to let Japan be among the countries with a fully codified legal system. He also believed that the interpretation of statutory law was the specialization of the French School, while the English School had some problems with it. If the English School jurists were going to learn the details of the positive law interpretation, he recommended that they enrol for a short specialist course.

Y. Okuda compared the silence that fell among the audience after saying these words to that "in a deserted village". He disagreed with R. Mitsukuri's argument,

[14] Okuda, 1889, pp. 4–10.

judging it as unfounded and unfair. In Y. Okuda's view, comparing judges from the French and English Schools was biased and unprofessional. He argued that the English School judges were in no way less intelligent than the French School ones. On the contrary, he believed his colleagues were often more precise and inquisitive. Y. Okuda generally did not support dividing lawyers into better and worse because of their legal education background (English or French law) since this would negatively impact the entire Japanese jurisprudence. He emphasized the fundamental and incomparable differences between the two legal systems and the lack of understanding of the difficulties faced by the English School of legal jurisprudence in Japan. Although the English School jurists did not feel offended by R. Mitsukuri, Y. Okuda recalled in a slightly malicious tone that he could not stop laughing because he knew the actual educational path of the English School lawyers. After completing their education in common law, they also studied statutory law. He tried to convince the reader that after reading the content of the regulations, English School lawyers could also interpret and apply the legal norm correctly. According to Y. Okuda, R. Mitsukuri's arguments (indicated as a French School representative) were ridiculous because to exclude the English School jurists from commenting on the provisions of legal acts, the Ministry of Justice should have forbidden them to read statutory law at all.

As a positive aspect of R. Mitsukuri's speech, Y. Okuda mentioned his awareness of the need to publish a commentary on the Codes. The Deputy Minister had a different view on the reasons for this statement, yet the author felt that the Codes in their current shape could cause harm to people so the commentary would be necessary. However, Y. Okuda's opinion focused on refuting the accusations against the English School that it should not interfere with the final shape of the Codes. Despite R. Mitsukuri's speech being far from depreciating the importance of the English School for Japanese jurisprudence, it was perceived as evidence of a lack of understanding of its profile among the French School representatives.[15]

4.1.6. Chū (Makoto) Egi's opinion (English School, postponement faction)

The subsequent opinion was presented by C. Egi, an advocate, a graduate of the Old University of Tokyo and one of the English School's key persons. His article "Criticism of the Book on Property Law in the Draft of Civil Code" was divided into three parts, published in *Hōri Seika* from October to December 1889 (Volume 4, Issue 19, Issue 21, Issue 22).[16]

[15] For the full opinion text, see Hoshino, 2014, pp. 22–25.

[16] Egi, 1889a, pp. 1–10; Egi, 1889b, pp. 1–5; Egi, 1889c, pp. 1–6.

C. Egi summarized the content of the Civil Code and the Commercial Code drafts and commented on the number of articles in both legal acts, identifying about 5,000 of them. He claimed that Japanese jurisprudence and scholars did not thoroughly discuss their content. Thus, the government's assurances that there were no reasons to worry about the Codes were insufficient for some jurists. C. Egi noted that the codification process had already taken ten years and could potentially be completed in another decade. For him, it was too soon to publish the Codes since preparing a commentary enabling their application was still necessary. The draft of the Civil Code, regardless of its French or English law foundations, should also refer to favourable Japanese customary law since history was an essential element of any legal system.

C. Egi expressed his astonishment that the Civil Code did not implement domestic customary law derived from Japanese legal history. According to him, the systematics of the Code was outdated, drafted like an academic textbook, and its content was as incomprehensible as ancient Chinese books. Fearing harmful consequences for Japanese society, he recommended refraining from publishing the Codes or preparing a commentary before they came into force. However, the best solution for him was to establish a joint position from the French, English and German Schools as they were the only ones with sufficient experience studying foreign legal systems. They could revise the content of the Codes to avoid introducing ineffective laws. The author understood and sympathized with global codification trends and wanted to avoid excessive criticism. Furthermore, he wanted to share his opinion on Property Law in the Civil Code.

C. Egi started his analysis with Article 1 and the definition of property rights, noting their patrimonial nature and imprecise meaning. He claimed that using the term *mukeijin* – an abstract person – in relation to a legal person may be incomprehensible to ordinary people without a legal education. He traced the origin of the term to an incorrect translation and cited as an example a straightforward word of a legal person in English law as part of a group of fictitious persons. He also argued that if the term "an abstract person" entered the Japanese legal terminology with the publication of the Code, it would be to the detriment of domestic legal scholarship, which should already use precise terminology at this stage.

In the next part, C. Egi criticized the formal division of rights into only two types: personal and real rights. He believed private law rights should be divided into three categories: personality, property and rights deriving from obligations. By personality rights, he understood the right to life, physical integrity, protection of reputation and a good name. For him, they were fundamental enough to be separated from personal and real rights, which had *kinsekiteki kakaku* – a measurable value. Additionally, C. Egi claimed a significant conflict of norms in Articles 2 and 3, which defined personal and real rights. Although the drafters of the Civil Code tried to present an exhaustive and clear division of rights based on French ideas, in reality, there were numerous factual situations in which personal and real rights were interwoven and hard to separate. Similarly, he assessed that including security in a separate book of a Civil Code was a mistake because it was a typical example of real rights. Despite C. Egi being aware that it was difficult to exhaustively separate personal and real rights, the division he postulated was supposed to be much more logical than that adopted in the French Civil Code.

C. Egi claimed that Article 6 of Property Law also contained a misinterpreted definition of a thing (good) borrowed directly from the Napoleonic Code, which was supposed to be contrary to global trends in legal scholarship. At the end of the 19th century, all material objects other than a human being were considered a thing. At the same time, the Civil Code retained the archaic division of things into *yūtaibutsu* – material goods that can be identified through the senses – and *mutaibutsu* – intangible goods. According to the Civil Code, material goods were products of human intelligence, which included: (1) rights directed towards things and a person, (2) copyrights, patent rights and rights vested in the inventor, and (3) common assets held after the liquidation of the enterprise or during its liquidation. C. Egi did not understand this solution and saw an apparent contradiction, particularly when juxtaposing it with the definition of real and personal rights provided by Articles 2 and 3. Although qualified lawyers prepared the draft, he feared the Code might be perceived as a work full of inconsistencies. He underlined the importance of legal terminology and called for introducing modern definitions of things and rights, avoiding discrepancies in the teaching of future law students once and for all. However, to agree on such details, he noticed that it was necessary to postpone the publication of the Code.

By referring to the enumeration of intangible goods from Article 6, C. Egi noticed that copyrights, patents and the inventor's rights are directed towards persons and things. Although he admitted that Article 4 defined them as special rights, subject to separate regulations, he argued that this norm caused additional confusion for people interpreting the Code. As he persuaded the readers, properly defining things and rights was the simplest way to avoid future confusion.

From beginning to end, the entire Book on Property Law was not to contain a single provision that would fully satisfy C. Egi. Some were illogical or too general for the Code because Property Law principles were regulated in only 12 articles. He wrote that a clear division of material and intangible goods would make it easier to define ownership and possession, which remained vague concepts. Based on the Civil Code, it was also necessary to separate the entitlement from the subject of the entitlement. For example, C. Egi mentioned servitude and the right to a way of necessity, which were legal terms related to limited real rights. He argued that ordinary people might find it too problematic to understand the definition of things adopted in the draft of the Civil Code. Beyond the general understanding of a thing as an object, it would be difficult for them to grasp the psychophysical nuances of a material good, which could be identified through the senses, much less an intangible good. The legislator should clearly define such basic terms because it was uncertain whether unbuilt land, residential property, animals and household goods were all material goods. C. Egi argued that it was not apparent whether the unbuilt land and residential property were material goods, even though their existence can be identified through the senses. Referring to scientists' findings, he mentioned five recognized and described senses. If the legislator intended to regulate the principles of understanding the external world by omitting even one of the senses, the capacity of human cognition would naturally be limited. However, introducing another sense into legislation, essentially the understanding of "products of human imagination", also led to a departure from the way of experiencing reality known to science. Consequently, C. Egi indicated that the Civil Code should not divide things into material and intangible goods identified by using an additional sixth sense because it exceeded the capabilities of natural human cognition and "belonged only to gods".[17]

4.1.7. Takuzō Hanai's opinion (English School, postponement faction)

T. Hanai was a School of English Law graduate from the 1888 cohort and an activist for Jiyū Minken Undō – the Movement for Freedom and Civil Rights. Parallel to the criticism of the Book on Property Law, he published his opinion on the Civil Code in *Hōri Seika* (Volume 4, Issue 20). His short text, "Ah, This Book of the Civil Code on Evidence…", was released on 15 October 1889.[18] Following C. Egi's commentary, it was another voice focusing on a particular book of the draft Civil Code.

By referring to the commonly known division into substantive and procedural law, T. Hanai reminded readers that the Civil and Penal Code belonged to the first category. In contrast, the Code of Civil Procedure and the Code of Criminal Procedure belonged to the second group. Thus, all legal norms concerning rights and obligations should be included in substantive law and norms concerning the course of proceedings in procedural law. T. Hanai argued that this division was understandable and should be preserved despite the lack of codes in the British and American legal systems. Meanwhile, numerous provisions of the Book on Evidence were procedural law included in the French Civil Code, which undoubtedly belonged to the category of substantive law. He named this solution peculiar and claimed that some jurists perceived it as an obvious mistake.

[17] For the full opinion text, see Hoshino, 2014, pp. 25–33.

[18] Hanai, 1889, pp. 15–18.

In the second part of the article, T. Hanai recalled essential allegations of the Association of Jurists: the codification process should consider such aspects as beliefs, folk customs, human nature and customary law. In addition, he emphasized that it was necessary to maintain the proper structure of the Code by separating substantive law from procedural law. He believed that the French Civil Code had lost its unique value in the eyes of global jurisprudence long ago, and he expressed the fear that Japan would only expose itself to ridicule by adopting the same flaws. As an English School representative, he was also exceptionally sceptical towards ideological principles adopted by drafters many years ago, which resulted directly from choosing French law as the basis for the Japanese Civil Code. Although T. Hanai knew this was not the right time to return to digressing about the past, he claimed that jurists involved in the codification process, which in fact was a painful translation of the French codes, also had numerous doubts and did not believe in overcoming the difficulties.

Finally, T. Hanai summarized his opinion in four points: (1) including the Book on Evidence in the Civil Code was an obvious legislative mistake; (2) since there was a separate Criminal Code and the Code of Criminal Procedure, placing the provisions on civil procedure in the Civil Code was provoking unnecessary chaos; (3) the work of Robert-Joseph Pothier[19] was destroyed by French legislators, who improperly copied it into their Civil Code; and (4) Édouard Bonnier[20] would also lament that French legislators had failed to prepare their national Code by mindlessly copying provisions.[21]

4.1.8. *Nihon no Hōritsu* editorial team's opinion on the succession system (postponement faction)

In November 1889, *Nihon no Hōritsu* editorial team published an opinion entitled "The Theory of Succession According to Feminist Activists".[22]

Based on rumours about the planned publication of the Civil Code, *Nihon no Hōritsu* editorial team expressed concern about establishing an entirely new succession system in Japan, contrary to well-established customary law. According

[19] Robert-Joseph Pothier (1699–1772) was a French professor in law of the Enlightenment era, lecturer at the University of Orléans, precursor of research on ancient Roman law and pandectic systematics in France, and author of numerous publications on civil law. His works about the nature of traditional French private law were incorporated into the Napoleonic Code.

[20] Édouard Bonnier (1808–1877) was a French professor in law, member of the Legislative Commission of Substantive and Procedural Criminal Law at the Faculty of Law of the University of Paris, and author of over 30 frequently cited monographs and articles on criminal law in the 19th century.

[21] For the full opinion text, see Hoshino, 2014, pp. 33–34.

[22] Nihon no Hōritsu, 1889, (original pages are unknown).

to the authors, the eldest son's exclusive succession was to be a widely recognized legal practice throughout the country, and revolutionary actions of feminist activists were seen as an attempt to eradicate it. The editorial team argued that since the activists understood the nature of the traditional succession system as harmful to women's status in society, they planned to eliminate this source of inequality in private law. The supporters of the draft of the Civil Code were accused of not being aware that their ideas were causing harm to Japanese society. The authors noted that without effective reform of the education system aimed at changing the mentality of older and younger sons, raising the status of women through private law would become fiction. They also wrote that although removing "old bad habits" was a positive motion initiated by the Meiji Revolution, it did not mean that all unwritten laws should be revised. If the eldest son's exclusive succession were to be abolished, the tremendous responsibility for implementing the law rested with the parents, who should have educated their sons and daughters in the spirit of the new succession system in advance. The editorial team argued that feminist activists were not to see this cause-and-effect relationship, which made their proposal to reform private law "devoid of any advantages".[23]

4.1.9. *Hōri Seika* editorial team's opinion (postponement faction)

On 3 January 1890, *Hōri Seika* editorial team published the collective opinion of the postponement party, entitled "*Hōri Seika* and the Legal Community in the 22nd year of the Meiji era [1889]" (Volume 5, Issue 25).[24]

After reminding readers of the scope of the journal's activity in 1889, the postponement faction paid particular attention to the links between the codification of law and the plan to revise unequal treaties. The authors recalled that 30 legal acts were promulgated in the country in 1889, including the Constitution, the Military Criminal Code for the Navy, Land Tax Exemptions for Hokkaido, and Rules for the Protection of Parliament Members. Naturally, most attention was devoted to the Constitution, reminding readers of the published articles and the moderate position of the journal's editorial team. *Hōri Seika* emphasized that throughout 1889, the codification project was the main subject of discussion for the postponement faction representatives and, simultaneously, a significant challenge since the editorial team also encountered opinions that they should not have published an open critique of the Codes. However, the authors eventually agreed that it was the jurists' and legal journalists' duty to keep the readers informed about the planned changes in the law and the resulting consequences. As they declared, the following

[23] For the full opinion text, see Murakami, 2008a, p. 306.

[24] Hōri Seika (ed.), 1890a, pp. 1–7.

year, they would not change the journal's publishing policy and would in fact increase activity in the debate on the Codes.[25]

4.1.10. *Nihon no Hōritsu* editorial team's opinion concerning the publication of Codes (postponement faction)

In January 1890, *Nihon no Hōritsu* editorial team published the opinion (Volume 2, Issue 1) entitled "The Codification of the Codes Must be Carried Out Properly".[26]

Despite the quite misleading title suggesting that the decisive faction raised its voice, the opinion contained a specific polemic related to the demands for a quick completion of the codification process. Wondering under what circumstances the Codes might be published, the editorial team recalled a close relationship between the plan to revise unequal treaties and introducing a new law. The authors also wondered if there should be less pressure to publish the Codes, considering the recent decline in the importance of revisions of unequal treaties. They described the mechanism of establishing unequal treaties as the lack of trust of Western powers towards Japan. The authors emphasized that the cabinet should have focused on gaining the trust if Japan intended to establish international agreements securing equal positions. Additionally, they envisaged that introducing the Codes would benefit judges, who would use them in practice. Still, it would not necessarily imply establishing an efficient justice system and international respect. Foreign countries were also not necessarily going to give up their special privileges to promote equality in official relations between states. Therefore, the law codification process should focus on guaranteeing public safety and protection of life, health, honour and property rights of Japanese citizens. The editors argued that, besides the political plan to revise unequal treaties, all those aspects mentioned above are equally important and could only be secured by introducing a flawless Civil Code.[27]

4.1.11. *Hōri Seika* editorial team's opinion of Evidence Law drafters (postponement faction)

On 3 January 1890, *Hōri Seika* editorial team published a collective opinion of the postponement faction representatives entitled "Discussion on the Evidence Law" (Volume 5, Issue 25).[28]

[25] For the full opinion text, see Hoshino, 2014, pp. 35–37.

[26] Nihon no Hōritsu, 1890b, pp. 84–85.

[27] For the full opinion text, see Murakami, 2008a, pp. 310–311.

[28] Hōri Seika (ed.), 1890d, pp. 8–31.

As in previous opinions, *Hōri Seika* journal editorial team drew attention to the artificial and borrowed language used by the drafters of the Codes. The word order and systematics of the Civil Code were considered unnatural for the Japanese language, which was particularly apparent after studying the Book on Evidence. The authors argued that combining procedural with substantive law, such as real rights and obligations, was copying the wrong solution. In accordance with the principles of dividing substantive and procedural law, a Book on Evidence should be included in the Code of Civil Procedure. They also indicated a growing discussion in France about separating procedural law from the Civil Code based on carefully studied German law at the time. Keeping the Civil Code provisions that are useful only to the courts to apply the rules to the case was defined as "sewing a fox's skin to a lion" and "duplicating erroneous French patterns". As the editorial team argued, its goal was to promote a state of the law in which the Civil Code, the Code of Civil Procedure and the Commercial Code would be statute law adequate to their official name. The issues about the Evidence Law mentioned above were the most significant practical flaw of the Civil Code.

By juxtaposing the Civil Code and the Code of Civil Procedure, the authors showed how to combine both legal acts to avoid unnecessary repetition. They also noted that law, like any other field of knowledge, was subject to the laws of logic, and therefore the legislator must obey them. As a deathly threat to the Code, which itself was to contain numerous logical and practical errors, they pointed to the loss of usability.

The editorial team concluded with digressions on substantive and procedural law. They proposed introducing, in their opinion, the "most secure" changes to Evidence Law, also discussing their construction in relation to the draft of the Code of Civil Procedure. Instead of the classification of evidence provided by the Civil Code, they suggested introducing a more precise division into written private evidence, oral evidence, written official evidence and witness statements and presented their characteristics.

Hōri Seika editorial team's opinion touched on several matters. They outlined the shortcomings of the systematics of the Civil Code and compared its provisions with the solutions adopted in the Code of Civil Procedure. In addition to the critical view on the Code, it contained specific proposals for amendments, supported by numerous arguments and commentary.[29]

[29] For the full opinion text, see Hoshino, 2014, pp. 38–47.

4.2. The decisive faction's first opinions and the postponement faction's polemic

4.2.1. S. Isobe's opinion (French School, decisive faction)

Although the decisive faction actively followed the publishing activity of the postponement faction, its representatives refrained from presenting official responses to the criticism of the Civil Code and the Commercial Code for a relatively long time. However, their attitude suddenly changed in January 1890. On 10 January, S. Isobe, a recognized graduate of the first cohort of the Law School at the Ministry of Justice and the University of Paris, a judge and one of the drafters of the Civil Code, presented in Hōsei Shigyō – *The Journal of Law and Politics* (Issue 99) issued by the Meiji Law School – his view concerning the first stage of the Controversy. His article, divided into three parts (the last part was published on 15 March), was entitled "Reading *Hōri Seika*".[30]

In his article, S. Isobe referred to C. Egi's criticism of Property Law, which he had read in *Hōri Seika* (Volume 4, Issue 19). By indicating C. Egi's limited experience and young age, he compared the postponement faction to "a group of dogs that bark in response to one howling". Although he did not consider the English School representative a worthy opponent, he felt obliged to refute his allegations. S. Isobe did not understand the arguments about the fear of introducing two pieces of legislation consisting of 5,000 articles that might cause great confusion among Japanese jurisprudence. He believed that all schools of legal jurisprudence would sooner or later have to adapt to the new law, but despite this awareness, he did not see them take any action to prepare for the new reality in advance. He also remarked on C. Egi's trivial error, as both Codes had over 1,500 fewer articles. S. Isobe admitted that although many jurists with various skills had participated in the drafting process, he did not have a chance to learn all the details about multiple legal systems from them.

Nevertheless, he knew that English law, based on centuries-old judicial decisions, was an unknown legal system in many countries. He even attacked C. Egi by arguing that if he were unaware of such a simple fact, he should return to the early stages of legal education. Additionally, he claimed that C. Egi's views led to the conclusion that the Japanese jurists' study of the English private law or French Civil Code was worthless since both legal systems also referred to the history of their development.

For S. Isobe, C. Egi was nothing more than "a law student who reads the rules aloud without making an effort to understand them". He compared the English

[30] Isobe, 1890, (original pages are unknown).

School representative's words to "an attempt to commit seppuku [ritualistic suicide] with a blunt sword". He dismissed C. Egi's concern about the ineffectiveness of the Code as *chimpu setsu* – a hackneyed idea – and expressed surprise that C. Egi did not know about such a simple thing as the fact that the current legal norms were not the same as a hundred years ago. S. Isobe could not see one valid argument in the opinion of his opponent, which he generally found absurd due to C. Egi's insufficient study of the Code. To understand it correctly, he recommended looking at it as a comprehensive work and carefully learning the content of each article.

Referring to the criticism of the definition of property rights, S. Isobe argued that the amendment proposed by C. Egi was also imprecise and seemed as if he ultimately did not understand that the Japanese language has its specificity resulting from the constraints of kanji characters. Similarly, in his opinion, the definition of an abstract person was flawless as the Code contained a sufficient explanation in the later part. He believed that since the current system of private law in towns and villages had already embraced the abstract person as a separate legal person, people would have no problem understanding the new concept. By comparing British India and the recent experiences of local lawyers with the interpretation of private law, S. Isobe argued that the term abstract person was intuitive, and the division into natural and legal persons was not exhaustive. Additionally, he claimed that some jurists allegedly did not grasp the meaning of the term natural person, which was supposed to reduce the whole debate to "re-inventing the wheel and undermining the achievements of global jurisprudence". He also assured his adversary that since 1880, the draft of the Civil Code, including the terms of the abstract person, rights and obligations, had been carefully corrected many times. S. Isobe was also ironic with C. Egi's suggestions and described them as a "courageous attempt", giving as an example defining a legal person not in Japanese but in English.

Regarding the proposal to divide the rights into three separate categories, S. Isobe considered that C. Egi again showed a lack of in-depth knowledge of the Code, which contained the necessary explanations in separate provisions. According to S. Isobe, the division into real and personal rights was the most natural and logical solution, and did not contradict the law principles. He explained that personality rights did not have to constitute a separate category because they concern a person. He expressed a similar opinion about the proposal to eliminate the term intangible good, accusing C. Egi of acting without "a larger and clearly defined plan". S. Isobe also disputed that the English School representative could not have known about the harmful social effects of the Code coming into force.

In the later part of the polemic, S. Isobe explained to C. Egi the rationale for separating the security provisions from the Book on Property Law, as a different division could cause even more significant damage to the creditors. As part of the discussion on the structure of Property Law in the Code, he cited possible cases that could cause legal issues. He argued that these problems were already well known to Roman law, while French and German law agreed to recognize the wisdom of the older generations of jurists. S. Isobe believed that security could not be classified uniquely as a real right since it was also related to an obligation, which in the Code was described as a personal right.

Having explained the essence of the Property Law and obligations in the Code, S. Isobe believed that the legislator had to maintain contractual freedom, understood as a joint declaration of will by both parties, as the essential feature of private law. All contractual freedom would lose meaning and importance if this consent were obtained by coercion or duress. He argued that a valid contract would not exist without a free declaration of will. Without a valid contract, there can be no transfer of ownership and things that have been transferred should be returned to the rightful owner based on a personal right, i.e. an obligation. Therefore, S. Isobe claimed that if anyone wanted to discuss the content of real and personal rights, he should also learn the provisions of Contract Law.

According to S. Isobe, C. Egi's division of property rights into three categories led to the annulment of an obligation between the rightful owner of a good and its temporary possessor. He explained possible complications resulting from the succession of the unlawfully owned good and saw it as a threat to the rightful owner, who would not be entitled to a compelling claim for the return of the good. The author argued that the right to demand the owned good was a characteristic feature of the real right and could not be categorized as a personal right. S. Isobe argued that C. Egi's mistake was a cursory reasoning that if a claim was made against another person, it was a personal right. He explained that the Romans understood this issue perfectly, and the French and Germans recognized their solution. Although S. Isobe admitted to having no in-depth knowledge of German law, based on his erudition of Roman and French law, he did not consider old provisions wrong. He also spitefully stated that if C. Egi had doubts about the achievements of great Roman and French jurists, he should first look for inaccuracies in his reasoning.

Concluding the polemic, S. Isobe confirmed his positive attitude to dividing goods into tangible and intangible goods and rights into real and personal rights. The existing regulations in the Code were to explain all C. Egi's doubts sufficiently. The French School representative also answered his assumption that the codified law should be understandable to the average citizen. He believed that the times of intuitive law were long gone because of the development of society, which forced the legislator to apply to a broader group of people and regulate more detailed matters. S. Isobe argued that in Japan and the civilized world, the law was to be universally recognized as a specialized science. Citizens must invest more effort and time to understand its principles and detailed regulations to comprehend any law during the first reading of the legal act. The need for people who specialized in reading and applying law was one of the reasons for the birth of professional jurisprudence. S. Isobe admitted that the Code included terms incomprehensible to the average citizen but felt this was inevitable. C. Egi's analysis of the Code through the prism of individual articles was also criticized and compared to ordinary people's misunderstanding of the legal text. The author regretted that C. Egi was "desperately poking holes" in Article 6 of the Property Law because only by looking at the Book's title could one guess that its provisions would concern the division of property rights and goods. To understand Article 6, it was also necessary to carefully read the five preceding articles, which, according to S. Isobe, C. Egi failed to do.[31]

4.2.2. Teijirō Torii's opinion (English School, postponement faction)

S. Isobe's strident critique of C. Egi's opinion and C. Egi himself met a swift and strong response from T. Torii, a graduate of the School of English Law and a lawyer from the younger generation of Japanese jurisprudence. His article "Evaluating the Five Arguments of the Great Professor and Jurist Shirō Isobe" was divided into three parts and published by 15 February 1890 in *Hōri Seika* (Volume 5, Issues 26–28).[32]

T. Torii expressed great disappointment about the attitude of S. Isobe, a recognized Japanese jurist of the older generation, towards the much younger C. Egi. The author did not understand the motives of one of the drafters of the Civil Code and spoke maliciously about his competencies. T. Torii also supported C. Egi's postulates, describing them as consistent with the direction of the development of law at the end of the 19th century, while S. Isobe was assessed as representing the generation of law professors from the previous century.

In what followed, T. Torii commented on the five main arguments of S. Isobe, juxtaposing them with the original content of C. Egi's commentary. After clearing up the misunderstanding related to the number of articles in both Codes, he argued that S. Isobe did not substantively refer to the allegation that Japanese customary law was not included in the Civil Code. He also expressed great surprise that the French School representative ignored the development of law over the centuries and missed the differences between the countries of Western Europe and the Far East. For T. Torii, S. Isobe treated the law extremely doctrinally, literally "like a stone", missing its natural evolution. T. Torii believed that the Code S. Isobe had drafted could be nothing else than "Eskimo law".[33] S. Isobe was criticized for com-

[31] For the full opinion text, see Hoshino, 2014, pp. 61–69.

[32] Torii, 1890a, pp. 1–7; Torii, 1890b, pp. 1–5; Torii, 1890c, pp. 25–29.

[33] Eskimo law (Inuit law) was cited as an example of the legal system (in fact, it was not a system, but a "set of laws") of primitive societies still existing in East Asia. It was also a veiled critique of the

paring the law to science and proving that "also a hundred years ago, two plus two equalled four".

In conclusion, T. Torii ironically asked S. Isobe from which country and century BC he came and whether he believed that studying the legal history of different countries was useless because all the knowledge about regional differences could be reduced to universal principles. He also argued that if, according to him, only private law was identical in all countries, excluding criminal law and other branches of law, then this rule was not "an attempt to prove that two plus two equals five". T. Torii also stated that if S. Isobe believed that private law was similar in all countries, he should have considered it unnecessary to draft a separate Civil Code for Japan. The author was critical of the adversary's vision, which reduced private law to simple obligations. T. Torii noticed, however, that the codes of different countries had significant differences, which experienced S. Isobe should not have overlooked.[34]

4.2.3. Misao Inoue's opinion (French School, decisive faction)

On 10 March 1890, *The Journal of Law and Politics* (Issue 103) published another opinion from the decisive faction, which was entitled "Pros and Cons of Law Codification".[35] Its author was M. Inoue, a graduate of the first cohort of the Law School at the Ministry of Justice, former lecturer of criminal procedure at the Old University of Tokyo and an appeals court judge in Osaka.

M. Inoue noted that the dispute between recognized law specialists and jurists regarding the advantages and disadvantages of law codification was an essential feature of the changes in the Japanese legal system in the second half of the 19th century, especially since the Codes started to be drafted. He acknowledged the arguments related to the adverse effects of codification, which included, among others, disturbance of the natural evolution of law. However, he also mentioned the undeniable benefits of the new Codes. Regardless of the degree of reception of foreign law in the Codes, M. Inoue believed that their introduction would only improve Japan's international position and prevent Western powers from intervention in domestic affairs. Although he admitted that some jurists wanted to avoid the publication of the Codes before the Imperial Diet's first meeting, scheduled for late 1890, he persuaded the reader that introducing amendments should be avoided to complete the codification project hastily.

natural law doctrine advocated by the French School.

[34] For the full opinion text, see Hoshino, 2014, pp. 47–54.

[35] Inoue, 1890, (original pages are unknown).

M. Inoue claimed that the postponement faction's allegations of disregarding customary law by drafters were unfounded, as the Codes implemented the old principle of equity and some customs. According to him, the purpose of the Codes was to reorganize the legal system for the government and citizens. He compared private law to public law and emphasized that people need to know the content of the provisions to obey legal norms. However, the Codes had to be published first to make provisions transparent for the public. M. Inoue tried to understand the arguments of the English School representatives but, at the same time, asked them not to obstruct the publication of the Codes because of their deficiencies regarding customary law. The author feared unnecessarily prolonging the codification process. Giving as an example the United Kingdom, he mentioned that some countries did not have codes due to numerous customary laws and judicial precedents. M. Inoue was convinced that statutory law was a pillar of the separation of legislative and judicial powers, which helped judges to focus more effectively on making judicial decisions. For him, the English common law system was far from this concept and contrary to trends in global jurisprudence. Regardless of different notions, M. Inoue argued that opposing the publication of the Codes would make Japan follow the path of the Tokugawa shogunate and the United Kingdom. He indicated that Japan should strive to embrace the French model, the best example of an effective statutory law system. Even if the Codes had shortcomings related to some provisions, he suggested using Article 38 of the Constitution of Japan to introduce amendments to them after they came into force.

The author convinced the readers again that the Codes would correspond to old Japanese customs. However, if the English School believed otherwise, he asked for a more precise indication of potential discrepancies. He also proved that since the breaking of isolation, all Japanese legal norms were based on natural law doctrine, which granted the legal capacity to every person after birth, claiming that this principle was permanently adopted in the Japanese legal system. Therefore, discussing the content of each article separately and seeking arguments for their faulty construction was, in his opinion, a waste of time. As specific examples of the application of customary law in the Japanese private law system, he mentioned Decree No. 103 of 1873 concerning the rules of concluding marriage between foreigners and Japanese citizens, Decree No. 1 of 1868 concerning the issue of family certificates, and some provisions from the Book on Personal Law. In the end, M. Inoue asked the postponement faction to reconsider in light of the need to publish the Codes to make them available to all citizens. He indicated that statute law had always been created for the middle and upper classes. Thus, its publication could not be made conditional on the lowest social class understanding the content of legal provisions.[36]

[36] For the full opinion text, see Hoshino, 2014, pp. 69–73.

4.2.4. *Nihon no Hōritsu* editorial team's commentary on Saburō Ozaki's opinion about the illegitimate child system (postponement faction)

In March 1890, *Nihon no Hōritsu* (Volume 2, Issue 3) editorial team published a commentary on S. Ozaki's opinion, who referred to the law regulating the status of illegitimate children adopted in the Civil Code. The article was titled "Mr Ozaki's Opinion Concerning the Status of Illegitimate Children".[37]

Referring to the statement by S. Ozaki, one of the members of the Chamber of Elders, the editorial team cited his critical opinion regarding the Book on Personal Law of the Civil Code. He did not understand why the drafters decided to remove the institution of an illegitimate child, characteristic of Japanese customary law. Although it did not exist in some Western countries, in his opinion, it had historical significance in Japan. According to the centuries-old tradition, illegitimate children had no right to inherit property. Regarding other rights and obligations, their legal situation was similar to that of legitimate children. S. Ozaki criticized drafters for adopting a foreign, namely French, model and listed possible conflicts of norms which would impact ordinary citizens and the imperial family, which could suffer from a revision of essential rights and duties between its members. He asked about the logic of the new family law provisions and expressed the view that the old illegitimate children system should be preserved at all costs.[38]

4.3. Publication of the Civil Code, the Commercial Code and the Code of Civil Procedure

At the time of publication of the Association of Jurists' opinion on the Codes, work on finalizing the Civil Code draft was at an advanced stage. By the end of December 1888, the Law Research Committee made a preliminary[39] and follow-up examination of the part prepared by G. Boissonade.[40] From 24 January 1889, the Chamber of Elders also provided additional analysis and suggested some

[37] Nihon no Hōritsu (ed.), 1890d, pp. 97–98.

[38] For the full opinion text, see Murakami, 2008a, p. 313.

[39] Detailed course of work during the preliminary examination of the Civil Code draft is covered by the following documents: from Mimpō Sōan Giji Hikki, Dai 1–5 Kai [meetings on 6, 12, 13 December 1887], Ref. XB300 N2-2a-1, to Mimpō Sōan Giji Hikki, Dai 82–84 Kai [meetings on 18, 24, 25 September 1888], Ref. XB300 N2-2d-3.

[40] Detailed course of work during the follow-up examination of the Civil Code draft is covered by the following documents: from Mimpō Sōan Saichōsa Giji Hikki, Dai 1–6 Kai [meetings on 4, 7, 14, 21, 28 July 1888], Ref. XB300 N2-6a-1, h, to Mimpō Sōan Saichōsa Giji Hikki, Dai 26–44 Kai [meetings on 28, 29, 30 November and 3, 4, 5, 8, 10, 11, 12, 13, 15, 17, 18, 19, 21, 22, 24, 25 December 1888], Ref. XB300 N2-6c-2.

corrections.[41] A detailed description of the course and the adopted methodology for introducing changes to the draft was presented in Japanese legal history monographs.[42] Due to the clearly outlined cabinet policy on introducing the Codes, the Chamber of Elders' examination process was characterized by excessive haste, which would help to publish the last missing parts of the codified legal system as soon as possible. The cabinet believed the Codes would impact the revision of unequal treaties and fill the gaps in the Japanese private law system.[43] Following this policy, the Law Research Committee, supported by G. Boissonade,[44] analysed 1,315 articles by 29 July 1889. After receiving the formal approval of the Chamber of Elders,[45] the part of the Code was submitted to Emperor Meiji as *jōsō* – an official report to the throne.[46]

In October 1889, a slightly revised plan of the Ministry of Justice for revising unequal treaties was openly criticized by political circles centred around the cabinet and the opposition. At the same time, the Japanese political scene was shocked by the unsuccessful assassination of the Minister of Foreign Affairs, Shigenobu Ōkuma. This event forced Prime Minister K. Kuroda to temporarily suspend the enforcement of the plan related to unequal treaties. Eventually, being pressured by all circles, K. Kuroda soon resigned. The cabinet crisis lasted almost two months and ended when A. Yamagata became prime minister in the final days of December 1889.

Japanese legal scholars did not mention to what extent the temporary chaos at the highest decision-making levels affected the course of work on the Civil Code draft. However, after the Law Research Committee submitted its positive opinion by the end of December 1889,[47] on 28 January 1890, the draft was passed directly to the Privy Council for additional analysis and final adjustments. The accelerated work took less than two months. On 25 March, the Privy Council voted to accept the part of the Civil Code drafted by G. Boissonade.[48] In the last days of March, the

[41] Kokuritsu Kōbunshokan: Ref. 01937100, Genrōin Kaigi Hikki.

[42] Ōkubo, Takahashi, 1999, pp. 197–216; Ishii, 1979, pp. 231–319.

[43] Ōkubo, 1977, p. 158.

[44] G. Boissonade presented his opinion on the suggested amendments to his Code in 13 parts published from 21 March to 9 April 1889. See more, Mimpō Hensan ni Kansuru Zassho (Vol. 1–2), Boasonaado-shi Mimpō Sōan Shūsei ni Kansuru Iken Hikki, Dai 1–13 Kai), Ref. XB300 N2-14, XB300 N2-15, XB300 N2-16.

[45] Mimpō Sōan Saichōsa Giji Hikki, Ref. XB300 N2-5.

[46] Hoshino, 1943, p. 102.

[47] Kokuritsu Kōbunshokan: Ref. 類00528100, Mimpō Zaisan Hen, Zaisan Shutoku Hen, Saiken Tampo Hen, Shōko Hen Hōritsu Torishirabe I'inkai Jōshinan.

[48] Kokuritsu Kōbunshokan: Ref. F00035100, Sūmitsuin Ketsugi.

cabinet began the preparation of the final version of the Code, which was to be published soon.[49]

On 21 April 1890, despite the postponement faction's negative comments on the Civil Code draft, which had been known in some circles for almost a year, Emperor Meiji, countersigned by ministers from the A. Yamagata cabinet,[50] promulgated Books Two, Three (without the part concerning succession and matrimonial property), Four and Five of the Civil Code, prepared directly by G. Boissonade.[51] On the same day, Minjisoshōhō – the Code of Civil Procedure – was also promulgated, followed by Shōhō – the Commercial Code – on 26 April.[52]

The draft of Book One and the rest of Book Three, prepared by a team of Japanese jurists and arousing the greatest controversy, went through a separate legislative path. From the end of January to 21 April 1890, it was studied by the Law Research Committee.[53] On 20 May, the Chamber of Elders began an additional analysis, which ended on 26 September.[54] Subsequently, the project was approved by the cabinet on 30 September.[55] Finally, it was promulgated on 7 October 1890, almost half a year later than the first part.[56]

[49] Kokuritsu Kōbunshokan: Ref. 類00531100 – Ref. 00532100, Mimpōchū Zaisan Hen, Zaisan Shutoku Hen, Saiken Tampo Hen, Shōkohen o Sadamu.

[50] Hoshino, 1943, p. 103.

[51] Meiji 23-nen Hōritsu Dai-28 Gō.

[52] Meiji 23-nen Hōritsu Dai-29 Gō; the Commercial Code was promulgated on 26 April 1890 (five days later than the Civil Code and the Code of Civil Procedure) due to considerable opposition from the Privy Council.

[53] Mimpō: Hōrei, Jinji Hen, Zaisan Shutoku Hen Hōritsu Torishirabe I'inkai Jōshinan, Ref. XB300 H1-3.

[54] Kokuritsu Kōbunshokan: Ref. 単01751100: Genrōin Gitei Jōsoan: Hōrei, Jinji Hen, Zaisan Shutoku Hen.

[55] Mimpō Jinji Hen Naikaku Shūseian, Ref. XB300 H1-3B.

[56] Meiji 23-nen Hōritsu Dai-98 Gō.

Table 2: The legislative path of both parts of the draft Civil Code.

DRAFT OF BOOKS TWO, THREE (PART), FOUR AND FIVE author: G. Boissonade	DRAFT OF BOOKS ONE AND THREE (PART) authors: Japanese team of jurists led by S. Isobe and B. Kumano
↓	↓
Law Research Committee preliminary examination (03.12.1887 – 25.09.1888)	↓
↓	↓
Law Research Committee follow-up examination (03.07.1888 – 28.12.1888)	↓
↓	↓
Chamber of Elders preliminary analysis (24.01.1889 – 07.03.1889)	Law Research Committee preliminary examination (04.02.1889 – the end of 1889)
↓	↓
G. Boissonade commentary on suggestion of amendments (21.03.1889 – 09.04.1889)	↓
↓	↓
Law Research Committee analysis of Chamber of Elders amendments (13.07.1889 – 23.07.1889)	↓
↓	↓
Chamber of Elders approval (24.07.1889 – 29.07.1889)	↓
↓	↓
Law Research Committee approval (by the end of December 1889)	↓
↓	↓
Privy Council final examination (28.01.1890 – 25.03.1890)	↓
↓	↓

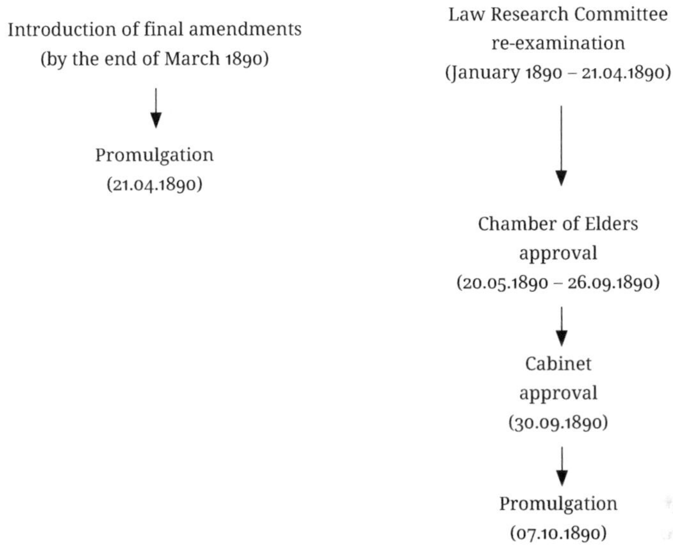

The entire Civil Code was to come into force on 1 January 1893. More than two years of interregnum, despite the plan to complete the work on the five fundamental codes rapidly, might indicate that the cabinet still left room for debate on a possible revision of the Civil Code. In contrast, the Commercial Code and the Code of Civil Procedure were to come into force on 1 January 1891 and therefore, their interregnum was much shorter.[57] If the opponents of the Civil Code wanted to push their postulates through, they had to do it by 1 January 1893. Otherwise, the Civil Code would become binding law in Japan, regardless of any mentioned flaws and the voices of disapproval.

According to G. Boissonade's vision of the systematics, the Code was divided into five books concerning personal law, property, acquiring property, security and evidence. Compared to the Napoleonic Code, loosely referring to the tripartite

[57] According to M. Fukushima, the earlier entry into force of the Commercial Code was planned as a testing ground before fully embracing the Civil Code. It was supposed to give the cabinet more time to deal with the undesirable effects of the sudden enrichment of some enterprises. Before commencing the negotiations on the revision of unequal treaties, the Japanese also wanted to secure the financial liquidity of domestic companies in commercial contracts with foreign companies. Fukushima, 1988, pp. 109–110; Tokutomi, 1933, pp. 22–23. The entry into force of the Code of Civil Procedure on 1 January 1891 resulted from the cabinet's earlier promulgation (10 February 1890) of Saibansho Kōseihō – the Ordinary Courts Organization Law. This act, constituting the culmination of work on establishing a unified judiciary in Japan, was to come into force on 1 November 1890. Meiji 23-nen Hōritsu Dai 6-Gō.

division in Gaius' *Institutes*, the Japanese version had two additional books. G. Boissonade extracted them from the original Roman systematics to increase the readability and usability of the Code. Still, according to some Japanese scholars, the Code comprised 1,762 articles and was considered an extensive legal act.[58]

The detailed systematics of the Civil Code was as follows:

Book One – *Jinji* (Personal Law)

- Chapter 1: Possession and Exercise of Personality Rights
- Chapter 2: Competence
- Chapter 3: Relatives and Family Relations
- Chapter 4: Marriage
- Chapter 5: Divorce
- Chapter 6: Parent and Child
- Chapter 7: Adoption
- Chapter 8: Termination of Adoption
- Chapter 9: Parental Responsibilities
- Chapter 10: Ward
- Chapter 11: Legal Capacity
- Chapter 12: Incapacitation
- Chapter 13: Head of Household and Family
- Chapter 14: Domicile
- Chapter 15: Missing
- Chapter 16: Civil Registration Certificates
- Total: 293 articles

Book Two – *Zaisan* (Property Law)

- Part 1: Real Rights
  - Chapter 1: Ownership
  - Chapter 2: Right to Benefits, Free Use and Domicile
  - Chapter 3: Rent, Usufruct and Superficies
  - Chapter 4: Possession
  - Chapter 5: Servitude
- Part 2: Different Categories of Rights and Obligations
  - Chapter 1: Source of Obligations
  - Chapter 2: Effectiveness of Obligations
  - Chapter 3: Expiry of Obligations
  - Chapter 4: Natural Obligations
- Total: 572 articles

[58] Miyakawa, 1963, pp. 201–228.

Book Three – *Zaisan Shutoku* (Acquiring Property)

Chapter 1: Usucapion
Chapter 2: Accession
Chapter 3: Purchase and Sale
Chapter 4: Exchange
Chapter 5: Settlement
Chapter 6: Company
Chapter 7: Speculative Contracts
Chapter 8: Life Estate
Chapter 9: Loan
Chapter 10: Deposit
Chapter 11: Agent
Chapter 12: Employment Contract
Chapter 13: Succession
Chapter 14: Donation and Bequest
Chapter 15: Matrimonial Property Agreements
Total: 435 articles

Book Four – *Tampo* (Security)

Part 1: Guarantor
Chapter 1: Surety
Chapter 2: Debtor and Joint Debtors
Chapter 3: Optional Indivisibility
Part 2: Real Security
Chapter 1: Right of Retention
Chapter 2: Pledge of Movables
Chapter 3: Pledge of Immovables
Chapter 4: Prior Right
Chapter 5: Mortgage
Total: 298 articles

Book Five – *Shoko* (Evidence)

Part 1: Evidence
Chapter 1: Judicial Evidence
Chapter 2: Direct Evidence
Chapter 3: Circumstantial Evidence
Part 2: Prescription
Chapter 1: General Provisions of Prescription
Chapter 2: Waiver of Prescription
Chapter 3: Interruption of Prescription
Chapter 4: Suspension of Prescription
Chapter 5: Prescription for Usucapion of Real Estate

Chapter 6: Prescription for Usucapion of Movables
Chapter 7: Exclusion of Prescription
Chapter 8: Special Type of Prescription
Total: 164 articles[59]

4.4. Summary of the first stage of the Civil Code Controversy

The first stage of the Civil Code Controversy, which lasted for 13 months (April 1889 – April 1890), was characterized by increased activity of the postponement faction centred around the English School. Its representatives, mostly practitioners and graduates of the Old University of Tokyo/Imperial University, raised their concerns about the Civil Code (when it was still a draft) individually or in groups. Their articles were published mainly in *Hōri Seika* journal, which in a short time gained great popularity among English School representatives.

The allegations raised by the postponement faction focused on three main aspects. Firstly, the Civil Code completely omitted Japanese customary law and excessively copied the French Civil Code, especially in Family and Succession Law. Secondly, the systematics of the Code adopted by G. Boissonade resulted in the merging of substantive and procedural norms in one legal act, and thus it negatively impacted the formal structure and lowered its value and significance as a Code. Thirdly, many provisions were written in too abstract and specialized language, which could lead to miscomprehension of the Code by ordinary citizens. As an undesirable effect of introducing the Civil Code in the proposed shape, the postponement faction indicated the potentially low effectiveness of private law, which would require numerous amendments in the near future.

From April 1889 to April 1890, the postponement faction commented on the draft of the Civil Code, which had still not been presented to the public despite the cabinet's plan to publish it soon. The English School jurists tried to prove that the drafters deliberately avoided legal debate and excluded them from codification. The opinions published in *Hōri Seika* also revealed a group of jurists opposed to the publication of the Codes motivated by the revision of unequal treaties. The postponement faction saw the old customs in private law as an element of Japanese culture and identity that should not be overlooked or removed under any pretext, particularly to modernize the country.

[59] The systematics of the Civil Code is based on Hoshino, 1943, pp. 108–109.

Initially ignored articles of the postponement faction finally met with a response from the decisive faction representatives. Published in January 1890, S. Isobe's criticism showed that French School representatives condemned the English School arguments and opposing views on the Code, causing great emotions and the willingness to justify the decision to adopt the proven French model for the Japanese Civil Code.

The Civil Code Controversy, initiated by the postponement faction, did not affect the policy of the cabinet, which did not wait for the Imperial Diet's first meeting scheduled for autumn 1890 and decided to promulgate three missing codes in April 1890, including the part of the Civil Code on Property Law, Security and Evidence. The work on the part concerning Personal and Succession Law was already advanced. After obtaining the approval of the Chamber of Elders, the cabinet promulgated it in October 1890, a couple of days before the Imperial Diet's first meeting.

CHAPTER FIVE

THE SECOND STAGE OF THE CIVIL CODE CONTROVERSY – THE TRANSITIONAL PERIOD

Abstract

This chapter presents the second stage of the Controversy, which lasted from May 1890 to March 1891. During this transitional period, A. Yamagata's cabinet promulgated the missing part of the Civil Code regarding Personal and Succession Law. It was also distinctive of the first victory of the postponement faction during the Imperial Diet's first meeting when the date of entry into force of the Commercial Code was extended by two years, until 1 January 1893.

Keywords: Civil Code Controversy, Japanese Civil Code, Codification in Japan

"I don't know whether without the Civil Code the nation and the society will be destroyed".

—Katsunan Kuga

5.1. The reaction of the postponement faction to the publication of the Civil Code and the decisive faction comments

The interregnum for the Civil Code established by the cabinet, which was to last until 1 January 1893, became an occasion for the postponement faction to present its views and put pressure on the cabinet (or possibly the Imperial Diet) to postpone the entry into force of the challenged Code. The decisive faction representatives, who noticed the group of influential Japanese jurists adamantly criticizing the Code, focused on making their points in the discussion. Equally important, they tried to persuade the cabinet that the codification project, initiated by the predecessor of the Ministry of Justice, should finally be completed after 20 years of struggle. Given the positive attitude of both factions towards the Code of Civil Procedure, the French School believed that a compromise could be reached with the English School, which would result in dropping the idea of postponing the entry into force of the Civil Code.

In addition to the numerous comments and opinions regarding the part of the Civil Code drafted by G. Boissonade, the period from April to October 1890 was also a time of waiting for the publication of the missing part of the Civil Code on

Personal and Succession Law. At the end of November 1890, the Imperial Diet's first meeting was convened, whose members included some of the jurists participating in the Civil Code Controversy. The issues concerning the Codes went beyond the framework of legal journals and thus became one of the most critical matters of Japanese domestic policy.

5.1.1. *Hōri Seika* editorial team's opinion on the new Codes (English School, postponement faction)

From 1 June to 15 July 1890, *Hōri Seika* editorial team[1] published their opinion (Volume 6, Issues 35–36) entitled "Commentary on the New Codes".[2]

The editorial team indicated that for many years, the English School jurists had tried to present the advantages and disadvantages of the codification. Since the opening of Japan to the outside world, launching the modernization process of the state and establishing the cabinet, the new Codes had finally been promulgated. Writing in an ironic tone, the authors noted that this was a triumph of the French School, a group which did not consider world trends and views of ordinary people. The English School jurists regretted that the publication of the Codes would be described in Japanese legal history textbooks as a breakthrough event with far-reaching consequences, while foreign scholars would perceive it as an incomprehensible step of the cabinet.

Referring to the authority of world-renowned jurists, the authors tried to convince readers that although the Codes were criticized for their harmful effect on the natural evolution of law, the opposition towards the codification process had failed. The English School highlighted the weaknesses of law codification, yet their arguments should have been better addressed. They also needed to understand why the cabinet omitted the discussion on the Codes in the Imperial Diet or did not go for public consultation despite the interpretation difficulties. Instead, the Meiji politicians sought advice from foreign governments, secretly preparing the Codes and prohibiting their drafts from being publicly available. In addition, the cabinet presented the opponents from the English School with a fait accompli, and after the promulgation of the Codes, their arguments became outdated. Although the decisive faction representatives might think that the promulgation had closed a chance for debate, the editorial team announced that the postponement faction would soon retake the floor, as it did not doubt the final victory.

In the second part, the opinion raised issues related to the impact of revising unequal treaties on the publication of the Codes. Despite the importance of this

[1] In fact, C. Egi was the main author of the opinion.

[2] Hōri Seika (ed.), 1890b, pp. 1–8; Hōri Seika (ed.), 1890c, pp. 1–27.

policy, the authors argued that the potential adverse effects of codification were known to some influential political circles. The cabinet was also criticized for believing that establishing equal relations with colonial powers would be sufficient compensation for adopting the wrongful law. As for the English School jurists, the cabinet's policy was well reflected in the old Japanese proverb that "one could only solve an urgent problem if sacrificing something significant in return". The authors claimed that such a determination was "one big puzzle" for them because the policy of revising unequal treaties had recently been suspended. Yet, the cabinet published the Codes without considering their harmful effects. The editorial team appreciated the efforts to protect sovereignty and avoid foreign intervention in domestic affairs. Still, they believed they had enough evidence to argue that the Codes were enacted only to revise unequal treaties.

Having returned to the discussion on the promulgation of the Codes, the authors wanted to persuade the readers that the best solution to address this issue was to refrain from any decisions until the convening of the Imperial Diet. Pursuant to the Constitution of Japan, the legislative body representing the citizens' views had already been scheduled for its first meeting by late 1890. The English School presented the simultaneous publication of three Codes as a deliberate undermining of the role of the Imperial Diet and a reckless action since the parliament could use its powers to review or even repeal the Codes.

The editorial team was concerned that the Civil Code was not based on any notable principle and became a misinterpreted version of Roman law. The English School representatives blamed G. Boissonade for this flaw and wrote that he introduced a few amendments to the French Civil Code. Although they appreciated his past commitments, especially as a legal adviser and lecturer, and respected his vast knowledge, they believed that his views needed to be updated since they did not correspond to the latest trends in jurisprudence. According to them, G. Boissonade was to be a jurist recognized primarily for his works on French law, but the Code he had drafted could not be applied in Japan. The editors dissociated themselves from the accusation of disrespect for French law. However, they argued that G. Boissonade's Civil Code would be a step back in introducing modern legal theories.

The authors indicated that the Code did not reflect any guiding principle, as they failed to apply French law on foreign soil. Quoting one of the opinions concerning the work of the famous English poet and writer John Milton, they also stated that such an indistinct code would be difficult to understand for most citizens. Even considering that G. Boissonade educated a large group of Japanese jurists who participated in the drafting process, the Code was still the French Civil Code that lost its unique character by introducing amendments to adapt it to Japanese conditions. Despite the effort to make it Japanese, the practical usefulness of the Code was assessed as negligible. As the reason for this statement, the editorial team highlighted the circumstances and ideas accompanying the drafting of the French Civil Code. Republicanism and the spirit of the Roman Catholic Church were supposed to make it fit perfectly into French society. For them, its principles were also perfectly understood by G. Boissonade, a French citizen born and raised in his birth country under the influence of French customary law. They admitted that G. Boissonade knew the advantages and disadvantages of French law. Regardless of his awareness, the Japanese Civil Code he had drafted was dominated by republican and Catholic ideas that could be discerned at first glance. If the Code came into force in this shape, Japanese society would inevitably be subjugated to foreign cultural and political patterns. The editorial team emphasized that the cabinet should refrain from implementing the Codes to complete the codification process. Otherwise, they would cause significant damage to the state, domestic legal scholarship and ordinary citizens.[3]

5.1.2. Tatsuo Kishimoto's opinion (French School, decisive faction)

On 10 May 1890, *The Journal of Law and Politics* (Issue 107) published an article by T. Kishimoto, a graduate of the first cohort of the Law School at the Ministry of Justice, a judge at the Cabinet Legislative Office and one of the founders of the Meiji Law School. The opinion entitled "About the Promulgation of the Codes" was a clear voice of the decisive faction supporting the cabinet in promulgating the Codes.[4]

Speaking at the spring semester academic meeting, T. Kishimoto congratulated and expressed his admiration for the publication of the Codes after many years of exhausting drafting work. He recalled the effort to prepare all projects and believed it was also an occasion for celebration for millions of Japanese people. However, he also indicated that a group of jurists opposed the codification and tried to persuade the public about the harmful effects of the Codes. As a jurist but also a Japanese citizen, T. Kishimoto wondered if any national should not be joyful of this legislative achievement. Referring to social sentiments in Tokyo and throughout Japan, he provided information about ordinary people's enthusiastic reception of legislative action. For him, the publication of the Civil Code was a natural consequence of the promulgation of the Constitution, as establishing civil rights should be followed by a legal act protecting the personality and private law rights. The author was confident that since the promulgation of the Constitution was widely celebrated, the English School's endeavour to convince people not to support the new Codes should be condemned. Arguing directly with the opponents, T. Kishimoto believed that despite their allegations, a legal act giving citizens numerous private law

[3] For the full opinion text, see Hoshino, 2014, pp. 54–60.

[4] Kishimoto, 1890, (original pages are unknown).

rights must be respected. He admitted that every opinion is valuable, yet the issues concerning the Code should be discussed from different angles without denying the reason to celebrate a national success.

Giving an example from the history of France, the author recalled that in his youth, he had read about King Francis I's invasion of the Kingdom of Savoy, which resulted in recognition of the new ruler by the conquered nation. T. Kishimoto did not understand the voluntary renunciation of one's sovereignty, and he was looking for logic in the attitude of the Savoyards for many following years. He finally realized that phenomenon during his legal education. Acceptance of the conquest of one's own country was an expression of recognition for Francis I and the superiority of French culture. Following Emperor Meiji's declaration concerning the aspiration to reform the state, the author considered that old customary law meant no law.

For him, the logical consequence was that the new law could not refer directly to Japanese customs. By asking a rhetorical question, he inquired how Japanese judges should pass their decisions in a legal system dominated by multiple customary law systems. He argued that in a system of fragmented customary law across the country, without the written law, judges could not even be guided by their reason and logic, which is why every sentence could be challenged. He called the debate about the rationale of the codified law system "treading on thin ice". As a French School representative, he identified himself as following logical thinking.

In contrast, he identified the opponents of the Codes, the English School representatives, as people who believed in the ability to shape the future contrary to facts. T. Kishimoto argued that the publication of the Codes saved the Japanese citizens from the inconvenience of many existing common law systems and helped the country to enter a new era with the codified law system, which secured private law rights. He also argued that if the Code principles were followed and all its provisions were known, one should not see any significant flaws. T. Kishimoto reminded the readers of the effort and fortitude required to develop thousands of articles. At the same time, he admitted that he had never seen the Codes to be *kanzen muketsu* – entirely perfect. Considering the aspects of the logic and legal argumentation, he indicated that publishing the Codes, thus securing specific private law rights, must be beneficial. He was convinced that different opinions on the content of the law were inevitable, as were the perceptions of judges and jurists. Nevertheless, he believed in establishing a stable core of a codified legal system, with "branches which would pass in individual leaves".

T. Kishimoto disagreed with the criticism of the Codes and allegations that they were primarily based on foreign law. He believed there was insufficient reason to deny the value of the Codes since the Japanese should know that the name of their country (Nihon) was also a combination of two foreign characters. He recalled that by borrowing the Chinese writing system, Japanese culture was able to make a civilizational leap many centuries ago. Additionally, in old Japan, adopted Chinese codes were equally imperfect because of their archaic form and superficial content, as they were translated versions of foreign law. The Japanese political elites had been aware of this and still did nothing to oppose it.

For this reason, he did not believe that the grammatical problems concerning the correct use of the Japanese language and the archaic stylistic form of the Codes should obstruct their publication. T. Kishimoto also argued that the language of legal acts was different from poetry, so the opponents of the Codes should focus on more serious things than preserving the beauty of the form and style in legal scholarship. Referring to his experience, he cited French laws, which were understood entirely differently by the average reader and an experienced jurist. In the last sentences of his article, he added that the promulgation of the Codes was the beginning of Japan's prosperous era, and the Codes themselves, being the Japanese citizens' cornerstone of the private law rights, must be defended as *kinjō teppeki* – an impenetrable castle.[5]

5.1.3. Hikoroku Morozumi's opinion (French School, decisive faction)

On 10 May 1890, *The Journal of Law and Politics* (Issue 107) also published an opinion of H. Morozumi, a third-cohort graduate of the Law School at the Ministry of Justice. His article was entitled "About the Publication of New Codes", and similarly to T. Kishimoto's statement, presented a resolute voice of the decisive faction.[6]

Referring to the words of the famous English jurist Henry Maine, one of the forefathers of modern legal history, H. Morozumi tried to predict the outcomes resulting from the reception of foreign law in Japan. Based on Maine's views, he argued that if the adopted foreign law was well analysed and deprived of its native elements typical for the country of origin, there is a possibility that it would function well in both countries and would emphasize cultural differences between them in appropriate proportions. The author claimed that if the government decided to adopt foreign law, it might help the state make a civilizational leap. H. Morozumi gave examples such as old Chinese codes that were in force in Japan and Roman law, adopted in many European countries. He expressed his opinion that in times of significant human progress and the transitional period of Japanese statehood, the reception of foreign law should be natural for society.

The French School representative argued that even though Japan had not experienced any notable foreign intervention and remained a sovereign country

[5] Opinion reprint, Hoshino, 2014, pp. 73–75.

[6] Morozumi, 1890, (original pages are unknown).

in the last 600 years, it had developed a non-functional system of customary law that differed in all the former 66 provinces. He indicated that the Edo government controlled the administration of justice and guaranteed the protection of life and property rights yet failed to overcome the fragmentation of the country and the unification of the customary law system after the opening of Japan's borders. By describing the complicated procedure of court rulings based on the search for appropriate customs and correcting them with the equity principle, he rhetorically asked the postponement faction representatives if they were opponents of the law codification. H. Morozumi also referred to French history as the best example for Japan. Before the publication of the Codes, France had at least 66 national and over 300 regional customs considered inconsistent and requiring unification. They were the main reason for the state authorities to codify the law.

The author confirmed the current stance of the decisive faction, calling for the publication of part of the Civil Code (Property Law), the Code of Civil Procedure and the Commercial Code to be the cornerstone for securing the citizens' private law rights. He also expressed joy and did not understand the English School's obsession with preserving the old system of customary law. H. Morozumi admitted that the new Codes were "a reception of Western laws" and "an imitation of the French law". However, he did not see anything wrong with this since France built its legal system on Roman law like other European countries. In his opinion, Japan did not have to oppose these trends. The author did not want to hide this fact from the public and insisted on transparency.

Having referred to the number of articles in each of the three published Codes, he argued that they should not be described as too complicated, especially compared to European countries. He mentioned that the Meiji Constitution, consisting of about a hundred articles, became the core of the new Japanese legal system. However, it still needed to be supported by further legislation. H. Morozumi also criticized the postponement faction's arguments regarding the complicated content of the Codes. He acknowledged that some terms, primarily created from traditional kanji characters, would be incomprehensible to the lower class. Still, he argued that the interpretation of the law was the task of jurists, who became specialized professionals due to developments in the law. For him, independent schools of legal jurisprudence were established for this purpose, where specialized kanji characters are taught to understand the content of the law thoroughly. Therefore, he rejected the postulate of the postponement faction regarding the need to draft bills "comprehensible to the ordinary citizen". This view was criticized as a strange notion among a part of Japanese jurisprudence. Referring to army and navy drills and early school education, H. Morozumi argued that public law was widely respected regardless of social class. Contrary to private law, no one has yet suggested simplifying its language and form.

In the final part of his article, H. Morozumi once again confirmed the nature of the new Codes drafted based on the reception of foreign law. He justified the legislator by attributing to him human characteristics, such as the tendency to make mistakes. At the same time, he believed that most of the Codes' defects could be removed by simple amendments. The attitude of the postponement faction was assessed negatively, as its representatives denied the value of the new Codes and tried to prevent their entry into force. H. Morozumi called it an incredibly irresponsible and despicable act.[7]

5.1.4. *Nihon no Hōritsu* editorial team's opinion on morality and law (postponement faction)

In May 1890, *Nihon no Hōritsu* editorial team published an opinion (Volume 2, Issue 5) entitled "Criticism of Moral Persons = Lawyers' Mockery".[8]

Referring to the codification project, the journal's editorial team reminded readers that the Codes had been attacked in numerous speeches, press articles and official inquiries for their systematics and style. The cabinet's stance was described as adamant since codes were promulgated despite the criticism and awareness that they would change the nature of the Japanese legal system. According to the editors, an axiologically contradictory Roman law replaced the well-known and well-established Chinese model. As an example of discrepancies, they cited the Civil Code legitimation of a child who could bring an action against its guardian. The editors commented on this private law right, raising doubts about whether providing for it was necessary. They believed that, although the drafters of the Code might see it as being morally right, it would undermine traditional family ties. The postponement faction representatives argued that the guardian, often the parent themself, cannot fear a lawsuit from their child. Although the authors did not negate the idea of children claiming their rights in court, they believed the lack of legal regulation regarding conflicts between a child and a parent was the best solution, as each person should decide whether to sue their guardian after considering the moral aspects. The attempt to interfere with the morality of society was strongly criticized and presented as short-sighted protection. The editors recommended that the drafters not focus on one aspect of human morality but also look at this problem from a more distant perspective.[9]

[7] Opinion reprint, Hoshino, 2014, pp. 76–78.

[8] Nihon no Hōritsu, 1890a, pp. 87–88.

[9] For the full opinion text, see Murakami, 2008a, p. 318.

5.1.5. Sentarō Hirayama's opinion (English School, postponement faction)

In June 1890, *Nihon no Hōritsu* (Volume 2, Issue 6) published an opinion entitled "What English School Jurists Should Do with the New Codes?". The author was S. Hirayama, a student of the Faculty of Law of the Old University of Tokyo/Imperial University.

Referring to the ten-year process of codification of Japanese law, which required the involvement of foreign jurists and the allocation of considerable financial resources, S. Hirayama emphasized the importance of the codes for each legal system. Although the recently promulgated Japanese Codes seemed to be an epochal work at first glance, he was worried that their effectiveness was debatable. As the reason for that statement, he referred to an archaic form and incomprehensible terminology, which might influence the public's insufficient understanding of private law rights. S. Hirayama also expressed his regret that despite the fact a large group of jurists initiated the discussion on the Codes, the cabinet treated the entire drafting process as a solely government project. It also did not give it the appropriate attention apart from establishing a codification committee. For him, the most visible disadvantage of the Codes was ignoring the national customary law, and this flaw resulted from setting aside the idea of cooperation between drafters and ordinary citizens.

S. Hirayama argued that codification should not be treated only as a legislative activity because the publication of new Codes and the Constitution had a considerable impact on the entire society by extending or limiting the rights of citizens. He believed that the Drafting Committee members should have paid more attention to social conditions, customs, history and spirit of the nation and be genuinely engaged in the process of drafting. As an example of the complicated nature of law, he mentioned the United Kingdom, where thousands of court decisions resulted in hundreds of legal norms, which required the work of many jurists to understand their nature. S. Hirayama accused the drafters of preparing the Codes in haste, motivated by the desire to appear on the pages of Japanese legal history textbooks. For him, copying a foreign law was not an honest attempt to develop a national code. He admitted that the Meiji Restoration, the opening of the country's borders, the establishment of a centralized government and the policy to eradicate feudalism positively affected society. He also understood that introducing the Codes was the only way to unify the customary law systems used in various domains. However, he also stated that this task turned out to be much more complicated than the political elites had initially expected.

The author explained the motives of the Association of Jurists, which reacted to rumours about the plan to publish the Codes. The English School representatives, who knew the issues related to the codification of law in the United Kingdom and

Germany, opposed accelerating the law codification process in Japan, as their old legal system did not have such a rich legacy compared to European countries. S. Hirayama supported the postulates of the Association of Jurists and called the cabinet to abandon the one-sided point of view on law codification, make the Code drafts publicly available and invite jurists for a debate about their content to develop a coherent view of the national jurisprudence. He also expressed regret that citizens in their country were still accustomed to a despotic way of pursuing domestic policy since modern legal thought was still developing.

According to S. Hirayama, the emergence of the postponement faction was a natural consequence of drafting the Civil Code only by French School representatives who adopted the well-known French model as the basis for the Japanese private law system. As he continued, the English School representatives saw the shortcomings of the French Civil Code and did not agree to duplicate its errors in the Japanese version. In addition to faulty systematics and artificial language, the author mentioned a vaguely outlined division between rights and obligations. He also disagreed with the French School representatives' claims that their opponents' competence was lacking in matters related to the interpretation of statutory law. S. Hirayama explained the differences in legal education between the two schools, underlining that the English School only criticized memorizing the content of each article as devoid of cognitive sense. At the same time, it promoted drafting provisions with understandable meaning, which did not require people to use commentaries. He argued that although the English School jurists were used to studying numerous judicial decisions with their justifications and then identifying legal norms based on them, reading the Code caused great difficulties in interpretation. For this reason, he believed that the postponement faction had to present the flaws of the Code to a broader audience and avoid the situation in which the new law would only be readable by the French School jurists.[10]

5.1.6. Kiyohiko Nakamura's opinion (English School, postponement faction)

In June 1890, *Nihon no Hōritsu* (Volume 2, Issue 6) published another opinion of the postponement faction. The author was K. Nakamura, a judge and an Old University of Tokyo/Imperial University graduate. The article was entitled "Discussion on the Gravity of the Codes".[11]

Referring to the publication of the Civil Code (part), the Commercial Code and the Code of Civil Procedure, the author stated that after almost 20 years, the uncodified Japanese private law had become history. According to him, however,

[10] For the full opinion text, see Murakami, 2008a, pp. 320–324.

[11] Nakamura, 1890, pp. 15–20.

the promulgation of the new Codes provoked a debate, which took the form of commenting on the advantages and disadvantages of the codification. He argued that among numerous questions, there were many doubts about the nature of the Codes and only jurists knew the actual reason for this issue. K. Nakamura tried to convince the readers that he was well acquainted with the problems concerning drafting the Code, which would not have significant flaws and gaps. At the same time, he postulated that the cabinet should not rush into the entry into force of the Codes because there was still room for improving them, especially in adapting them to Japanese social conditions.

K. Nakamura argued that although society will be granted numerous private law rights after the entry into force of the Civil Code, it will also have to obey equally abundant new obligations. He predicted that by negating the existing customs, people would not be able to follow the path of evolution of Japanese culture. He believed that the Civil Code's systematics, form and nature, criticized for the sake of the greater good of the Japanese law, needed a more critical view. He also stated that the simultaneous publication of three codes without carefully considering their advantages and disadvantages was a severe mistake. As a jurist, he felt responsible for informing society, who did not understand the complicated nature of the law, about the possible negative consequences of the entry into force of the new Codes. He actively followed the previous opinions of the postponement faction and favoured its position as the voice of reason against excessive haste. K. Nakamura wanted to avoid criticism of the drafters, and he believed that the code should have a special place in every legal system. In his opinion, the policy of revising unequal treaties should not be the main reason for the promulgation of the Codes, which would become "amorphous law" for society. He also criticized the postulates of the subsequent amendment of the Codes, which he considered complicated to do in practice and negatively affecting the perception of the new law. K. Nakamura was aware that public criticism of the Codes was undermining their authority in the eyes of society. Yet, he emphasized that speaking out loud about the shortcomings was necessary to make them visible to the cabinet and legislators.

The author admitted that he knew about the effort related to the need to invent a specialized legal language from scratch, although he considered the level of its development to be low. Using as an example J. Bentham's rejected offer to President J. Madison related to the drafting of Codes for the United States, K. Nakamura argued that in some societies, the law remained uncodified for various impartial reasons. However, he considered the emergence of "three or even four" schools of legal scholarship as a positive aspect of Japanese jurisprudence. He also indicated that Japanese jurists learned about their strengths and weaknesses by studying foreign legal systems. This knowledge could be used to revise the Code. Still, the cabinet must delay its entry into force. As a model of ideal legislation, the author mentioned the Danish Code of King Christian V of 1683, which was respected by people due to preserving Danish customary law. K. Nakamura hoped that the newly published Civil Code could also earn a favourable reputation among Japanese citizens.[12]

5.1.7. Hideo Itō's opinion (English School, postponement faction)

In October 1890, *Nihon no Hōritsu* (Volume 2, Issue 11) published H. Itō's opinion entitled "One Doubt Concerning the Provisions on the Validity of Marriage".[13]

H. Itō's article was written in response to the promulgation of part of the Civil Code concerning Personal Law and Succession Law in early October 1890. The author argued that the Minister of Justice, A. Yamada, did not consider the English School's objections and published the missing part of the Code. Although H. Itō was not a supporter of the new Civil Code, he simultaneously expressed his admiration for the boldness and determination of the cabinet, which elevated Japan to a group of countries with a fully codified legal system.

In the next section, the English School representative partially distanced himself from the previous criticism of the postponement faction. He appreciated the value of the four books of the Civil Code concerning Property Law published six months earlier. Additionally, he was particularly interested in Personal and Succession Law, which in his opinion had the most significant impact on society due to their connections with folk customs. He claimed they were the most native spheres of the Japanese private law system. Their importance for Japanese legal scholarship was confirmed when G. Boissonade entrusted Japanese jurists with drafting this part of the Code. Therefore, he felt that Personal and Succession Law should be based on simple and proven customs to avoid creating complicated law theories. H. Itō admitted that although he had no choice but to celebrate the publication of the Civil Code as a Japanese citizen, he also wanted to convey that several hundred Personal Law articles did not exhaustively describe the private law relationships between people. He again expressed his concern that the Japanese legislator should strive to harmonize the Code with domestic customary law at all costs.

As the most critical defect of the Book on Personal Law, H. Itō pointed out Article 38, which introduced the obligation to receive the father's and mother's consent by a child willing to enter into marriage. He stressed the importance of marriage not only as the cornerstone of every family but also from the national perspective, as each society was mostly built up from families. For him, it was also a specific type of contract between a woman and a man, concluded with the

[12] For the full opinion text, see Murakami, 2008a, pp. 324–328.

[13] Itō, 1890, pp. 29–33.

genuine intention to last the entire life, in which both spouses had essential rights and responsibilities towards each other. Referring to this theoretical model, H. Itō also mentioned marriages concluded by emotionally immature persons, where the spouses' decision was not based on rational grounds. He believed that if a marriage was designed to be a permanent contract, the law had to contain a mechanism to protect young men's and women's interests.

While agreeing with the restriction related to the marriage of people who have not attained full legal capacity, H. Itō criticized the obligation to receive the father's and mother's consent to enter into a valid marriage if both spouses had full legal capacity. He assessed that Article 38 limited each person's freedom since the obligation to obtain parental consent for a 30-year-old or even 40-year-old man to marry was contrary to logic and the natural social order. As he continued his analysis, if a parent wanted their child's happiness, they should give consent regardless of their views on the future marriage. He also argued that the Civil Code restriction described as a lack of parental consent should only protect the child from entering into a highly unfavourable marriage until they attain the age of majority. H. Itō claimed that children always struggled to obtain their parents' approval of their life choices. Therefore, there was a risk, assuming the worst-case scenario, parents could never agree to their child's marriage. The author also believed that an adult was capable of making rational decisions, and family law should not restrict their legal capacity in the most private sphere of human life. The solution adopted in Article 38 was detrimental to the child and their relationship with the parents since Japanese society was familiar with a relatively common phenomenon of parents interfering in the child's marriage despite their superficially positive intentions.

H. Itō believed Article 38 might become antagonistic to Japanese society as he found no traces of the requirement to acquire parental consent for marriage in old customary law. The drafters of the Code also did not fully adopt the French model they had been most familiar with. According to the Napoleonic Code, only men under 25 and women under 21 had to obtain parental consent to conclude a valid marriage. In the author's opinion, establishing the principle of lifelong child protection in matrimonial law had the opposite, harmful effect. He did not doubt that the Japanese legislator knew the French model. Thus, he tried to convince him that introducing more strict requirements for parental consent in Article 38 lacked proper justification.[14]

[14] For the full opinion text, see Murakami, 2008a, pp. 361–364.

5.2. The controversy during the Imperial Diet's first meeting

In June 1890, in reaction to the publication of three codes and the emerging Civil Code and the Commercial Code Controversy among Japanese jurisprudence, Tamotsu Murata presented a proposal that the Civil Code and the Commercial Code would enter into force on 1 January 1893. T. Murata was one of the members of the Chamber of Elders and the Law Research Committee, the dedicated postponement faction representative.[15] His initiative was supported by more than 50 distinctive lawyers, politicians and entrepreneurs. Despite some objections and suggestions to withdraw from this idea, it was approved by the Chamber of Elders. Subsequently, the proposal was passed to the cabinet. The friction between the supporters and opponents of the Codes was already visible, even to the people outside the Controversy. On 22 July, Prime Minister A. Yamagata rejected Murata's proposal and soon submitted his decision to the emperor as a report to the throne.[16]

The increased activity of the postponement faction became a legal and political issue for the cabinet, requiring extraordinary measures to carry out the legislative plans without any hindrance. Among the Japanese law community, one of the greatest and most influential adversaries of the Codes was *Hōri Seika*. In June 1890 alone, the English School journal published seven long articles criticizing the Civil Code and the Commercial Code in two issues (Volume 6, Issues 35 and 36).[17] At the end of July, just after the release of Issue 38, the cabinet, hoping to limit the activity of the postponement faction, imposed censorship on the journal, banning it from further publishing activity.[18]

On 29 November 1890, the Constitution of Japan entered into force. Pursuant to Article 41, the Imperial Diet's first meeting began on the same day. Shūgi'in – the House of Representatives – consisted of 300 members elected in general elections held four months earlier in 214 single-member and 43 double-member constituencies throughout the country. The first elections to the legislative body in Japan (also in Asian history) coincided with a bad harvest and widespread panic in the domestic rice market, directly resulting in the overrepresentation of anti-government and lower-class factions in the lower house.[19] Once the agreement between political circles was established, the House of Representatives was finally dominated by the Civil Coalition (Liberal Party and Constitutional Reform Party), which had

[15] Dai Nippon Suisan Kai, 1919, pp. 26–28.

[16] Ōkubo, Takahashi, 1999, pp. 292–293.

[17] Hōri Seika (ed.), 1890d, https://dl.ndl.go.jp/info:ndljp/pid/1493319, (access: 18.01.2021); Hōri Seika (ed.), 1890e, https://dl.ndl.go.jp/info:ndljp/pid/1493320, (access: 18.01.2021).

[18] Hoshino, 1943, p. 126.

[19] As many as 191 elected members of the House of Representatives were of plebeian origin.

171 members compared to only 84 members supporting the cabinet (Taiseikai and Kokumin Jiyūtō).[20] Four decisive faction representatives, S. Inoue, S. Isobe, S. Kōmyōji and K. Miyagi, and three postponement faction representatives, M. Hajime, K. Okayama and M. Tsuda, also got seats in the lower house. Notably, M. Tsuda was elected Vice President of the House of Representatives.

On 10 December, during the House of Representatives plenary session, Matsūemon Nagai, a businessman from Aichi Prefecture, submitted a bill to unify the interregnum of the Civil and Commercial Code. The proposal assumed that both Codes would enter into force on 1 January 1893, the same as T. Murata's plan from June, which was rejected by A. Yamagata's cabinet. On 15 December, a committee chaired by Noboyuki Nakayama started thoroughly examining M. Nagai's bill.[21] It soon triggered the first parliamentary dispute between the decisive faction, represented by S. Inoue, S. Kōmyōji and K. Miyagi, and the postponement faction, represented by M. Hajime and M. Tsuda. Although the decisive faction initially had the upper hand in the House of Representatives, the arguments concerning the need to postpone the date of entry into force of the Commercial Code were positively assessed by most lower house members. R. Mitsukuri, then the Deputy Minister of Justice and a cabinet delegate to the Imperial Diet, also became involved in the discussion, trying to convince the audience that postponement of the entry into force of the Commercial Code would be a blow to the authority of Emperor Meiji.[22] However, the lower house members still remembered the cabinet's unfavourable policy for entrepreneurs and R. Mitsukuri's speech had the opposite effect. Therefore, they were more likely to support the position of the postponement party, whose bill was passed by a 189–67 vote.[23]

Subsequently, on 20 December, the bill on postponing the date of entry into force of the Commercial Code became the subject of analysis at Kizokuin – the House of Peers – where it provoked a fierce debate on the merits of Nagai's proposal.[24] Tosuke Hirata, Kōhei Sufu and Masamoto Watari represented the decisive faction in the upper house. The postponement faction was represented by K. Hiroyuki and N. Hozumi and moderately supported by the Chairman of the House of Peers, H. Itō.[25] The members' statements revealed fundamental differences in views regarding the date of entry into force of the Commercial Code and its nature. Based on press releases, it can be assessed that N. Hozumi's speech was crucial in convincing the

20 Tomita, 1986, pp. 66–93.

21 Record on the House of Representatives committee session on 15 December 1890 regarding the change of the date of entry into force of the Commercial Code.

22 Record of R. Mitsukuri's speech during the House of Representatives session on 15 December 1890.

23 Hozumi, 1980, p. 335.

24 Hozumi, 1980, p. 335.

25 Hoshino, 1943, p. 123.

House of Peers. On 22 December, it eventually approved the bill on postponing the entry into force of the Commercial Code by a 104–62 vote.[26]

The following day, the bill approved by the House of Representatives and the House of Peers became an essential subject of the cabinet agenda. Referring to Article 55 Section 2 of the Constitution, the Minister of Justice, A. Yamada, and the Home Minister, Jūdō Saigō, refused to sign the bill sanctioning the postponement of the entry into force of the Commercial Code. They also insisted on submitting the veto by a separate route, preferably as a report to the imperial throne. However, A. Yamagata's cabinet was internally divided. The Minister of Trade and Agriculture, Munemitsu Mutsu, explicitly objected to turning down the bill on the Commercial Code and referred to Article 37 of the Constitution, which gave the Imperial Diet the right to decide on legislative initiatives in Japan.[27] The dispute among the ministers was not resolved by the Prime Minister, who did not take a clear stance. Finally, on 25 December, A. Yamada resigned under the pretext of health problems, yet feeling responsible for the legislative failure. The Chairman of the Privy Council, T. Ōki, was temporarily appointed as the Minister of Justice and signed M. Nagai's bill.[28] Eventually, it was passed directly to the emperor for his sanction, who following Article 6 of the Constitution, also signed and promulgated it as binding law on 27 December.[29]

Publishing the bill on delaying the entry into force of the Commercial Code was the first postponement faction victory party in the Civil Code Controversy. The debate in the Imperial Diet revealed that the relatively influential decisive faction did not have a majority in any house. Adequate reasoning was enough to convince the members of parliament to support M. Nagai's proposal. The postponement faction predominance was evident in the House of Representatives, where many entrepreneurs were keenly interested in the new law directly influencing their businesses. As for the discussion at the House of Peers, two factors caused the unexpected postponement faction victory. Firstly, the surprised decisive faction referred only to the authority of the government and the need to complete the law codification process and failed to mobilize its group to gain new supporters among the hesitant members of parliament. Secondly, N. Hozumi, an experienced advocate with great oratory skills, spoke on behalf of the postponement faction and clearly presented not only theoretical but also practical issues concerning the

[26] Hoshino, 1943, p. 123.

[27] Fukushima, 1988, p. 121.

[28] This resignation was not formally accepted. Ultimately, A. Yamada continued to serve as Minister of Justice in Yamagata's cabinet. Nihon Daigaku, 1963, pp. 788–799.

[29] Meiji 23-nen 12-gatsu 27-nichi Hōritsu Dai 108-Gō: Shōhō oyobi Shōhō Shikō Jōrei Shikō Kigen Hōritsu.

Commercial Code. His voice of reason became the decisive factor for winning in the House of Peers dominated by cabinet supporters.

The Imperial Diet's first meeting focused on the struggle to postpone the date of entry into force of the Commercial Code. It resulted from the fact that on 1 January 1891, less than a month from the submission of M. Nagai's bill, the Commercial Code interregnum was about to end. Since the postponement faction still had two years before the entry into force of the Civil Code, it concentrated on the most pressing issues of Japanese legislation. Increased activity in one field did not mean the Civil Code Controversy was utterly put aside. In December 1890 and January 1891, various legal journals published numerous texts commenting on the advantages and disadvantages of the Civil Code. The October 1890 promulgation of the missing part concerning Personal and Succession Law enabled the postponement faction representatives to familiarize themselves with all the Civil Code provisions and thus have a comprehensive view of its principles, systematics and content. At the same time, members of the Japanese legal system watched the legislative endeavour in Germany with great attention. In December 1890, the Bundesrat established the Second Codification Commission to review and amend the first draft of the national Civil Code.[30]

On 7 March 1891, during one of the last sessions of the Imperial Diet's first meeting, Umashine Obata, a distinguished judge and former member of the Chamber of Elders, on behalf of the postponement faction, submitted to the House of Peers the first proposal to amend the Civil Code. As expressed in the project's justification, he argued that the Civil and Commercial Codes did not consider Japanese customary law. Thus, they should not only be delayed but also thoroughly amended. On 13 February 1891, during the House of Peers plenary session, he proposed establishing a Review Committee to re-examine the Codes and provide necessary corrections.[31] Pursuant to Article 40 of the Constitution, the legislative project required a favourable cabinet opinion. However, A. Yamagata soon rejected U. Obata's initiative, explaining there was no time to introduce additional amendments to the Civil and Commercial Codes. The equally essential part of the cabinet's feedback was that it strongly disagreed with the negative assessment of the Codes and underlined that they should come into force on 1 January 1893.[32]

30 Iwamura, 1996, p. 172.

31 Record of the House of Peers session on 13 February 1891.

32 Ōkubo, Takahashi, 1999, p. 294.

5.3. Summary of the second stage of the Civil Code Controversy

Once the cabinet promulgated the part of the Civil Code related to Property Law in April 1890 and Personal and Succession Law in October, the postponement faction focused on preparing for the debate in the Imperial Diet. Although in the first half of 1890, the increased activity of *Hōri Seika* indicated that the public discussion with the decisive faction regarding the revision of the Civil Code would be continued for the rest of the year, the cabinet's censorship led to the forced shutdown of the postponement faction's largest and most influential journal. After that, the position of opponents of the Civil Code was presented in other periodicals, especially in *Nihon no Hōritsu* which was gradually gaining popularity.

In the second stage of the Controversy, the decisive faction took a firm stand to complete the codification project. They argued that introducing the last missing codes would have measurable positive effects on Japan's internal and external affairs. Its representatives referred to the policy of revising unequal treaties to a lesser extent, focusing on demonstrating the outdated nature of Japanese customary law and the inefficiency of a legal system lacking two of the five key codes. For most of 1890, the decisive faction did not see a significant threat from the postponement faction. The course of the Imperial Diet's first meeting perfectly reflected their unawareness. Members of the House of Representatives and the House of Peers who belonged to the postponement faction showed more determination and presented more convincing arguments related to practical issues. They also skilfully used the public mood among the Japanese entrepreneurs and politicians in both houses to pass a bill postponing the date of entry into force of the Commercial Code. This success not only partially thwarted the adamant policy of the cabinet, undermining its authority in the eyes of parliamentarians and society, but also showed the effectiveness of the Japanese Constitution concerning the rule of law and separation of powers in the legislative process. As M. Fukushima indicated, among the far-reaching effects of postponing the date of entry into force of the Commercial Code, which was only one of the fronts of the Controversy, one should also include the consolidation of both parties.[33] Despite achieving the first remarkable victory, the postponement faction still intended to press for revising the Civil Code and Commercial Code.

The decisive faction, suffering its first unexpected defeat which in turn negatively affected the prestige of the Ministry of Justice and the French School, finally noticed the real threat from the opponents of the Codes almost two years after the publication of the Association of Jurists' opinion. The proposals of the postponement faction representatives presented at the House of Peers in February 1891

33 Fukushima, 1988, p. 124.

proved that by the time the Civil Code and Commercial Code entered into force on 1 January 1893, the subject of their revision would undoubtedly be discussed at the Imperial Diet's second meeting which had to be convened by the end of 1891 according to Article 41 of the Constitution. Regardless of those expectations, the second stage of the Civil Code Controversy ended with the closing of the Imperial Diet's first meeting on 7 March 1891.

CHAPTER SIX

THE THIRD STAGE OF THE CIVIL CODE CONTROVERSY – ESCALATION AND CONCLUSION

Abstract

This chapter describes the last stage of the Controversy from April 1891 to June 1892. Due to numerous publications of both parties before the Imperial Diet's second and third meetings, the dispute escalated from a scholarly debate between jurists to a crucial national matter discussed by various influential circles. Finally, the Civil Code Controversy (including the issues related to the Commercial Code) was resolved by the Imperial Diet's third meeting at the turn of May and June 1892. The House of Peers and the House of Representatives passed a bill postponing the date of entry into force of both codes by another four years, until 31 December 1896.

Keywords: Civil Code Controversy, Japanese Civil Code, Codification in Japan, Meiji Parliament

"Because it's not the Civil Code for all of us".

—Yoshitarō Hirano's comment on the Civil Code

The postponement of the entry into force of the Commercial Code during the Imperial Diet's first meeting revealed to both factions the importance of legal argumentation for gaining supporters among parliament members. To convince the largest possible group of future parliamentarians and influential circles of Japanese entrepreneurs and politicians, the opponents of the Codes focused their activities on publishing short but expressive opinions. They directly attacked the Civil Code as harmful to society and called for the new law to be revised during the Imperial Diet's second meeting. At the beginning of April 1891, in response to the ban on the publication of *Hōri Seika*, the English School representatives, graduates of the Old University of Tokyo/Imperial University, founded a new magazine entitled *Hōgaku Shimpō – The Jurisprudence News*.[1]

[1] Hoshino, 1942, p. 126.

Severe criticism of the Codes soon met with a violent reaction from the decisive faction, which mobilized its supporters to speak out publicly and present numerous advantages of the entry into force of the Civil Code and the Commercial Code on 1 January 1893. Even though the decisive faction succeeded in consolidating the jurisprudence around the Ministry of Justice and the largest academic centres recognizing the importance of the Codes, in the final stage of the Controversy, some French School representatives supported the postulates of the opposing faction. The period from March 1891 to June 1892, was also characterized by more significant activity of a small group of German School representatives, who were divided between postponement and decisive factions.

6.1. New publications of the postponement faction – Opinions published in 1891

6.1.1. *The Jurisprudence News* editorial team's declaration concerning the goals and purposes of founding the journal (postponement faction)

On 25 April 1891, in the first issue of *The Jurisprudence News*, the editorial team published a declaration entitled "The Main Importance of Founding *The Jurisprudence News*". The text presented the motives for establishing a new legal journal and their main goals for the upcoming fierce debate on the Codes.[2]

The editorial team assured the readers that they founded the new journal only to inform the public about legal matters. As the main subject of interest, they indicated that they would comment on legislative activity and educating citizens about the possible harmful consequences of the law that had been promulgated recently. The editors believed that they had a duty to protect present and future generations from the "spreading tide of misfortune" as they presented the Codes. By using the allegory of a doctor knowingly using the wrong medicine leading to the death of a patient, they asked a rhetorical question of whether reckless legislation could not have had a similar effect on society.

The Jurisprudence News referred to the words of Herbert Spencer, who stated that the British parliament could adopt a system of statutory law only after promoting a different vision of social morality and using forcible methods and huge funds. According to Spencer, a supporter of historical evolutionism, the publication of any law must have disturbed the social order because people were firmly attached to their customs. The editors believed that Spencer's words were relevant to Japan, where the government wanted to eliminate all customs by bringing the Civil Code into force. They were also sceptical about the political situation in the country,

[2] Hōgaku Shimpō (ed.), 1891, pp. 1–3.

as the cabinet denied citizens participation in the legislation despite the newly established constitutional rules of the law-making process. As for the editors, the concern related to the Codes became evident during the Imperial Diet's first meeting, which decided to take a closer look at them and not ignore doubts about their advantages and disadvantages. Referring to the sincere desire to fight for the nation and its legal system, *The Jurisprudence News* encouraged readers to join the criticism of the mindless westernization of Japan.[3]

6.1.2. Yatsuka Hozumi's opinion concerning the nature of the Civil Code (German School, postponement faction)

On 25 April 1891, *The Jurisprudence News* also published Y. Hozumi's short opinion entitled "The National Code of Civil Law".[4] The author was an Old University of Tokyo/Imperial University and Berlin University graduate and the younger brother of N. Hozumi.[5]

At the start of his article, Y. Hozumi stated that the drafters of the Civil Code should have paid more attention to its national character. Referring to the lectures of the German lawyer and theologian Rudolph Sohm, he argued that private law regulates the distribution of society's wealth because by combining labour and capital, it allocated goods to people in a balanced manner. Sohm described the societal consequences of it and advocated a return to the original understanding of social wealth. For Y. Hozumi, "the right to property" was in fact "the mere excuse of the rich to take food from the poor". He wondered if the biblical Adam and Eve had such a thing as "the right to property" since it was a concept artificially created by private law and became a dangerous weapon of uneven distribution of goods used by the courts, thus creating social inequalities. Y. Hozumi believed that all schools of legal jurisprudence in Japan should read the theory of Ferdinand Lassalle, accurately describing this issue.

The author indicated that the Civil Code contained an idea of a natural person, an individual human being, pointed out as a basic unit of the division of goods in society. According to him, such a solution completely ignored the aspect of concern for the collective interest and was "contrary to the natural order and did not necessarily have a long-term positive effect". Y. Hozumi believed that the private law system based on guaranteeing individual rights obviously led to deepening social differences: the rich freely accumulated more capital, and the poor became even poorer. He considered the Civil Code as such an unjust law. Therefore, he

[3] For the full opinion text, see Hoshino (red.), 2014, pp. 80–81.

[4] Hozumi, 1891a, pp. 8–10.

[5] Ushiomi, Toshitani, 1975, p. 99.

openly enquired whether society should be divided into a wealthy and a poor class that could be described as "a nation". Referring to the socio-political situation in Western Europe at the end of the 19th century, he argued that pro-worker legislation should also greatly interest private law jurisprudence. The author claimed that the economic postulates of Carl Menger and Gustav von Schmoller shook the Austrian and German legal scholarship, undermining their theoretical foundations.[6]

In the summary of his opinion, Y. Hozumi explained that he took the opportunity to present his short manifesto addressed to the public in *The Jurisprudence News*, hoping that it would become the subject of a wider discussion. Using the allegory of not being able to see the wood for the trees, he wanted to show that lawyers should not only read individual Civil Code provisions but also try to catch its overall picture. This did not lead to a favourable assessment of the Code, but, as he tried to persuade, dissenting opinions on it should not be rejected.[7]

6.1.3. Zenjirō Tsuboya's opinion (English School, postponement party)

In July 1891, *Nihon no Hōritsu* (Volume 3, Issue 7) published Z. Tsuboya's opinion entitled "On the Book on Personal Law of the Civil Code".[8]

Z. Tsuboya argued that family law was the part of private law in which the legislator should pay special attention to avoid discrepancies between statute and old customary law. He thought that from the very beginning Japanese customary law should be the basis for the codification process, but for various reasons the Meiji government chose a different path. According to him, the use of various formal divisions of social groups in the Civil Code – such as into married couples, parent and child, and citizens – did not refer to customary law, because it was more similar to European private law systems. Z. Tsuboya indicated that in many other fields, the Civil Code scrapped the customary law and adopted foreign norms without a significant reason. He pointed out that the reception of foreign private law was absolute, as it also included Property Law, Security and Evidence. The author did not negate the value of foreign private law but was trying to demonstrate that the new family and succession law aroused the most tremendous controversy. Thus, their entry into force should be postponed.

[6] Carl Menger (1840–1921) was an Austrian economist, founder of the Austrian school of economics, and known for his theory of value and price and the development of the concept of marginal utility, which criticized the labour theory of value of Adam Smith and David Ricardo. Gustav von Schmoller (1838–1917) was a German economist, the main representative of the historical school in economics, which treated economics as an empirical science and based on experience and opposing the concepts of Carl Menger and Max Weber.

[7] For the full opinion text, see Hoshino (ed.), 2014, pp. 81–82.

[8] Tsuboya, 1891.

Referring to rumours circulating among the public concerning the involvement of the French School and then the English School representatives in the drafting of the Book on Personal Law, Z. Tsuboya expressed doubts regarding the methods of its approval. He mentioned that despite reading the Code's provisions several times, he still had numerous interpretation queries, which did not result from the legislator's lack of due diligence.

First, the Japanese discussed Article 41, which stipulated that if the father and mother were unknown, a child under 20 had to obtain the consent of a guardian to conclude a valid marriage. Z. Tsuboya noticed the legislator's intention to protect minors from entering marriage under the influence of irrational premises. At the same time, he indicated that Article 42 was a *lex specialis* since children under 20, whose father and mother were unknown and who were fostered by an orphanage, had to obtain permission from the head of the facility. Taking as a basis the consent of the guardian regulated by Article 41 and the head of the facility described by Article 42, Z. Tsuboya commented on the complicated process of selecting a guardian. In the case of abandoned children, their status was easy to determine according to Article 42, but children whose parents died simultaneously could not enjoy the trouble-free appointment of a new guardian. Pursuant to the provisions of the Civil Code, the guardian could be appointed by a parent in the will. In practice, this meant that the second line of kinship ascendant was usually the first candidate to become the guardian. If there were no ascendants, the head of the household became the guardian. However, if the guardian did not agree to accept their new role, the decision was to be made by the family council based on information about other blood ties [according to Article 167].

Z. Tsuboya reminded readers that in the customary Japanese family law, adopting and raising an abandoned child until it reached the age of majority were standard practices. He sought the reasons for this phenomenon in the lack of offspring and the simple desire to do the right thing. Quoting the folk tales, he argued that adoption was a permanent element of Japanese culture, which numerous restrictions in the Civil Code have strongly revised. Also, for him, the complicated nature of the relations between adoptive parents and children was contrary to the existing practice. It could lead to numerous conflicts over priority between blood and adoption ties. Z. Tsuboya felt that the new law was also particularly inconvenient for adoptive parents, who could not fully exercise parental authority and thus failed in finding a suitable heir.

Subsequently, the author criticized the content of Article 162, which stipulated that in one household, regardless of the number of minors, only one guardian could be appointed. According to him, this provision was contrary to Article 164, as in the case of the deceased guardian appointing in their testament another guardian for one of the children, many guardians could be appointed in one household. The author also believed that the law regulating the status of a guardian should not cover meticulous aspects of daily life, only the most critical issues.

In conclusion, Z. Tsuboya argued that regardless of the French and English School representatives' efforts to introduce a comprehensive legal act in Japan, few apparent contradictions in the Civil Code require a more detailed explanation from the legislator.[9]

6.1.4. Y. Hozumi's opinion on the European pre-Christian family system (German School, postponement faction)

On 15 August 1891, *Kokka Gakkai Zasshi – The National Scientific Society Journal* (Volume 5, Issue 54), published by the National Scientific Society at the Old University of Tokyo, released another of Y. Hozumi's opinions. "The European Family System before Christianity" sparked a debate on the similarities between the old European and Japanese family law systems.[10]

Y. Hozumi accused private law jurists of following the path of radical individualism and equality, which violated the traditional Japanese social order and disturbed the harmony of the old legal system. He claimed that the Civil Code drafters perceived the promulgation of the Constitution as a pretext to carry out ground-breaking social reforms in line with their private views. Instead of a unilateral codification of law, he proposed a more thorough study of the legal history and the selection of the guiding principles of private law using the comparative law method.

The author was of the opinion that equality and individualism constituting the core of the Code were contrary to the nature of Japanese society. Y. Hozumi argued that it was based on the family and the nation, which functioned harmoniously thanks to the authority of the head of the family and the emperor. According to him, this system derived from the traditional beliefs in the spirits of deceased ancestors, influencing the shape of national customary law. He indicated that this phenomenon was also noticeable in ancient Europe, but with the spread of Christianity, faith in ancestors was completely forgotten.

Referring to the latest research on the old Germanic law system, Y. Hozumi argued that ancient Greek and Roman law had a shared principle before Christianity: the belief in the spirit of the dead ancestors who took care of the living descendants. One of the effects of this widespread notion was the emergence of a family law system based on patriarchal relationships. He claimed that the dominant position of the head of the family, accepted by all generations, regardless of

[9] For the full opinion text, see Murakami, 2008b, pp. 232–235.

[10] Hozumi, 1891b, pp. 2–5.

gender, had its source in the consensual transfer of power from deceased ancestors to descendant to ensure the safety and continuation of the family line. Y. Hozumi stated that a similar system had been in force in Japan for ages, and the promulgation of the Civil Code was to mark its definitive end. He was convinced that the new family law system would destroy the belief in family and loyalty to deceased ancestors, weakening relations even between blood relatives. Among other threats to the family, he mentioned changes in the relationship between the spouses, who became a couple of people bound to each other only by a civil law contract. Y. Hozumi strongly criticized the Civil Code for giving women the right to divorce if a man was sterile.

The author eventually agreed that the family system in ancient Rome and Greece best reflected the traditional Japanese family law. Y. Hozumi argued that by promoting equality and individualism, Christianity irreversibly changed the nature of the European family law systems, destroying their native elements, such as faith in ancestors and loyalty to the head of the family. For him, if the Civil Code came into force, Japanese society would be forced to follow the path of an incomprehensible Christian ideology. Opting unequivocally against individualism and equality promoted by the decision-making party, Y. Hozumi tried to convince readers that the native belief in ancestors and the old family system resulting from it was not only beautiful but also created the foundations of the Japanese nation.[11]

6.1.5. Y. Hozumi's opinion on the harmful effects of the entry into force of the Civil Code (German School, postponement faction)

On 25 August 1891, *The Jurisprudence News* (Issue 5) published Y. Hozumi's opinion: "The Entry Into Force of the Civil Code Means the Collapse of Loyalty and Filial Devotion".[12] This short text by the German School representative was a continuation of an earlier opinion on the European family system in the pre-Christian era. The article quickly stirred up the legal community and became the subject of numerous public opinion comments. Although Y. Hozumi's text was initially intended to strongly criticize the Civil Code and the decisive faction, during the editing process of the magazine, there was an accidental typographical error involving the exchange of kanji characters that had a similar reading. Thus, the opinion received an even more critical connotation. It went down in history as "a collapse comparable to the death" (亡フ, hōfu), not a "collapse through degradation" (滅ブ, hōbu). In the context of "loyalty and filial devotion", a value particularly

11 For the full opinion text, see Hoshino (ed.), 2014, pp. 85–87.

12 Hozumi, 1891c, pp. 8–13.

appreciated in the traditional Japanese family system, the fierce criticism forced the decisive faction to defend the Code more actively.

Y. Hozumi argued that the Civil Code should be analysed not only through the prism of benefits but also through the damage it could bring to Japan. He accused French School representatives of following the path of radical individualism and equality, which had a negative impact on the existing social order. He also claimed that they attached too much importance to political aspects characteristic of public law while neglecting to follow global trends in legislation. The author believed that securing the harmony of the Civil Code with the old customs was necessary, creating a "beautiful national legal system" that would end the debate on the misunderstood idea of reforming Japanese society initiated by the Meiji Revolution. He additionally indicated that the Constitution of Japan did not have points of convergence with French legal thought. For him, this fact would be noticed and criticized by future historians.

The author wrote that before Christianity, ancient Greece and Rome were typical examples of native European culture. Their rich legal tradition could be learned from the works of Fustel de Coulanges,[13] Theodor Mommsen[14] and Rudolf von Jhering.[15] Y. Hozumi also added that comprehensive research on ancient Germanic law gave scholars more evidence to say that Greek and Roman law had multiple common elements. They revealed the truth about the general Indo-Germanic (Indo-European – author's note) legal thought before the era of Christian domination. The author called for recognizing them as one group. For him, the native European legal system was initially based on worshipping the spirits of dead ancestors, ultimately leading to nationhood. He emphasized that from the point of view of legal scholarship, it was the moment when the family system was born and paternal authority was recognized. The German School representative sought the origins of the family and the establishment of the patriarchy in the adoption of a coherent model of beliefs in the nation, which consisted in entrusting the protection of the household to the spirits of the deceased ancestors, commonly referred to as the "god of the family". He also believed that the head of the family,

[13] Fustel de Coulanges (1830–1889) was a French historian researching the socio-religious aspects of ancient states, whose monograph entitled *The Ancient City* (*La Cité Antique*) was assessed as a model description of relations between property and political and religious institutions in the ancient era.

[14] Theodor Mommsen (1817–1903) was a German historian and lawyer, winner of the Nobel Prize in Literature in 1902, researcher of Roman law and author of the fundamental three-volume work *History of Rome* (*Römische Geschichte*).

[15] Rudolf von Jhering (1818–1892) was a German lawyer and scholar in Roman law, representative of legal positivism and founder of sociological jurisprudence; he was also the author of the famous four-volume work *The Spirit of Roman Law* (*Der Geist des römischen Rechts auf den verschiedenen Stufen seiner Entwicklung*).

being the direct link between family generations, represented the spirits of the ancestors in the world of the living. Obedience and respect towards the head of the family, regardless of gender and age, guaranteed the satisfaction of the "god of the family" and thus the safety of the household.

According to Y. Hozumi, the original European family model was destroyed by adopting the Great Commandment principle promoted by Christianity. He believed that the entry into force of the Civil Code in Japan would result in the abolition of traditional family ties based on respect for previous generations and obedience to the head of the family. Among the most harmful solutions of the new family law, he pointed to the new way of understating a marriage. For him, too much personal freedom of the spouses would lead to the breakdown of family bonds. Y. Hozumi also criticized the wife's right to demand a divorce due to the husband's infertility and the introduction of the system of separate surnames of the child and parent, which in the case of adopted children could lead to the unfair extinction of the family line. The author argued that the pre-Christian family law system was similar to the customary law system in Japan. He wrote that the contemporary European model of the family was deprived of the element of faith in ancestors due to the existence of a "god full of pride, who was the only one deserving the love and respect from people".

Later on in the article, Y. Hozumi asked rhetorically whether introducing formal equality should be accepted with a threat of the dissolution of traditional family ties and the creation of barriers between blood relatives. He felt that the legislator intended to create a society composed only of individuals by establishing the natural person as a critical part of the private law system. Referring to the words of F. de Coulanges, he stated that people, regardless of generation, worshipped their dead ancestors. He noticed that the ancient Greeks and Romans naturally understood this fact, but the faith in ancestors was challenging to accept among Christians. Thus, Y. Hozumi warned that the native system of values would also be superseded by the Civil Code principles, which promoted individualism incomprehensible to society despite the declaration to preserve the Japanese terminology related to family law. The author argued that over 3,000 years of tradition should not be compromised, primarily if the worldview revolution was based on the teachings of Christianity, without prior education of citizens. The lack of logic in the actions of the Japanese legislator became the object of Y. Hozumi's ridicule.

Sharing his observations related to the scope of power of the head of the family in the French private law system, Y. Hozumi stated it was a "misunderstanding" compared to the old provisions in Roman law. He wrote that the spread of Christianity in France (as well as in Europe) negatively affected the bonds and respect between blood relatives, as the new faith promoted the equality of women and men before God and the Great Commandment principles. According to him, the natural consequence of the development of legal scholarship in close relation to Christian teachings was the weakening of the role of the family and the elevation of the individual to the pedestal. Consequently, this all led to the collapse of the European moral system. Y. Hozumi spoke positively about Japan in the context of its unique features: the uninterrupted line of divine emperors and the steadfast spirit of a society loyal to its monarch and deceased ancestors. He was afraid that the entry into force of the Civil Code would destroy this beautiful system of values and would not necessarily result in the reception of Western ideas in Japan.[16]

6.2. Decisive faction responses – opinions published in 1891

6.2.1. *The Association of Constitutionalists Journal* editorial team's article regarding the motives of journalistic activity (decisive faction)

On 12 July 1891, in the inaugural issue of *Hōchi Kyōkai Zasshi – The Association of Constitutionalists Journal* (Issue 1) – founded by Hōchi Kyōkai at the Association of Constitutionalists at the Meiji Law School,[17] the editorial team published an opinion entitled "Explaining the Most Important Ideas of the Association of Constitutionalists Related to the Publication of the Journal".[18]

The editorial team informed the readers about the motives behind the founding of the Association of Constitutionalists at the beginning of 1891 and the admission of over 1,500 members throughout Japan. The authors denied the rumours about the commercial nature of the journal's activities in connection with membership fees. They argued that their mission was only to promote values beneficial to the state and the nation. They wrote about the significance of the Association for educating the masses on the importance of law and reminding them of the internal situation before the Meiji reforms. According to the editors, Japan was a seemingly independent country, struggling with a high degree of decentralization of power and division into independent regions ruled by clans. In addition to the anachronistic system of administration, they also pointed to the existence of more than a hundred different systems of customary law, which in the first years after the Meiji Revolution were closely examined. The editors commented on the accusations of the postponement

16 For the full opinion text, see Hoshino (ed.), 2014, pp. 82–85.

17 The Association of Constitutionalists was founded in February 1891 by a group of French School representatives to promote the idea of the rule of law and the immediate entry into force of the remaining codes. T. Ōki was appointed its chairman, and Taizō Namura vice-chairman. The members of the Chancellor's Council included K. Imamura, S. Inoue, S. Isobe, S. Kameyama, T. Kishimoto, Seigo Kurizuka and R. Mitsukuri. Hoshino, 1943, p. 126; Ōkubo, 1977, p. 170.

18 Hōchi Kyōkai Zasshi (ed.), 1891, pp. 1–5.

party regarding the lack of consideration of customary law during the drafting process by referring to its true nature. The authors did not negate the existence of old Japanese customs but criticized the attachment to them as they needed to be changed. The rejection of the majority of customary law, described as unsuited to modern times, was presented as the only way to modernize the country. They recognized that repealing customary law was of particular interest in various regions of Japan, but at the same time, argued that it was wrong to believe that the legislative goals could be achieved by leaving customs to their natural evolution.

The editors wrote that in the last 20 years, Japan had made dramatic progress due to the reception of the achievements of Western civilization. However, they warned that citizens still did not have the guarantee of their private law rights. This inconvenience, highlighted as the greatest issue of both modern and ancient Japan, caused damage to the state and society that was difficult to estimate. The authors stated that the Code drafters had a moral right to change this situation by breaking with old bad habits and guaranteeing citizens their private law rights. They also believed that the haste in this matter was justified because by precisely indicating the rights and obligations of society in the sphere of private law, Japan was to become a state entirely governed by the rule of law. The editors argued that this was why the Association and its journal were established. Their goal was to study law and promote knowledge about the global trends of the constitutional state. Regarding the legislative actions, they also indicated two most important points: promoting the coming into force of the Civil Code and protecting its principles, which were necessary to follow the path of national development.

Regardless of the disputes about the nature of the law and the profile of the journal's activity, the editors believed that it was their duty to act for the benefit of society by telling the truth about the importance of the rule of law principle. Finally, they announced the struggle to reform the old customary law system and expressed the hope of gaining many supporters who would help to undertake this task.[19]

6.2.2. Kōsaku Handa's opinion (French School, decisive faction)

The inaugural issue of *The Association of Constitutionalists Journal* also covered other important decisive faction opinions. One of them was drafted by K. Handa, a graduate of the second cohort of the Law School at the Ministry of Justice and a judge at the Tokyo Court of Appeal. The text was entitled "About Native Customs from a Legal Point of View".[20]

[19] For the full opinion text, see Hoshino (ed.), 2014, pp. 88–89.

[20] Handa, 1891, pp. 38–43.

K. Handa began his digressions by reminding the readers that law codification had been a significant issue for the last two decades. Since other jurists had previously explained the detailed aspects related to the codes, the author did not consider it necessary to start another debate on this subject. He indicated that the drafting of the codes was the basis of the policy of successive governments and was expected by most citizens. He based his view on observing unequivocally positive social moods after the publication of the Constitution in 1889. It united people and shaped the nation, giving citizens and the government various rights and obligations. K. Handa emphasized that the codification process had to be completed to the very end because the new codes removed the contradictions and loopholes in the legal system. He argued that the legal system was incomplete without codes as it failed to protect the citizens or the government. In his opinion, the cabinet should strive to promote the rule of law principle by supporting the entry into force of all codes.

The author identified jurists who criticized the Commercial Code and the Civil Code with people who are generally against the codification of the law. He argued that the intention to prevent the entry into force of the Codes on the pretext of protecting old customs and criticizing the principles of the new law was an insufficient justification. K. Handa emphasized that from the beginning, the intention of the drafters was to preserve beneficial customs and eliminate those that had a harmful impact on the state and society. As an example of harmful practices that the legislator revised, he cited the introduction of a ban on torture in the course of criminal proceedings, the abolition of social classes and the introduction of formal equality of all citizens before the law. He rhetorically asked the adversaries whether they did not consider the old customs terrifying, stating that the beneficial customs were preserved in the codes since the drafters intended to preserve the national character of the Japanese legal system. K. Handa wrote that old customs were selected and applied with great care in the Civil Code by the reformist policy of the Meiji Revolution. He reminded the readers that the legislator's goal was to complete the legal system reform, which would be associated with the most negligible possible negative social consequences. He highlighted that the gradual changes, initiated in the seventh/eighth year of the Meiji era (1874/1875), were based on the French legal system, as English and American law did not have codes and were based on precedent. According to K. Handa, this decision was made after careful analysis of differences and similarities in foreign legal systems and the efficiency of the judiciary.

As another argument against maintaining the old customs, contrary to the Civil Code norms, K. Handa reminded readers about the circumstances of their drafting. He argued that old customs were norms established in China, and after a long time, they acquired a Japanese character. For him, the role of the legislator during the codification process was to study the existing customs and identify unfavourable ones. The author knew that a sudden change in the customary law system could negatively affect the social order. Still, he believed that possible negative consequences could not stop reforms, which had been discussed many times. He wrote that people attached to the old customs could also appreciate the new ones, speaking about the old law as antiquarians about antiques. According to him, the absence of some old customs in the Civil Code should not be a reason to deny the need to introduce new customs and complete the codification process.[21]

6.2.3. Kentarō Ōi's opinion (French School, decisive faction)

On 12 August 1891, *The Association of Constitutionalists Journal* (Issue 2) published an article by K. Ōi, a lawyer, former student of R. Mitsukuri and the Daigakuminami School, and one of the founders of the Liberal Party. His article was entitled "What Are the Advantages and Disadvantages of the Codes in Our Empire?"[22]

K. Ōi focused on presenting the legitimacy of law codification from the point of view of state policy, regardless of the disputes between jurists. He stated that the purpose of the Civil Code, the Commercial Code and generally all codes was to protect the interests of citizens by introducing an effective legal system. He asked rhetorically how these postulates could be implemented based on the old system of customary law. The author emphasized that he was aware that the dispute between the two schools of legal jurisprudence related to the legitimacy of law codification and its implementation. He also believed that the stubborn discussion of jurists on the state policy was not beneficial because the public should focus on more serious issues.

The author reminded the readers that Japan began to codify its legal system because it was widely agreed that the state without a written code was an objectively unfavourable phenomenon. For him, this decision was in line with global trends and supported by a plan to establish a state governed by the rule of law. While he recognized the advantages of the English legal system and its positive impact on the nation's wealth, he also argued that the codification of law must envisage the unification of a divided society. K. Ōi expected that radical reforms might provoke widespread reactions, yet felt that Japan should not follow the example of the United Kingdom, a country with a specific legal tradition. According to him, an attempt to imitate the English model, to a greater or lesser extent, was promoting the vision of a country with a completely shapeless legal system. He argued that the United Kingdom and Japan were countries with entirely different legal cultures, and he compared the postulates of adopting customary law in an uncodified form to transplanting plants from a tropical to a polar climate. It was an

21 For the full opinion text, see Hoshino (ed.), 2014, pp. 96–98.

22 Ōi, 1891, pp. 3–7.

obvious allusion to earlier allegations of similar content by representatives of the English School that were directed at the French School representatives in 1890. K. Ōi also believed that English law would not contribute to the country's unification, unlike French law, which effectively reconciled the customs of the northern and southern parts of the country. He saw in this phenomenon a similar opportunity to unite the western and eastern parts of Japan, whose customs, culture and even language differed significantly despite establishing a central government focused around Emperor Meiji.

In the following part of the opinion, K. Ōi argued about the anachronism and defects of the customary law system in former Japan, which became particularly visible after opening the country's borders. He believed that in the era of the Industrial Revolution and international contacts, the arrival of foreigners in Japan and the first conflicts between them and residents were inevitable. For him, the fair settlement of any disputes by civil and criminal courts was not possible without a major reform of the legal system. He wrote that relying on dismembered customary law would prove that Japan does not belong to the group of civilized countries. He also argued that without the publication of the codes, the effectiveness of the law would depend only on the degree of experience of judges. Considering the national character of Japan and its legal culture, he tried to persuade the reader that the state's role was to adopt a coherent system of statutory law.

K. Ōi concluded his argument by stating that regardless of analysing and comparing various legal systems of civilized countries, the laws promulgated in Japan, like the Law on the Organization of the Work of Courts or the Code of Criminal Procedure, would never reconcile the views of all jurists. He asked rhetorically how the Commercial Code and the Civil Code were supposed to make up two different opinions on the nature of law. He stated that French School representatives naturally referred to the ideas adopted in the French Civil Code. By contrast, he did not understand how the English School representatives intended to emphasize the role of English law, knowing that there were no codes in force in the United Kingdom. In such circumstances, K. Ōi believed that the most natural solution was a thorough study of the specificity of Japan and adapting the legal system to its actual socio-political conditions. The author addressed the English School representatives with the same accusations that had previously been directed at the French School: ignoring the historical background of their country during the law codification. The experience of the last three decades allowed him to present his thesis that since the opening of the borders, the Japanese government had been struggling with the threat of intervention by foreign powers under the pretext of the lack of a uniform legal system. Looking further at the importance of a trade policy to help the nation's wealth, he thought it was necessary to support Japanese entrepreneurs through the promulgation of the Commercial Code. Thus, K. Ōi could not imagine advocating the idea of an uncodified legal system in the international situation in which Japan found itself. The opinions focused on showing the negative aspects of law codification, primarily spread among the public by English School representatives, were described by him as "a bolt from the blue".[23]

6.2.4. The opinion of Michito Shirome (French School, decisive faction)

On 15 September 1891, *The Association of Constitutionalists Journal* (Issue 3) published M. Shirome's opinion entitled "Codes and Revision of [Unequal] Treaties". M. Shirome was in fact a pseudonym for Seikon Koshino but as per the publication, this book references M. Shirome.[24]

In the opening words of his article, M. Shirome reminded the readers about an argument often raised by the decisive faction: codes were necessary to unify the legal system for all citizens. According to him, their role was primarily to secure all private contracts and protect society from the stagnation characteristic of the old times before the Meiji Revolution. He also argued that the equally crucial significance of the Codes should be recognized. He gave as an example the government's plan to revise unequal treaties. M. Shirome felt that there should be no doubt about the rightness of this policy because fighting for sovereignty meant saving the honour of the state. He emphasized that sovereignty was the most important political factor for citizens regardless of race, literally described as "white or yellow". The author claimed that in the case of Japan, one cannot speak of full sovereignty, as the unjust, illogical and inhumane law of extraterritoriality limited the state. He expressed dissatisfaction that foreign legal systems and Japanese courts protected white residents in Japan and did not have the power to judge them for their crimes. He mentioned that this issue was also for transactions concluded by Japanese citizens and foreign residents, as citizens often complained about the inability to enforce their rights through domestic courts.

The author appealed to the opponents of the codes that the situation in which a foreign resident could not be convicted of committing crimes in any other way than before their own consular court was an apparent injustice. Since the consular court deliberated on the case based on its own national criminal law, he saw no element of legal guarantee for Japanese citizens and no chance to apply Japanese criminal law. For him, the potential contradiction in the enforcement of criminal law norms was unacceptable and could lead to deliberate attempts to violate the Japanese legal system with a sense of impunity.

[23] For the full opinion text, see Hoshino (ed.), 2014, pp. 106–108.

[24] Shirome (Koshino), 1891, pp. 40–48.

M. Shirome argued that the principle of extraterritoriality was equally troublesome in the case of private law, where all legal disputes with foreign residents had to be settled by consular courts. He claimed that they looked more favourably at their own citizens, who could count on additional financial and institutional assistance from the state during the appeal process. The author highlighted that deliberating on cases by the court of the second instance was time-consuming and costly, and therefore obviously less favourable to Japanese citizens who had repeatedly encountered this problem.

The matter discussed by the author was well founded in relation to Article 24 of the Constitution of Japan, which granted every citizen the right to pursue their claims before the court. The cited civil right was naturally limited by the law of extraterritoriality, as any attempt to claim one's right against a foreigner required bringing an action before a consular court. M. Shirome additionally referred to Article 57 of the Constitution, which stipulated that judicial power was exercised by the courts bounded by law in force and in the name of the emperor. He alleged that in the case of trials before consular courts, justice was administered on behalf of a foreign monarch and based on foreign law. Therefore, he wondered how the state intended to protect the rights of Japanese citizens and argued that promulgating the Constitution, despite the apparent benefits and widespread joy of this fact, was insufficient to safeguard the effectiveness of the private law rights and national interests.

The French School representative wrote that Japanese citizens had sincerely wanted an immediate revision of the unequal treaties for over 20 years, and the government's current policy was not accidental. He believed that the political situation at that time was a "classic struggle for the survival of the stronger" and that Japan's goal should be to "establish a state where its citizens and their enterprises, not white residents, would be the most privileged social group". As a negative example of succumbing to the influence of stronger countries, he mentioned China, which experienced a foreign invasion and became an arena of struggle for influence between world powers. According to him, a damaging aspect of the inequality in relations between the Western powers and China was that the Americans passed a federal law that altogether prohibited the immigration of Chinese workers.[25] M. Shirome empathized with the Chinese situation in relation to the "rivalry between the white and yellow races". At the same time, he argued that it was a warning to the Japanese willing to follow the path of the neighbouring country. As an extreme

[25] The Chinese Exclusion Act was a federal law signed by President Chester A. Arthur on 6 May 1882. It completely prohibited the immigration of Chinese labourers to the United States for a period of ten years. This Act was an extension of earlier American domestic and foreign policies aimed at stopping Chinese labour immigration, especially in California. Despite numerous cases of non-compliance with this law, it was officially repealed only in December 1943 by the so-called Magnuson Act.

example of the harmful domination of the Europeans and Americans, he referred to the situation of the Indians in North America, whose land was gradually taken away and their population was deliberately reduced.

The author knew that several groups opposed the revision of unequal treaties, but he considered their arguments senseless. He did not want to abandon the government policy and rhetorically asked whether its adversaries really did not see clear links between the unequal treaties and the codification of law. He claimed that without the introduction of all Japanese codes, foreign residents would never give up their right of extraterritoriality for fear of securing their property. M. Shirome could not imagine the legal system based on customs and wondered about its application in a situation where national customs varied from region to region and were often incomprehensible, especially to foreign visitors. As an example of such a custom, he referred to the old principle of equity, which was understood in a completely different way in Japan, the United Kingdom, the United States, Germany and France, as evidenced by Japanese jurists educated in the spirit of the above systems of law. He argued that if the equity principle would be interpreted differently by both parties to the dispute, the court of first instance would be forced to refer the case to a higher court, which would lead to low effectiveness of law and undermine the credibility of private law. He also compared the situation to Japan having to navigate a ship on high seas without a compass.

Referring to external information, M. Shirome explained that the Western powers indicated the lack of a codified Japanese legal system as the most important reason for the existence of unequal treaties. Therefore, he claimed that by codifying the law, the Japanese could turn this argument against their enemies. At the same time, he criticized the main idea of the postponement faction pushing for the gradual publication of short bills, as they would still constitute a large collection of illegible laws after some time. Again, he rhetorically asked his adversaries about their preferences, juxtaposing comprehensive codes with numerous statute laws. The author wrote that the codes would force the Western powers to revise unequal treaties and that any benefits resulting from their publication would outweigh their possible disadvantages. At the end of his article, he stated that any delay in the entry into force of the Codes would mean more days of disgrace for the nation. M. Shirome did not fully understand the motives of the postponement faction and believed that it was an evil that did not result from the adversary's ignorance.[26]

[26] For the full opinion text, see Hoshino (ed.), 2014, pp. 120–123.

6.2.5. Kōzō Miyagi's opinion (French School, decisive faction)

On 10 November 1891, *The Association of Constitutionalists Journal* (Issue 5) published K. Miyagi's opinion "The Codes Preservation Doctrine Has Its Origins in English School".[27] The author was a graduate of the first cohort of the Law School at the Ministry of Justice and the University of Lyon and a Supreme Court prosecutor.

In the introduction to his opinion, K. Miyagi indicated the motives for establishing the Association of Constitutionalists, pointing to the intention to provide research on the advantages and disadvantages of the Japanese legal system to promote the state's development. He argued that due to the cooperation of over 1,000 members of the Association, it would be possible to present different opinions on the law, which in the long run will enable its constant improvement. As one of the most important goals of the Association in the near future, he announced the fight to preserve the Codes.

The author wrote that Codes' role should be strongly emphasized in the ongoing dispute over the Codes. He argued that the Constitution, the Civil Code, the Commercial Code and the Code of Civil Procedure constitute an integral part of the legal system. K. Miyagi claimed that the majority of Japanese society understood the need to introduce the Codes. For this reason, the Association of Constitutionalists should actively support their entry into force. As the first argument in favour of the Codes, he indicated the Japanese legislator's intention to establish the rule of law principle to the full extent. First, the Constitution was promulgated, followed by the publication of the Ordinary Courts Organization Law, the Civil Code, the Commercial Code and the Code of Civil Procedure, thus establishing a complete and uniform legal system. This was an essential argument for him, as regardless of the postponement faction's criticism for including procedural provisions in the Civil Code, the Civil Code and the Code of Civil Procedure nevertheless formed a coherent private law system.

K. Miyagi argued that all legal systems borrowed part of their law from another country. Knowing about the French, English and German Schools of legal jurisprudence in Japan, he was of the opinion that the differences between them would be mainly reflected in the functioning of the judiciary in the process of appealing to a higher court. Therefore, the French School representative believed that from the point of view of the public interest, it was necessary to fight for the Civil Code and the Commercial Code to come into force at all costs. He recalled that the arguments supporting codification were sufficient to promote the universal law codification as a natural way of the law development process in the last century. K. Miyagi criticized the English School representatives who published in *The Jurisprudence*

[27] Miyagi, 1891, (original pages are unknown).

News opinions against the Civil Code and the Commercial Code because their criticism provoked the creation of two opposing factions and a doctrine seeking to reject both Codes.

In closing, the author enumerated the allegations of the postponement faction against the Codes: inconsistency with native customary law and content not being sufficiently legible. Due to these imperfections, the postponement faction insisted on postponing the entry into force of the new law and instead wanted to gradually introduce amendments. K. Miyagi also claimed that their views were limited to the assessment that the current legal system was already so complicated that there was no need to pass numerous laws at the same time, and in the case of the Civil Code, it was enough to implement the necessary part without making any additional changes to family and succession law.

The author argued that the postponement faction had socially harmful views that required a strong response. He stated that by seeking a way to reject the Codes, English School representatives provoked part of the jurisprudence to defend them. M. Miyagi directly claimed that the postponement faction was the original reason for establishing the Association of Constitutionalists, a centre of legal scholarship supporting the doctrine of preserving the Codes.[28]

6.3. Issues during the Imperial Diet's second meeting and the House of Representatives election in 1891

A new Japanese cabinet led by Count Masayoshi Matsukata, a distinguished politician and military man, was established on 6 May 1891. Initially, the post of Minister of Justice was retained by A. Yamada. However, he soon resigned after a series of dismissals in the cabinet and the Privy Council due to the assassination attempt on Nikolai Alexandrovich, the heir to the Russian throne, during his trip to Japan.[29] A. Yamada, who stepped down under the pretext of health issues and then was assigned as the Secretary of the Privy Council,[30] was replaced by F. Tanaka, appointed on 1 June. Notably, F. Tanaka had served as the Minister of Justice a decade earlier and supervised the first unsuccessful attempts to draft the Civil Code.

On 26 November 1891, the Imperial Diet's second meeting began. During the House of Representatives session on 10 December, Matasaburō Watanabe, a lawyer from Hiroshima Prefecture affiliated with the decisive faction, submitted a bill providing for the immediate entry into force of a part of the Commercial Code.

28 For the full opinion text, see Hoshino (ed.), 2014, pp. 134–136.

29 Ōkubo, 1977, p. 172.

30 Nihon Daigaku (ed.), 1963, p. 794.

In the explanatory notes, he referred to the historical aspects and the necessity to complete the codification of private law in Japan. As a result of his proposal, a lively debate ensued, which the Minister of Justice joined. F. Tanaka did not criticize M. Watanabe's project but intended to use the bill to push through in the House of Representatives the entry into force of the entire Commercial Code at an earlier date.[31] The vote held on 17 December ended in an unexpected stalemate (64 to 64). Pursuant to Article 47 of the Constitution, on the basis of the consent given by the Chairman, the Deputy Chairman of the House of Representatives, M. Tsuda, decided on the further course of the legislative process. Since he was a postponement party representative and did not see sufficient grounds to speed up the date of entry into force of the Commercial Code, he decided to reject M. Watanabe's bill.[32]

On 22 December, the House of Representatives held the long-awaited discussion on revising the budget plan for the following year. The Minister of the Navy, Vice Admiral Sugenori Kabayama, demanded that more funds be allocated to develop Japan's naval shipbuilding industry and openly spoke out against parliamentary democracy.[33] Despite warnings from cabinet members, the House of Representatives passed a draft budget unfavourable to the Navy. In response to the policy of the parliament aimed directly at confrontation with the cabinet, on 25 December, Prime Minister M. Matsukata exercised his constitutional power and decided to dissolve the House of Representatives.[34]

The first dissolution of the House of Representatives in Japan's history meant not only the need to organize early elections within the next two months but also a temporary truce in the fight for the Civil Code. At the end of December 1891, the Home Minister, Yajirō Shinagawa, presented a plan to mobilize the Japanese police to forcefully intervene in the elections to the House of Representatives. In response to the cabinet's anti-democratic stance, the Japanese ruling elites split into the "hawk" wing centred around the former Satsuma domain and former Prime Minister A. Yamagata and the "moderate" wing represented by the former Chōshū domain led by former Prime Minister H. Itō.[35] The ambiguous attitude of the emperor, who initially expressed concern about the dissolution of the House of Representatives but soon conveyed to Prime Minister M. Matsukata his expectation of going smoothly through the elections, made the cabinet believe that they had received official permission to intervene.[36] In reality, however, the further devel-

[31] Record of the House of Representatives session, 10 December 1891.

[32] Record of the House of Representatives session, 17 December 1891.

[33] Record of the House of Representatives session, 22 December 1891.

[34] Sekiguchi, 2021, p. 49.

[35] Ōkubo, 1977, p. 177.

[36] The emperor's attitude and his orders towards M. Matsukata's cabinet are quoted in more detail by Sueki, 2018, pp. 244–246.

opment of the situation depended on the influence that both parties had in the provincial police offices.

The general election for Japan's House of Representatives was held on 15 February 1892. A total of 300 parliamentarians were elected in 214 single-member and 43 double-member constituencies throughout the country. Despite the generally peaceful atmosphere, five prefectures saw violent clashes between citizens and police officers trying to detain some of the voters. In total, 25 people died and 66 were injured. In some constituencies, the police received reports suggesting that the ballots were not counted accurately, but this probably did not affect the overall shape of the House of Representatives.[37] Although the pro-democratic parties were victorious for the second time with 132 seats won, they lost the majority and held only a narrow margin over the 124 parliamentarians supporting cabinet policy. This meant that each party had to individually solicit support from a group of 44 unaffiliated members of the House of Representatives. Nevertheless, the unsuccessful attempt to intervene in the election ended with the "hawk" wing's defeat, leading also to Y. Shinagawa's resignation as Home Minister in March.[38]

6.4. Postponement faction's opinions in 1892

6.4.1. T. Okuda's opinion on the inaccuracies in Personal Law (English School, postponement faction)

On 25 April 1892, *The Jurisprudence News* (Issue 13) published T. Okuda's opinion entitled "Repetitions and Contradictions in the Book on Personal Law".[39]

T. Okuda, who was a lecturer in personal law at the Doctoral School of the Old Tokyo University/Imperial University, briefly presented his allegations against the Civil Code by commenting on the adopted natural law doctrine.

The author presented the apparent discrepancies between Articles 162 and 164 of the Book on Personal Law. While Article 162 established the rule of only one guardian, 164 allowed the father or mother to appoint a guardian for the minor from the closest family or unrelated persons. According to T. Okuda, selecting a guardian separately by the father or mother could lead to a situation of multiple guardians. He also argued that separating the will of the father and mother was

[37] Japanese historians do not agree on the nature of the riots between citizens and the police and their impact on the outcome of the House of Representatives general election. Sueki, 2015, pp. 105–135; Sueki, 2010, pp. 120–130.

[38] Cabinet Bulletin from 11 March 1892 on the Home Minister's resignation.

[39] Okuda, 1892, pp. 33–36.

contrary to Japanese customary law, which treated a married couple as a family jointly exercising parental authority. As the reason for departing from the traditional solution, T. Okuda indicated the Civil Code drafters' plan to copy European legal culture based on individualism.

Continuing his criticism, the English School representative wrote that the content of Articles 135, 155 and 245 was, in fact, a repetition of the same legal norms defining the right related to inheritance, including the position of the adopted child. He suggested the unification of those provisions by removing redundant sentences and rhetorically asked the legislator whether he had noticed this defect in the supposedly perfect Civil Code.[40]

6.4.2. K. Takahashi's opinion (English School, postponement faction)

On 25 May 1892, *The Jurisprudence News* (Issue 14) published an article by K. Takahashi, an Old Tokyo/Imperial University student and director of the *Official Cabinet Gazette*. His article was entitled "The Proponents of the Theory of Immediate Entry into Force of the Codes Confession".[41]

K. Takahashi noted that despite the primarily fair and open discussion between the postponement and decisive factions, there were also dishonest personal attacks on the supporters of postponing the entry into force of the Codes. He informed readers that regardless of the feelings of the attackers, the public felt an aversion to such behaviour. He supported his opinion with comments from three recognized jurists who assessed the possible benefits of attacking the postponement faction representatives.

In the first commentary, the decisive faction point of view was quoted, which identified the opponents of the Codes as mostly English School representatives, jurists known for having legal education in the law system without codes. According to the commentator, the decisive faction accused their adversaries that they saw the need to introduce the Codes yet criticized the legislative policy to protect particular interests. The decisive faction believed that the English School jurists, recognized as experts in the field of judicial decisions, allegedly opposed the entry into force of the Codes, as they feared that their profession would become redundant and they would lose their earning capacity. In a malicious tone, the author of the commentary concluded that this particular opinion resulted from the decisive faction's fears that without the immediate introduction of the Codes, they would lose their professional position.

[40] For the full opinion text, see Hoshino (ed.), 2014, pp. 160–161.

[41] Takahashi, 1892, pp. 50–52.

The second commentary criticized the decisive faction's argument suggesting that the opponents of the Codes wanted the entire legal community to be involved in the codification process, as they were jealous of the fact that the Codes had been drafted only by the French School jurists. The author of the second comment argued that such statements meant that the decisive faction's main motivation for the entry into force of the Codes was their professional prestige.

The third commentary discussed another decisive faction allegation, namely that the majority of the opponents were entrepreneurs who feared that the entry into force of the Codes would lead to bankruptcy. The author of the third commentary concluded that this time those words of contempt were directed towards all businessmen who make rational decisions by calculating possible profits and losses.

In the summary of his short article, K. Takahashi expressed the hope that by citing all non-substantive arguments of the decisive faction, he fairly presented their actual views on the issue of the entry into force of the Codes.[42]

6.4.3. T. Hanai's opinion concerning the relation between the Codes and the revision of unequal treaties (English School, postponement faction)

On 25 May 1892, *The Jurisprudence News* (Issue 14) also published T. Hanai's opinion entitled "Codes and the Revision of Unequal Treaties".[43]

By assessing the attitude of the Minister of Foreign Affairs, Shigenobu Ōkuma, T. Hanai reminded the readers of his primary mission to revise unequal treaties. Referring to the hitherto unsuccessful attempts to change the international position of Japan, the author expressed doubts about the "Western doctrine" approved a few years earlier by the Ministry of Justice and the Ministry of Foreign Affairs, which was based on introducing the five most essential codes characteristic to civil law systems. T. Hanai asked whether S. Ōkuma had any evidence to support the theory that the revision of unequal treaties could be achieved by establishing a codified law system. He also wondered if the cabinet saw a threat that foreign powers would not perceive the implementation of the provisional and flawed codes as a simplistic diplomatic manoeuvre.

The author claimed that he had closely observed the Japanese legal history and argued that most of the time it was a system based on customary law or judicial decisions, and therefore the Codes were not a necessary element for its proper functioning. According to him, the unequal treaties were not necessarily related to the lack of codes in Japan but to other crucial factors. Among them, he indicated

[42] For the full opinion text, see Hoshino (ed.), 2014, pp. 188–189.

[43] Hanai, 1892, pp. 58–61.

the flaws of the judiciary system and the distinct nature of old national norms that forced foreigners to seek protection in the consular courts. He also claimed that if the above-mentioned concerns were the reason for concluding the unequal treaties, they should have been revised more than ten years earlier.

T. Hanai did not notice the general link between the codified legal system and unequal treaties, which was the subject of the Ministry of Foreign Affairs' detailed analysis for a few years. He believed that, in the first place, the codes should be introduced to provide citizens their private law rights and help them understand the complicated nature of law. He criticized the codification of the law under the pretext of revising unequal treaties because he saw that society would become the victim of this policy. Additionally, he wrote that the rest of the world assessed the Japanese government's actions as irrational.

In the conclusion of his article, the author rhetorically asked the adversaries whether they really believed that with the entry into force of the Codes on 1 January 1893, the unequal treaties would be automatically revised.[44]

6.4.4. *The Jurisprudence News* editorial team's opinion related to the arguments for postponing the date of entry into force of the Codes (postponement faction)

On 25 May 1892, *The Jurisprudence News* (Issue 14) editorial team published their opinion entitled "Opinion on the Postponement of the Date of Entry Into Force of the Code[s]".[45] The article was signed by 11 jurists (C. Egi, K. Takahashi, Y. Hozumi, Tei'ichirō Matsuno, Yasuji Hijikata, Teiji Itō, Tomotsuke Asakura, Tokugorō Nakahashi, Y. Okuda, T. Okamura and K. Yamada), but later it was confirmed that C. Egi prepared the draft. The publication of the text was preceded by a great social campaign by the postponement faction, which tried to arouse the interest of influential personalities throughout Japan. The English School representatives also agreed with the famous Tokyo daily gazette *Nichinichi*, who reprinted the opinion in ten parts for a wider audience.[46] Japanese legal historians emphasize that due to seven carefully presented objections to the Codes and expressive language, which once again forced the decisive faction to take a stance, *The Jurisprudence News* article was one of the most profound and opinion-forming texts of the postponement faction.[47]

In the first point, the editorial team alleged that the new codes (actually the Civil Code) would lead to the "corruption of common morality" (*rintowa o kairan*

[44] For the full opinion text, see Hoshino (ed.), 2014, pp. 189–191.
[45] Hōgaku Shimpō (ed.), 1892, pp. 1–35.
[46] Fukushima, 1988, p. 127.
[47] Hoshino, 1943, p. 128.

su). As the reason for this opinion, they indicated that the complete rejection of national customary law and the adoption of a foreign Christian ideology, which was accompanied by harmful individualism, would harm particularly valued family relations. Among the most criticized provisions of the Civil Code, they mentioned establishing separate paternal and maternal parental authority and dealing with spouses as two individuals only bonded by a civil law contract.

In the second point, the editorial team criticized the Civil Code for limiting constitutional executive power (*kempōjō no meireiken o genshuku su*). Although the Civil Code should belong only to private law, they claimed that it also contained provisions of public law limiting a large amount of imperial authority, which was an issue of national sovereignty. According to them, the priority of property rights over the broadly understood public interest was characteristic of French individualism and economic capitalism, contrary to the spirit of the old Japanese private law system.

In the third point, the authors noticed that the Civil Code's guiding principles differed from those declared by its drafters (*yosan no genri ni chigau*). As justification for this statement, they referred to contradictions between the provisions of the Constitution and public law, which resulted from relying on the French private law model, as opposed to the reception of English and German constitutional law models.

In the fourth point, the editorial team argued that the Civil Code did not implement the national ideas (*kokka shisō o kaku*); rather, it referred to the democratic state with a republican form of government. Once again, the authors invoked the lack of harmony between the Civil Code and the Constitution, which introduced the system of national sovereignty centred around the emperor. For them, the Civil Code did not sufficiently emphasize the superior role of the nation in the private law system but promoted the natural law doctrine, opposing universally accepted Japanese ideas.

In the fifth point, the authors warned that the Civil Code would bring chaos to the economic life of the entire society (*shakai no keizai o kakuran su*). They spent a few pages explaining the negative impact of individualism promoted by the new law on the functioning of the economy. Numerous defects were noticed in the construction of legal persons and property law provisions and in a significant part of the Commercial Code.

In the sixth point, the English School representatives wrote that the Civil Code revised the basis of tax law (*zeihō no kongen o hendō su*). By introducing concepts unknown to the tax law in property law and establishing a solid guarantee of protecting individual private law rights, the Code influenced the effectiveness of tax laws that had previously entered into force.

In the seventh point, the editorial team concluded that the Civil Code implemented purely academic legal theories using state authorities (*seiryoku o motte gakuri o kyōkō su*). The authors suggested that reading the Civil Code was like having to learn from an academic textbook, making it difficult for ordinary people to understand. Its drafters were also accused of relying on national institutions to introduce ideas contradictory to widely known customary law.

The arguments collected by *The Jurisprudence News* were not new in the context of the previously published postponement faction's allegations against the Civil Code. However, they provided a valuable discussion summary that reached a broader audience before the Imperial Diet's third and decisive meeting.[48]

6.5. Decisive faction's opinions in 1892

6.5.1. *The Meihō Journal* editorial team's opinion on the goals of establishing the Meihō Association (decisive faction)

On 21 March 1892, in the inaugural issue of *Meihō Shisō – The Meihō Journal* (literally *The Clear Law Journal*) – the editorial team published an opinion piece that indicated the reasons for establishing Meihō Kai – the Meihō Association. The article was entitled "Purpose of Establishing the Meihō Association and Its Members".[49]

By indicating the names and academic titles of the 14 founding members (including K. Handa, B. Kumano, S. Kurizuka, M. Tomii and K. Ume), the authors presented their group to the public and the reasons for establishing the Meihō Association at the Japanese-French Law School at the end of February 1891. They also mentioned researching broadly understood legal, political and economic topics.[50]

Overall, 20 board members and 69 ordinary members signed the founding declaration. The following jurists were elected to the board: S. Inoue, M. Tomii, S. Kameyama, K. Ume, S. Kōmyōji, T. Kishimoto, K. Handa, B. Kumano, S. Kurizuka, K. Miyagi and T. Takagi.[51]

The Meihō Journal editorial team's declaration was an unambiguous attempt to demonstrate the size of the decisive faction and its permanent unification in the face of the expected decisive clash in the defence of the Civil Code before the Imperial Diet's third meeting.

[48] For the full opinion text, see Hoshino (ed.), 2014, pp. 171–185.

[49] Meihō Shisō (ed.), 1892, pp. 67–80.

[50] T. Hoshino argued that advocating for the removal of old customary law and promotion of further reforms of the Japanese legal system was an additional goal of the Meihō Association. Hoshino, 1943, p. 126.

[51] For the full opinion text, see Hoshino (ed.), 2014, pp. 232–233.

6.5.2. G. Boissonade's opinion (decisive faction)

Speaking up in the Civil Code Controversy, on 30 April 1892, G. Boissonade submitted his legal opinion to the Minister of Foreign Affairs, Takeaki Enomoto, addressing the allegations of the postponement faction.[52] At this stage, the Japanese jurists mostly already knew the content of *The Jurisprudence News* editorial team's opinion (officially published on 26 March 1892), which also reached G. Boissonade during his recovery stay in one of Hakone's famous resorts. Unlike other texts published by opponents of the Codes, his opinion was a private commentary for M. Matsukata's cabinet, as its publication in any legal journal could be considered political activity and thus a violation of the contractual conditions of his stay in Japan.[53] Nevertheless, G. Boissonade's opinion was a valuable source of his personal views on the Civil Code Controversy and one of the decisive faction's voices, which the cabinet could have used during the Imperial Diets' third meeting.

G. Boissonade divided his opinion into three main parts. In the first, he identified the opponents of the Codes as a faction composed of four smaller groups: (1) state officials and attorneys, (2) lecturers in state and private law schools, (3) some entrepreneurs and (4) some journalists. He wrote that they all looked at the Codes through the prism of potential personal gains and losses. He criticized this approach and added that people in the postponement faction used the controversies around the Civil Code and the Commercial Code as a pretext to attack the cabinet.

In the second part, G. Boissonade wrote that the postponement faction was wrong by claiming that the Civil Code contradicted old customary law. He argued that this accusation was without foundation as the books on property law, security and evidence were drafted on the basis of legal, economic and moral theories universally recognized in civilized countries. He believed that the preservation of native customary law could only harm Japan. He further commented that establishing a unified basis of private law was essential to the abolition of Edo-era feudalism and support for the centralized government. Despite his general view, G. Boissonade stated that in the Civil Code, particularly in the part concerning the succession law, some old feudal customary law norms, like the eldest son's

[52] Ōkubo, 1977, pp. 174–175.

[53] The Japanese scrupulously monitored G. Boissonade's activities, especially his sources of income, requests for additional funds and any internal and foreign trips. The special care for his supervision can be evidenced by numerous documents that were drafted during almost 30 years of his stay in Japan: Kokuritsu Kōbunshokan: Ref. 太00717100; Kokuritsu Kōbunshokan: Ref. 太00838100; Kokuritsu Kōbunshokan: Ref. 公02571100; Kokuritsu Kōbunshokan: Ref. 公02692100; Kokuritsu Kōbunshokan: Ref. 纂00034100; Kokuritsu Kobunshokan: Ref. 記00570100; Kokuritsu Kobunshokan: Ref. 別00007100.

exclusive succession, were retained. He also believed that Family Law was drafted with great care to preserve most Japanese customs.

In the third part, the author commented on the reasons why the date of entry into force of the Civil Code should not be postponed. Firstly, he argued that acceding to the postponement faction postulates would negatively affect the national authority since the emperor had promulgated the Codes. He recommended that the Codes should come into force, and only after a few years could they be amended, based on the opinions collected from judges exercising the law. Also, G. Boissonade was worried that postponing the Codes would have detrimental effects on Japanese businesses and citizens, as it would slow down the economic development and unification of the country and would prolong the process of revising unequal treaties. The latter matter was also raised in point three, which indicated the direct link between the entry into force of the Civil Code and the Commercial Code and supporting the negotiations carried out by the Ministry of Foreign Affairs. He condemned the postponement faction for adhering to the idea of revising the unequal treaties while pressing for the postponement of the date of entry into force of the Codes, which was an apparent contradiction for G. Boissonade.[54]

6.5.3. Kenjirō Ume's opinion (French School, decisive faction)

On 21 May 1892, K. Ume, a graduate of the second cohort of the School of Law at the Ministry of Justice, Doctor of Laws at the University of Lyon,[55] Dean of the Japanese-French Law School and Associate Professor at the Faculty of Law of the Old University of Tokyo, published his opinion on the Civil Code just before the beginning of the discussion at the Imperial Diet's third meeting. Nowadays, he is unanimously recognized as one of the fathers of the Japanese Civil Code. Japanese scholars often describe him as the most outstanding jurist during the Meiji era. The exceptional position of K. Ume may be evidenced by the process of drafting the revised Civil Code. Prime Minister H. Itō addressed him by his professorial title (Ume Sensei), while the other two members of the Project Team – M. Tomii and N. Hozumi, also generally recognized as legal authorities with academic titles – were treated as junior associates (Tomii-kun, Hozumi-kun). Additionally, N. Hozumi, the undisputed leader of the English School and K. Ume's greatest adversary during the debates on doctrinal issues, also admitted after some time that his rival was an outstanding figure with extraordinary intellectual abilities.[56]

[54] For discussion on G. Boissonade's opinion submitted to T. Enomoto, see Ōkubo, 1977, pp. 174–176.

[55] Shichinobe, 2009c, p. 66.

[56] Hozumi, 1980, pp. 325–326.

K. Ume's article was entitled "Opinion on the Entry into Force of the Code[s]".[57] In nine points, he presented the most important reasons for supporting the entry into force of the Civil Code and the Commercial Code by the initially agreed date, summarizing the arguments of the decisive faction.

The first point emphasized that the Codes should enter into force as soon as possible (*hōten wa kyū ni kore o jisshi suru no jūyō ari*). As the reason for this statement, K. Ume referenced the duty to complete the codification process and introduce a comprehensive system of statutory law. He believed that due to the recent history of Japan and the establishment of a constitutional monarchy, it was not possible to maintain the customary law system, which was based on two traditional ideas: feudalism and isolationism. Notwithstanding the lack of a codified system of private law in the United Kingdom and Germany, he argued that neither school of legal jurisprudence in Japan questioned the need for drafting a Civil Code and a Commercial Code. He argued that the entry into force of both Codes would make citizens aware of their rights and responsibilities. Despite all their substantive and formal flaws, there was no better solution than introducing them soon.

In the second paragraph, K. Ume indicated that if Japan intended to revise unequal treaties, it should first introduce the Codes (*jōyaku o kaisei sento horiseba kanarazu sakizu hōten o jisshi sezaru bekarazu*). He cited the main arguments of the decisive faction concerning this issue, adding that the codified legal system is one of the most objective and representative indicators of a civilized state. He believed that by establishing a complete system of statutory law, Japan would be able to return to negotiations with the Western powers from a different position.

In the third point, the author wrote that it was impossible to roughly predict whether reliance on an outdated or modern legal doctrine actually made any code good or bad work of jurisprudence (*gakuri no shinko o motte sumiyaka ni hōten no ryō o uranasu bekarazu*). According to him, over the centuries, legislators had applied many different doctrines that have undergone further evolution and modern interpretations. For this reason, the Japanese legislator analysed 12 Western legal systems to pick the most suitable one.

In the fourth point, K. Ume argued that the authors of the statement about the contradiction of the Civil Code and the Constitution norms were wrong (*Mimpō ga Kempō to teshoku su to iwaku wa gokai nari*). As a counterargument, he pointed out the opponents' lack of sufficiently in-depth knowledge of the provisions of the Civil Code and their reading of the content without a broader understanding of the entire legal act. By explaining the legal definitions of property law and the scope of their application, he tried to show that there was no collision between private and public law norms.

[57] Ume, 1892, pp. 1–21.

The fifth point had a similar construction and stated that the Civil Code did not restrict law enforcement by the public administration (*Mimpō wa gyōsei meirei o sokubaku sezu*). The author referred to the legal theory basics and explained the relationship between generally applicable law, which included acts such as the Civil Code, and special ordinances related to administrative law.

In the sixth point, K. Ume denied that the Civil Code amended the provisions of the tax law (*Mimpō wa zeihō o aratamezu*). For him, this was one of the most important arguments of the postponement faction during the last stage of the Controversy. It resulted, however, from the incorrect understanding of the Codes and tax law position within the Japanese legal system. Thus, he argued that the entry into force of the Codes neither changed the tax law nor negated the fiscal obligations of citizens towards the state.

In the seventh point, the French School representative wrote that attacking the Civil Code under the pretext of allegedly bringing about the decline of morality was nothing more than slander (*Mimpō wa rinjō o kairan su to iwaku wa zambu nari*). In particular, K. Ume criticized Y. Hozumi's article, widespread among the postponement faction, concerning the disastrous influence of the Civil Code on traditional family ties. The author felt that Y. Hozumi did not understand many Christian moral obligations. According to him, the German School representative also did not notice global trends, as in other countries, there were no significant objections to the transition from the old Roman law system emphasizing the superior role of the family to gradual individualism (*zenji kojinshugi*). K. Ume claimed that the Japanese legislator struggled (*rippōsha no kushin*) not to introduce revolutionary changes in the private law system. For him, the evidence of concern for protecting old customary law was visible in preserving such institutions as the head of the household, the family as the basic unit of family law, traditional divorce, adult adoption, and the position of illegitimate children. He was of the opinion that the essence of the old Japanese family system and the traditional understanding of morality were perfectly reflected in Article 19, defining relatives as persons related by consanguinity, and in Article 26, imposing a responsibility of mutual support between relatives. Overall, K. Ume tried to persuade the readers that the Civil Code was, in many respects, a significant improvement on the customary family law system.

In the eighth point, K. Ume wrote that the Civil Code protected honour and good faith (*Mimpō wa eiyo shin'yō o mo hogo su*). For example, he cited Article 323 related to the nullity of the obligation, in which one party does not receive any measurable financial profits, despite their contractual consent. In his opinion, the party is not bound by an obligation detrimental to their interests. The author also mentioned Article 170, which imposed the obligation to repair damage caused by unlawful action.

In the last, ninth, point, K. Ume argued that the assignment of claims was not necessarily contrary to old customs (*saiken no jōto wa aete kanshū ni motorazu*).

He claimed that this instrument, criticized by the postponement faction, was actually not a foreign solution adopted in Japan, as it was similar to the old merchant practices. According to him, the opponents of the assignment were terrified of modifying the contract concluded between relatives. K. Ume reminded them that in the past, the obligations could also be revised depending on the contractual provisions.[58]

6.5.4. S. Isobe's opinion (French School, decisive faction)

On 15 April 1892, *The Association of Constitutionalists Journal* (Issue 10) published S. Isobe's opinion entitled "Necessity of Entry into Force of the Code[s]".[59]

S. Isobe addressed the readers with the conviction that the postponement faction only sought a pretext to question the system of minors' protection adopted in the Book on Personal Law. He felt that a return to the old customs was unfavourable for guardians and minors, especially when protecting their property rights. He criticized the opponents for referring to the inconsistency of legal norms with the old customs in family law, yet they did not notice that it allowed for such injustice as, among others, the succession of the biological family's assets by an adoptive child from a different family. According to him, this traditional right could result in children leaving the adoptive family too hastily to acquire additional benefits from their biological family.

The imperfection of Japanese customary law was, for S. Isobe, harmful to a large part of society. He condemned the supporters of the non-codified legal system for ignoring the most essential ideas of the Meiji Revolution, which included the abolition of feudalism, the promotion of self-governance at all levels of the country's administrative division and the introduction of the Constitution and the Codes. By pointing to the establishment of the Imperial Diet, the author wondered whether this fact was also a violation of ancient customs for his adversaries. He believed that maintaining the widely accepted elements of the old customary law system was unfeasible since many people supported the creation of a parliament under the constitutional rule of law. S. Isobe also indicated that a natural consequence of this decision was guaranteeing private law rights.

The French School representative recalled the debate on the annual expenses of the Japanese treasury, the circumstances of the dissolution of the House of Representatives and the holding of extraordinary elections. Despite the chaos associated with the temporary reorganization of the legislative power, he called for calmness, not succumbing to opposition slogans, and sticking to the critical goal: guaranteeing private law rights. He emphasized that the Codes are equally

[58] For the full opinion text, see Hoshino (ed.), 2014, pp. 233–241.

[59] Isobe, 1892, (original pages are unknown).

important components of the legal system as the Criminal Code, the Code of Criminal Procedure and the Code of Civil Procedure. S. Isobe argued that the reliance on customary law in the private law system had been abandoned in France and Germany, and the existing resistance to introducing the codes in Japan was a great mistake solely made by the English School.

Through observing three European legal systems – English, German and Italian – the author wanted to draw attention to different views on the functioning of the justice system while exercising private law rights. He claimed that without a codified law, solving issues related to the acquisition and loss of property and the establishment of new enterprises was challenging. He felt it was difficult to properly balance the native customary law in the new legal system. As a reason for that, he pointed out keeping a firm distance from the outside world for the last 2,000 years and the Tokugawa shogunate period, which led to the country's strict isolation, the decentralization of power and the creation of numerous domains managed by clans. Consequently, internal trade was limited by customs chambers, and only the Meiji Revolution helped to eliminate unnecessary barriers and enabled the country to join world trade. Thus, S. Isobe saw no possibility of preserving a customary law system as it was not adapted to the global economic requirements at that time. For him, the entry into force of the Civil Code and the Commercial Code was the only way to secure the entire society's private law rights and resolve future potential issues. He wondered how the difficulties related to the bankruptcy of enterprises and various legal disputes should have been solved in a constitutional system, which limited the cabinet's powers in line with social expectations.

At the end of his article, S. Isobe argued that the choice of French law as the basis for the Japanese Civil Code was only intended to help overcome codification difficulties. He supported the claim that the opposition of the jurists brought up in the spirit of English and American law was motivated mainly by jealousy. However, since the Codes became a fact, he believed that regardless of their shortcomings, it was necessary to balance the advantages and disadvantages and introduce them according to the initial plan by defying the plot to reject them.[60]

6.5.5. *The Journal of Law* editorial team's opinion on the position of the Ministry of Justice and the Imperial Diet's third meeting (decisive faction)

On 25 April 1892, *The Journal of Law* (Issue 881), a journal founded by the French School representatives at the Meiji Law School in 1890 and focusing on periodic commenting on legal acts and reviewing various events in Japanese jurisprudence, published the editorial team's opinion about the Ministry of Justice and the

[60] For the full opinion text, see Hoshino (ed.), 2014, pp. 147–149.

upcoming meeting of the new parliamentary term. The article was entitled "The Imperial Diet's Meeting and the Ministry of Justice".[61]

The authors cited the emperor's edict, which established a 40-day extraordinary meeting of the Imperial Diet. They expected parliamentary sessions to be dominated by the rivalry between the cabinet and the lower house members over the new bills. At the same time, they predicted that the dispute between the two parties would be much more severe compared to previous meetings. Among the legislative initiatives the Ministry of Justice submitted before the debate's opening, the editorial team mentioned draft amendments to the Penal Code, the People Registration and Records Law, and the Bar Association Law.

In the later part of the opinion, the editorial team firmly stated that considering the expected coming into force of the Civil Code and the Commercial Code on 1 January 1893, the Ministry of Justice should avoid proposing any amendments to both legal acts. It was believed that admitting the postponement faction was right, even in some part, could weaken the position of the Ministry of Justice, which would result in postponing the date of entry into force of the Codes. As the prominent negative consequence of this scenario, the authors indicated keeping the Japanese judicial decisions inconsistent and varying by region. Referring to the data related to the courts throughout the country, they additionally argued that the number of judges who graduated from the French School and thus supported the immediate entry into force of the Codes was more significant than the number of judges who graduated from the English School and supported the postponement faction. The authors directly accused the adversaries of having deceived part of the Imperial Diet (*gikai no ichibu o manchaku shite*) and securing the most votes necessary to support postponing the entry into force and revising the Codes. At the same time, they criticized the Ministry of Justice for failing to halt the actions of the adversaries despite the cabinet's solid political position. This setback was called "an insult to all supporters of Codes". Accusations of a lack of will to fight were also directed at people holding senior positions in the Ministry of Justice. By referring to the passive attitude of the Deputy Minister of Justice, R. Mitsukuri, the editorial team feared that the ministry might face even more problems defending the Codes during the next Imperial Diet meeting.

In conclusion, the authors regretfully stated that A. Yamada's resignation as the Minister of Justice was a great problem for the decisive faction. According to them, the judges should theoretically bear the responsibility of fighting for the entry into force of the Codes, but the situation was not so obvious since the Tokyo Court of Appeals was dominated by graduates of the German School. The domination of French School graduates was apparent only in the Supreme Court, yet some judges supported even

[61] Hōritsu Zasshi (ed.), 1892a, pp. 1–6.

the most radical postulates of the postponement faction, which called for the rejection of the Codes. The editorial team thanked A. Yamada for his effort and regretted that no one could have predicted that the initial slight opposition to the Codes would lead to the creation of the "bandit postponement doctrine" (*enchōron naru hito*). Furthermore, they expressed disapproval of the current Minister of Justice, F. Tanaka, whose conciliatory attitude provoked even greater friction between the two factions.[62]

6.5.6. The Association of Constitutionalists' opinion concerning the arguments for the entry into force of the Codes (decisive faction)

On 15 May 1892, the first part of the Association of Constitutionalists' opinion was published in *The Journal of Law* (Issue 883). The article was entitled "Opinion on the Immediate Entry into Force of the Codes".[63] Despite the text being released ten days before a similar article by the postponement faction in *The Jurisprudence News* (Issue 14), the authors had acquired their adversaries' opinion through numerous personal connections and had read it before it was available to the public. Thus, in advance of the postponement faction's article being published, the Association of Constitutionalists provided a wider audience with a systematized response to most of the allegations directed towards the Codes. The second and third parts of the Association of Constitutionalists' article appeared in subsequent issues of *The Journal of Law* (Issues 884–885), just after the conclusion of the Civil Code and the Commercial Code Controversy at the House of Peers.[64]

As the most critical argument against postponing the entry into force of the Civil Code and the Commercial Code, the authors mentioned the violation of public order in the state (*kokka no chitsujo o binran suru mono nari*). As explained, the purpose of the codification of private law was to guarantee the peaceful functioning of society based on stable and publicly available statutory law, which guaranteed a number of individual rights. For the Association of Constitutionalists, the lack of codes meant denying the current reformist policy and returning to feudalism. They also believed that the opponents of the Codes were working to the detriment of the nation, calling for solutions promoting chaos and disorder.

In the second point, the authors claimed that the desire to postpone the entry into force of the Codes led to the decline of morality (*rinri no kairan o kitasu mono nari*). They argued that old customary law was inadequate for social conditions at that time, and therefore the legislator should strive for thorough modification. The Association of Constitutionalists defended the Codes against accusations of

[62] For the full opinion text, see Hoshino (ed.), 2014, pp. 214–215.

[63] Hōchi Kyōkai (ed.), 1892a, pp. 110–118.

[64] Hōchi Kyōkai (ed.), 1892b, pp. 166–172; Hōchi Kyōkai (ed.), 1892c, pp. 228–234.

weakening traditional ties between relatives, as drafters addressed the most critical issues in family law. They argued that the right to exercise one's rights in a civil dispute between a parent and a child or between siblings could not be considered a violation of public morality, because family disputes also occurred in the past, and the Codes were intended to solve them more efficiently.

In the third point, the Association of Constitutionalists claimed that the idea to postpone the date of entry into force of the Codes would cause damage to internal sovereignty (*kokka no shuken o gai shi*) and destroy the current achievements in the struggle to preserve independence on the international arena (*dokuritsukoku no mi o ushinawashimuru mono nari*). It was highlighted that the introduction of the Civil Code and the Commercial Code, regardless of their Franco-German nature, was a necessary element of the Japanese legal system and a matter of preserving the pride of the independent state.

In the fourth point, the authors indicated that the absence of both Codes would negatively affect the Constitution (*Kempō no jisshi o gai suru mono nari*). They wrote that a legal system that was not fully codified was an obstacle to applying the basic law effectively. For them, the mechanisms of exercising administrative power without establishing guarantees to protect citizens' private law rights would be limited. Consequently, they argued that the rapid introduction of the Civil Code would strengthen the cabinet's position in the eyes of the public.[65]

In further parts of the opinion, the Association of Constitutionalists argued that abandoning legislation at this stage meant entrusting this matter to judges (*rippōken o hōki shi, kore o saibankan ni i suru mono nari*). They also claimed that the postponement faction slandered the Codes because they did not understand them correctly (*hōten o gokai shi kore o zambu suru mono nari*). The authors warned that the absence of the Codes would introduce much confusion into the court proceedings (*koshō konran o shite sō kiseshimuru mono nari*). They feared that implementing the adversaries' demands would turn the whole of society off the road to "spiritual peace and enlightenment" (*anshin ritsumei no michi o usshinawashimuru mono nari*). Attention was also drawn to the prediction that without the Codes, the national economy would significantly suffer (*kokka no keizai o kakuran suru mono nari*).

6.5.7. The Japanese-French Law School Alumni Association's opinion (decisive faction)

On 25 May 1892, *The Journal of Law* (Issue 884) published the first part of the Japanese-French Law School Alumni Association's opinion (*Wafutsu Hōritsu Gakkō*

[65] For the opinion text until the fourth point, see Hoshino (ed.), 2014, pp. 218–225.

Kōyūkai), entitled "Opinion on the Immediate Entry into Force of the Code[s]".[66] Its release coincided with the beginning of the debate on the Codes in the Imperial Diet. The second part of the article was presented on 5 June 1892 in the next issue of *The Journal of Law* (Issue 885) after a debate in the House of Peers and the defeat of the decisive faction.[67]

The Association noticed that despite the ongoing dispute over the Codes, the decisive faction invariably stuck to its ideas. Yet, it did not thoroughly explain the reasons why the Codes should enter into force. Since this was not an easy task, the authors intended to depict the positive and negative aspects of the postponement and decisive parties' stances using objective and comprehensive commentary.

In the first point, the Association analysed the argument concerning the urgent need for the entry into force of the Codes. It agreed with this statement in general, pointing out, among others, the need to establish a unified judiciary and to show citizens their own rights and responsibilities. Additionally, the authors did not support the postponement faction's accusation that the new law, contrary to old customs, could adversely affect the social order. Regardless of the nature of the new regulations, the French School representatives claimed that citizens showed a patriotic attitude and were aware that they could always count on amendments to the Codes. The Association also tried to prove that the successful development of the Japanese economy based on trade, industry and private businesses strongly depended on establishing the codified private law system. The authors rejected the proposal to revise the Codes to consider customary law, as in their opinion, it had a feudal character and had been partially replaced by modern law in the last 20 years.

In the next paragraph, the Association discussed the postponement faction's allegation that the Codes were inconsistent with Japanese social conditions. The authors referred to the opponents of the Codes wishing to postpone the entry into force due to the need to provide substantial changes. The Association admitted that the Civil Code was largely based on foreign law, but despite this, they emphasized that the drafters acted in accordance with the government's instructions. Furthermore, they claimed that books on Personal and Succession Law significantly differed from the solutions adopted in other countries. The Association criticized the opponents of the Codes for not recognizing this fact and calling for the rejection of law codification under the pretext of defending national customary law. They also did not support the argument concerning the potentially adverse social effects of the Codes. As an example of an incorrect understanding of European legal culture, the authors cited Y. Hozumi's attack on individualism and glorifying Roman law in pre-Christian legal thought. They argued that respecting the father and mother was equally crucial in

[66] Wafutsu Hōritsu Gakkō Kōyūkai (ed.), 1892a, pp. 166–172.

[67] Wafutsu Hōritsu Gakkō Kōyūkai (ed.), 1892b, pp. 228–234.

Christianity. Additionally, they claimed that family law differed significantly from Western law, retaining its Japanese nature by keeping such institutions as the family household, adoption, the illegitimate children system, and the eldest son's exclusive succession. The Association wrote that returning to classical Roman law had become impossible in the modern world. They felt the postponement faction's fear of reversing the social order by destroying family ties and promoting individualism was groundless. By pointing to numerous legal loopholes in the customary law system, the authors indicated that the Civil Code comprehensively regulated the complicated relations between relatives without negatively impacting the perception of morality.

In the opinion of the Association, introducing the Codes was an essential element of a clear distinction between public and private law. The authors disagreed with the postponement faction's claim that the Codes limited executive power since, through the completion of the codification project, people would learn to distinguish between administrative and private matters and grasp the essence of their rights and responsibilities. They also explained that despite some warnings, there was no conflict between the Civil Code and the tax law. They believed that in economic terms, the Codes would not create the environment for the survival of the fittest, as the uncodified legal system promoted inequalities and law violations. It was emphasized that the Civil Code was designed to protect the creditor's rights and broadly understood private law rights, which could not be assessed as social injustice. For this reason, all the inaccuracies mentioned by the postponement faction were for the Association "making a fuss in a matter that required deeper study".

Subsequently, the authors again analysed the postponement faction's preference related to postponing the date of entry into force of the Codes to introduce amendments to them. They wondered how the opponents of the Codes intended to improve the Civil Code by including customary law, which was known for its imperfection and internal contradictions. The Association was very disappointed about the Imperial Diet's decision to pass the act on postponing the entry into force of the Civil Code and the Commercial Code, asking whether it would actually be possible to introduce amendments to both legal acts on time. The French School representatives did not know how to effectively revise the Codes when the relationships between the legislative and executive powers were more than complicated. They also could not imagine a debate on each of the more than 2,800 articles in parliament, which is why they recommended at least a partial introduction of the Civil Code as an expression of the people's will. In reality, the Association was most afraid of rejecting the Codes in the future under the pretext of making amendments to them.

In the summary of the article, the authors confirmed that since the postponement faction's allegations were invalid, the Codes should come into force on 1 January 1893. They also claimed that the adversaries' demands were impossible to implement and that delaying the entry into force of the Civil Code and the

Commercial Code could not last indefinitely. It was generally assessed that the Imperial Diet had made a fundamental mistake as the Codes' shortcomings could have been gradually eliminated through careful re-examination by a wider group of experts.[68]

6.5.8. *The Journal of Law* editorial team's opinion on the last determination (decisive faction)

On 5 June 1892, after the debate in the House of Peers, which ended with the defeat of the decisive faction, but in the course of the still ongoing dispute in the House of Representatives, *The Journal of Law* editorial team (Issue 885) published an opinion piece entitled "Our Last Determination".[69]

The editorial team revealed the circumstances of voting on T. Murata's bill concerning the postponement of the date of entry into force of the Civil Code and the Commercial Code at the House of Peers. They also informed readers about the House of Representatives debate and establishing a Special Committee. Although the matter was not yet decided, the authors expected that the lower house could support the upper house resolution. Therefore, they wanted to convey their latest message to the readers. It included emphasizing the need for the entry into force of the Codes and supporting the cabinet's effort to push through the legislative policy. The editors referred to Minister of Justice F. Tanaka's speech at the House of Peers to show that the goals of the journal and the cabinet were identical.[70]

The authors tried to predict the further course of the legislative path in the event of the approval of the bill postponing the entry into force of the Codes by both houses. They also reminded readers that the necessary condition for the entry into force of any bill was the emperor's sanction and publication. They still believed that the emperor's opinion on this matter should be listened to, and he might not sanction the postponement. Regardless of the events in the Imperial Diet, the editors believed that not everything had been lost yet, and therefore the cabinet should also be open to all possible options.

As an argument for the entry into force of the Codes, the authors mentioned the lack of a uniform judiciary, largely based on the private opinions of judges and not on stable statutory law. They also felt that if the date of entry into force of the codes were postponed, judges would be exposed to a lack of transparency of the entire legal system because they would not know whether the new provisions of the Civil

[68] For the full opinion text, see Hoshino (ed.), 2014, pp. 224–232.

[69] Hōritsu Zasshi (ed.), 1892b, pp. 213–216.

[70] Details on F. Tanaka's speech and other events at the House of Peers and the House of Representatives are presented in the next subchapter (6.6.).

Code should be applied or whether they should rely on the existing equity principle. Theoretically, the havoc could be avoided by instructions from the Ministry of Justice. However, the authors claimed that any action from the cabinet could be perceived as violating the separation of powers. They wrote that this issue might be more severe and difficult to solve than the alleged harmful social effects of introducing the Codes, which were constantly repeated by the postponement faction.

The editorial team noticed that although the House of Peers passed a bill postponing the date of entry into force of the Civil Code and the Commercial Code, two decisive faction members submitted a separate bill in the House of Representatives. It provided for postponing the entry into force of only part of the Civil Code, namely Personal and Succession Law. The authors were convinced that this solution could address the issues of revising the Civil Code concerning adopting customary law. Thus, they believed that in the worst-case scenario, the Civil Code could be saved at least partly, as the entry into force of Property Law should not encounter significant obstacles.

At the end of the opinion, the editorial team envisaged a possible plan for the supporters of the Codes. Supposing the postponement bill was passed in both houses of parliament, the cabinet must do everything to avoid granting them the emperor's sanction, which was necessary for the promulgation and entry into force according to the legislative procedure.[71]

6.6. Conclusion of the Civil Code and the Commercial Code Controversy during the Imperial Diet's third meeting

On 6 May 1892, the long-expected Imperial Diet's third meeting began. Due to the cabinet's dissolution of the House of Representatives at the end of December 1891, thus shortening the Imperial Diet's second meeting to only one month (from the three required by Article 42 of the Constitution), the upcoming meeting had an extraordinary character. The lack of binding decisions on many issues concerning domestic policy, as well as the temporary dispute between the House of Representatives and the cabinet over an attempt to intervene in the election,[72] resulted in a decreased interest in matters related to the Civil Code and the Commercial Code. However, the Controversy was still one of the most important issues of the postponement faction, which wanted to solve it by the end of the year, before the initially established date

[71] For the full opinion text, see Hoshino (ed.), 2014, pp. 241–243.

[72] The dispute concerned a resolution passed by the House of Representatives that criticized the cabinet's intervention in the elections held in February 1892. In response to the resolution, Prime Minister M. Matsukata decided to suspend parliamentary sessions for a week. Fukushima, 1988, p. 126.

for the entry into force of the Codes. Although the Imperial Diet's fourth meeting was to be held at the turn of 1891 and 1892, the postponement faction representatives expected that the fight for postponing the entry into force of two Codes, including the Commercial Code for the second time, might meet with great resistance. They were especially concerned about the debate in the House of Peers, where the decisive faction had the best organized and determined group of parliament members. For this reason, the postponement faction decided to act rapidly and focused on convincing the House of Peers, while trying to secure victory in the House of Representatives, which traditionally leaned more to their postulates.

6.6.1. Debate in the House of Peers

The first debate on the bill related to the postponement of the entry into force of the Civil Code and the Commercial Code was held during the session of the House of Peers on 26 May.[73] Its author was a well-known postponement faction representative: T. Murata.[74] In the justification, he indicated five short allegations against the Codes: violation of social morality, contradictory nature with old customs, inappropriate legal language, failure to implement the basic principles of law, and discrepancies with other legal acts.[75]

On that day, all members of the cabinet except the Minister of the Army, Lieutenant General Tomonosuke Takashima, participated in the House of Peers session.[76] Although the cabinet recognized the seriousness of the threat related to delaying the entry into force of the Codes, since the failed attempt to intervene in the elections to the House of Representatives, its position had been very unstable and had prevented active politics. Additionally, as indicated by Yū Shigematsu and Yasuo Ōkubo, the decisive faction was particularly weakened by the resignation of A. Yamada as the Minister of Justice in June 1891. In May 1892, only three members of the cabinet (Minister of Justice F. Tanaka, Minister of Education T. Ōki and Home Minister T. Enomoto) were sturdy supporters of the entry into force of the Codes in their original shape on 1 January 1893.[77] Even worse, the Ministry of Justice led by F. Tanaka had ultimately lost the initiative in recent months and could only react to the postponement faction's strategy.

[73] Record of the session of the House of Peers, 26 May 1892; for a timeline of the debate on a bill related to the postponement of the date of entry into force of the Civil Code and the Commercial Code in the House of Peers, see Ōkubo, Takahashi, 1999, pp. 297–300.

[74] T. Murata submitted the bill on 13 May. Its first reading was scheduled for 16 May, but due to the suspension of parliament sessions, it did not begin until 26 May. Fukushima, 1988, p. 126.

[75] Shigematsu, 2007, pp. 125–139.

[76] Nakamura, 1956, p. 156.

[77] Shigematsu, 2007, pp. 126–127; Ōkubo, 1977, p. 172; Hoshino, 1943, p. 136.

The Ministry of Justice's unwillingness to fight for the legislative policy was apparent to the opponents of the Codes from the very beginning of the third meeting of the Imperial Diet. On 26 May, the debate with the postponement faction was initiated by the Minister of Education, T. Ōki, who received support only from a few members of the House of Peers from the decisive faction. Apart from T. Murata, H. Katō also spoke on behalf of the opponents of the Codes. He emphasized that he spoke as a person who did not have in-depth knowledge of legal matters yet noticed fundamental contradictions between the Civil Code and the Constitution. H. Katō argued that in the justification of the Civil Code, its drafters used the wording about granting citizens their natural private law rights, referring directly to the natural law doctrine. He also noted that the Constitution did not strictly separate private rights from civil rights, containing only the "concept of national sovereignty" (*kokka no shuken to iu mono*). Finally, he expressed the opinion that the French natural law doctrine had led the civilization of the West to degeneration and that it could be considered outdated at that time, and thus it should never be applied in Japan.[78]

In response to these allegations, Koyata Torio, a major general of the Japanese Army and a Conservative Party representative, spoke after the statutory break. He said that it should be evident that citizens possessed rights in social relations between themselves, otherwise known as private law rights, regardless of the guiding principles of the Civil Code.[79] Until the beginning of the Imperial Diet's second meeting, K. Torio was known as one of the most active postponement faction representatives in the Commercial Code Controversy. His change of view gave the cabinet hope that some opponents of the Codes were definitely against the collective vision of society in the Japanese private law system.[80]

However, the most tremendous stir was caused by T. Ōki's speech, which combined legal arguments and concern for the good of the nation emotionally, yet with an appropriate distance. Although the Minister of Education was known for his poor oratorical skills, his words were quoted by Japanese newspapers as an example of the perfect voice for the decisive faction. The main part of his speech focused on showing that "national sovereignty" is based on granting private law rights to each citizen. He also argued that the universal protection of the property right of every person by the private law system is the most crucial principle of the natural law doctrine. Referring to H. Katō's foreign experience, the Minister of Education claimed that this relationship between the right to property and natural law was also recognized in Germany, where his adversary had once studied.

[78] Record of H. Katō's speech during the session of the House of Peers, 26 May 1892.

[79] Record of H. Torio's speech during the session of the House of Peers, 26 May 1892.

[80] Shigematsu, 2007, pp. 129–130. Shigematsu referred to the following newspapers: *Asano Shimbun*, Yokohama *Mainichi Shimbun* and *Kokumin Shimbun*.

T. Ōki emphasized that limiting private law rights under the pretext of adopting the idea of "national sovereignty" made citizens "slaves of the nation". As he said, fortunately for people, neither Germany nor Japan had accepted such a solution.[81]

The postponement faction was surprised by the Minister of Education's speech, who with great energy swore that he was defending the vital interests of Japan and its citizens by appealing to the rationality of parliamentarians. During his exchange of views with T. Murata, R. Mitsukuri also appeared on the lectern, reminding him of the importance of both Codes for legal order.[82] The discussion in the forum of the House of Peers became extremely fierce and soon escalated to a general dispute about the rationale of the Codes.[83] As a result of T. Ōki's speech, as well as the observation of the mood in the upper house, some Conservative Party members, centred around Tateki Tani, switched allegiances and decided to support K. Torio and the decisive faction. This unexpected shift met with great indignation among the postponement faction representatives, who accused recent allies that their leader had secretly been offered the position of Minister of Justice by the cabinet. In response to this gossip, K. Torio openly criticized H. Katō for his nationalist stance.[84] As K. Mizuno argued, the volte-face of several House of Peers members was primarily motivated by the rumours about the will of the emperor himself, who allegedly favoured no delays in the coming into force of the Codes. According to the Japanese press, which reported on the proceedings of the House of Peers, the first public debate on T. Murata's bill ended in a defeat of the opponents of the Codes due to the fierce resistance of three ministers.[85]

The next day, 27 May, the postponement faction regained the initiative in the debate at the House of Peers due to numerous concerns about general views on the natural law doctrine. T. Tani raised his doubts, negatively assessing the "natural human rights" doctrine (*tempu jinken*) constantly referred to by the Minister of Education. In his opinion, T. Ōki and K. Torio, educated in the traditional legal spirit, did not understand Western European ideas.[86] T. Tani's statement met with R. Mitsukuri's detailed explanation of the natural law doctrine. He was supported then by F. Tanaka and Shigetoshi Okauchi, a Supreme Court judge and one of the most active decisive faction representatives.[87] By contrast, the natural law doctrine

[81] Record of T. Oki's speech during the session of the House of Peers, 26 May 1892.

[82] Record of T. Mitsukuri's speech during the session of the House of Peers, 26 May 1892.

[83] Fukushima, 1988, pp. 124–125.

[84] Shigematsu, 2007, p. 128.

[85] Nakamura, 1956, p. 157.

[86] Record of T. Tani's speech during the session of the House of Peers, 27 May 1892.

[87] Record of R. Mitsukuri's, T. Tanaka's and S. Okauchi's speeches during the session of the House of Peers, 27 May 1892.

was subsequently criticized by T. Murata and H. Katō, who were mainly afraid of disharmony between the Japanese public and private law.[88]

The debate in the House of Peers on 27 May lasted until the evening, and its turning point was M. Tomii's speech. This recognized French School representative had not actively participated in the parliamentary discussion for health reasons. By rejecting the decisive faction's arguments based on emotions and emphasizing his neutral stance, he presented a number of reasons why the Civil Code should not come into force.

First, M. Tomii shared his opinion that the Code was more like a draft than a complete work, which was particularly visible in the inconsistent systematics and unclear content of many provisions. He criticized the definition and division of real rights adopted in the Book on Property Law and the complicated nature of contracts. The French School representative argued that contrary to the drafters' declarations, the Code only partially referred to the natural law doctrine and, in many fields, it was far from adopting this idea. He did not agree with the optimistic vision of the decisive faction that the new law would not cause major social damage and could be easily analysed by jurists. For him, even the interpretation of the Code's formal division into procedural and substantive law, internal systematics and legal definitions would be cumbersome in most law schools in Japan. M. Tomii suggested that there was a need to conduct additional research on old customary law, as he was concerned about the decline of the comparative law method in Japanese legal scholarship.

From the point of view of the Controversy, M. Tomii's decisive argument against the Civil Code was the allegation that the drafters intended to promote radical reform in the family law system at a time when gradual changes were already taking place in Japanese families anyway. He considered adopting the Code a hazardous idea and disagreed with legislators testing the new law's effectiveness on society. According to him, the introduction of amendments, even if it would delay the entry into force of the Civil Code by three or four more years, was "an obvious thing" (*tōzen no koto*). M. Tomii understood the determination of the Ministry of Foreign Affairs to revise unequal treaties, but argued that the drafting of the Codes should be a part of a domestic policy aimed at improving the lives of all people. At the end of his speech, he estimated that an additional four years would be sufficient to introduce amendments to the Civil Code. He persuaded the audience that if the Imperial Diet decided to assist the process, the Code could be passed without additional delays and come into force immediately. He also felt that the introduction of the Civil Code and the Commercial Code was a tremendous breakthrough in the

[88] Record of T. Murata's and H. Katō's speeches during the session of the House of Peers, 27 May 1892.

history of Japan. For this reason, he insisted on providing appropriate amendments to the Codes and securing a large majority of votes in the legislative process.[89]

Japanese legal historians agree that M. Tomii's speech was one of the most important factors in the final victory of the postponement faction in the Civil Code Controversy in the House of Peers, which also influenced the further events in the House of Representatives. M. Tomii's arguments broke the previous resistance of T. Ōki, F. Tanaka, R. Mitsukuri, T. Enomoto and K. Torio and convinced some French School representatives to introduce amendments to the Code.[90] Numerous observers of the debate at the House of Peers on May 27 were moved by his performance to such an extent that Chairman Mochiaki Hachisuka had to ring the bell repeatedly to keep silence and allow the debate to continue.[91]

On 28 May, the discussion continued on postponing the date of entry into force of the Civil Code and the Commercial Code. However, the debate quickly descended into accusations of other cabinet members' attempts to intervene behind the scenes. T. Murata complained that the decisive faction representatives publicly perceived him as the greatest enemy, and there were rumours at the House of Peers that he had been publicly assaulted. Moreover, the cabinet was blamed for assigning a police escort only to parliament members from the decisive faction, while K. Takahashi, the director of the government newspaper *Kanhō*, had to personally ask for identical protection for the postponement faction representatives.[92] Despite those odds, the House of Peers finally approved T. Murata's bill during the first reading, and after a short break, the second reading began.[93] The vote on T. Murata's bill was called immediately after its completion. Overall, 184 members of the House of Peers took part in it: 123 voted for the postponement faction's proposal, while only 61 were against it. The polarization of the Japanese political scene on Codes was well illustrated by the fact that no one abstained from voting despite a secret ballot.[94]

At the end of the debate at the House of Peers on May 28, the postponement faction proposed to add a clause to T. Murata's bill that allowed for the immediate entry into force of part of the Codes which were amended within the original deadline (*Tadashi shūsei o owaritaru mono wa honbun kigen-nai to iedomo kore*

[89] Record of M. Tomii's speech during the session of the House of Peers, 27 May 1892.

[90] Sugiyama, 1936, pp. 79–80. Sugiyama also mentioned the names of two other decisive faction representatives, Keigo Kiyoura and Tsunahiko Kuroda, but their speeches during the debate at the House of Peers on 26 and 27 May were not presented.

[91] Shigematsu, 2007, p. 125.

[92] Hoshino, 1949, p. 212. Hoshino indicated that the postponement faction was afraid of acts of violence since the cabinet officially recognized the danger of possible minor casualties related to social unrest.

[93] Record of the House of Peers session, 28 May 1892.

[94] Record of the House of Peers voting on T. Murata's bill, 28 May 1892.

o dankō suru koto o e). This proposition was formally submitted by M. Hachisuka and soon the majority of members accepted it.[95] The Civil Code and the Commercial Code Controversy at the forum of the House of Peers ended with the victory of the postponement faction.

Without waiting for further developments in the House of Representatives, on 4 June, U. Obata submitted a proposal to establish a Review Committee for the Civil Code and Commercial Code (*Mimpō Shōhō Shinsa I'in o mōkuru no kengian*).[96] Since the subsequent sessions of the House of Representatives were held as soon as on 6 and 7 June,[97] this initiative met with a moderately positive reaction from the decisive faction and was finally approved on 8 June.[98] The following day, U. Obata's bill was promulgated and handed over to the cabinet to execute.[99]

6.6.2. Debate in the House of Representatives

Compared to the events in the House of Peers, the Civil Code Controversy had a completely different course in the House of Representatives. On 24 May, a group of eight lower house members from the postponement faction (H. Genda, K. Hatoyama, K. Misaki, Sanae Takata, Naohiko Seki, Manjirō Suzuki and Susumu Sasada) submitted a separate bill related to the postponement of the entry into force of the Civil Code and the Commercial Code to Chairman Tōru Hoshi. However, the drafters decided to introduce a certain modification compared to T. Murata's bill by adding a provision enabling the entry into force of the Commercial Code on 1 April 1893, excluding the part concerning company and insolvency law.[100]

In response to this move, on 27 May, two decisive faction representatives, Hironaka Kōno and Saburō Shimada, submitted a bill regarding postponing the date of entry into force of part of the Civil Code (*Mimpōchū ichibu enchō ni kansuru hōritsuan*).[101] Being aware that the most controversial part of the Civil Code was the Book on Personal Law, both jurists believed there was still a chance to keep

95 Record of adding amendments to T. Murata's bill during the House of Peers session, 28 May 1892.

96 Ōkubo, Takahashi, 1999, pp. 299, 323. The authors indicate that it was U. Obata's old initiative from February 1891, and it was raised during one of the speeches at the House of Peers on 1 June. However, it formally became one of the agenda items only three days later. Record of the House of Peers session, 4 June 1892.

97 Record of the House of Peers discussion on U. Obata's bill, 6–7 June 1892.

98 Record of the House of Peers voting on U. Obata's bill, 8 June 1892.

99 Record of the House of Peers proceedings on U. Obata's bill, 9 June 1892.

100 Ōkubo, Takahashi, 1999, p. 297; Fukushima, 1988, p. 126; Shigematsu, 2005, p. 189. Some Japanese scholars wrongly claim that the bill was submitted on 26 May 1892. Record of the House of Representatives proceedings, 24 May 1892.

101 Record of the House of Representatives proceedings, 27 May 1892.

the books on Property Law, provided that certain concessions were made to the postponement faction.

Although all the parties of the House of Representatives comprised supporters and opponents of the Codes, Y. Ōkubo emphasized that the decisive faction had the advantage initially, as the leaders of three of the five parties (Pro-Cabinet Party, Liberal Party and Constitutional Reform Party) strongly opposed the bill from 24 May.[102] The apparent predominance of the supporters of the Codes, however, changed suddenly when just before 6:30 pm on 30 May, the House of Representatives announced the result of the vote of the House of Peers on T. Murata's bill on the postponement of the entry into force of the Civil Code and the Commercial Code.[103]

Following the approval of T. Murata's bill by the House of Peers, the House of Representatives began its first reading on 3 June. Since the lower house had to analyse three bills on the Codes simultaneously, the Special Committee (*Tokubetsu I'inkai*) was established. It received the task of examining all projects and submitting the combined proposal for further process within ten days.[104] On 4 June, during the next session, nine members of the Special Committee were elected, which included four decisive faction representatives (K. Kōno, S. Shimada,[105] Kōki Watanabe and M. Watanabe) and five postponement representatives (H. Genda, K. Hatoyama, Naomas Maki, K. Misaki and N. Seki).[106] On the same day, the Special Committee was also given an additional task to draft a coherent bill, considering the proposal to delay the entry into force of part of the Civil Code.[107] During the deliberations on 6 June, the House of Representatives also confirmed the appointment of its Chairman (K. Kōno) and Secretary (K. Misaki) by the Special Committee.[108]

The critical debate on postponing the entry into force of the Civil Code and the Commercial Code in the House of Representatives took place on 10 June. Under the

[102] Ōkubo, 1977, p. 180.

[103] Record of the House of Representatives proceedings, 30 May 1892. The House of Peers was known to be more conservative than the House of Representatives on legislative matters; thus, naturally it was more in favour of the entry into force of the Civil Code and the Commercial Code in accordance with the cabinet policy. The information about the defeat of the decisive faction in the House of Peers was a great shock for many members of the House of Representatives and significantly influenced the further course of events.

[104] Record of the House of Representatives proceedings on the Special Committee, 3 June 1892; for detailed explanations of the ten-day period, see Ōkubo, Takahashi, 1999, pp. 298–299.

[105] S. Shimada, a graduate of the English School, was a decisive faction representative in the Civil Code controversy and a postponement faction representative in the Commercial Code controversy.

[106] Record of the House of Representatives proceedings on electing the Special Committee members, 4 June 1892.

[107] Ōkubo, Takahashi, 1999, p. 299.

[108] Record of the House of Representatives proceedings on electing the Special Committee Chairman and Secretary, 6 June 1892.

legislative procedure, after a week's break, the first reading of T. Murata's bill passed by the House of Peers was resumed on that day.[109] On the first item on the agenda, K. Misaki replaced K. Kōno as Chairman of the Special Committee.[110] Subsequently, K. Misaki announced the results of the findings of the Special Committee, stating that most of its members supported T. Murata's bill.[111] In response to this declaration, Minister of Justice F. Tanaka appeared on the lectern. He gave a long speech concerning the importance of the Civil Code and the Commercial Code for the entire Japanese legal system and once again cited the decisive faction's arguments.[112] His address went down in history as "extremely firm" (*dandanko*) due to the phrase used by *The Jurisprudence News* in their article, which emphasized the relentless stance of the Minister of Justice.[113] F. Tanaka's speech was soon commented on by Iwane Abei, a postponement faction representative whom K. Misaki and Kenchō Suematsu next supported.[114] In response, S. Shimada, M. Watanabe, K. Miyagi and Masanosuke Katō spoke in favour of the decisive faction postulates.[115]

Regardless of the decisive faction's determination to protect the Codes, the House of Representatives approved the first reading of T. Murata's bill, moving to the second reading in the next item on the agenda.[116] Since it was agreed that the subject of postponing the date of entry into force of the Codes had been thoroughly discussed so far, and the necessary quorum was present in the lower house, the second reading was skipped in favour of proceeding directly to the vote. It was attended by 275 members of the House of Representatives: 192 voted for and 82 against postponing the entry into force of the Codes. Only one member of parliament abstained from voting.[117] T. Murata's bill was passed according to the postponement faction's plan. The opponents of the Codes secured almost 70% of the votes, significantly more than initially expected by the greatest optimists.

Subsequently, the House of Representatives proceeded with the next item on the agenda: the debate on the bill on the partial entry into force of the Civil Code. This

109 Record of the House of Representatives proceedings on T. Murata's bill, 10 June 1892.

110 Ōkubo, Takahashi, 1999, p. 299.

111 Ōkubo, Takahashi, 1999, p. 299; the authors indicate that this decision was made by the postponement faction representatives, as one of the decisive faction representatives always presented a dissenting opinion.

112 Record of F. Tanaka's speech at the House of Representatives, 10 June 1892.

113 Ōkubo, 1977, p. 180. The author included in his book a piece from *The Jurisprudence News* article (Issue 15).

114 Record of I. Abei's, K. Misaki's and K. Suematsu's speeches at the House of Representatives, 10 June 1892.

115 Record of S. Shimada's, M. Watanabe's, K. Miyagi's and M. Katō's speeches at the House of Representatives, 10 June 1892.

116 Record of the House of Representatives proceedings on T. Murata's bill, 10 June 1892.

117 Record of the House of Representatives voting on T. Murata's bill, 10 June 1892.

discussion began in highly unfavourable circumstances for the decisive faction, which suffered a strategic defeat and irreversibly lost the initiative in the lower house. In the wake of the postponement of both Codes by the Imperial Diet, adopting at least part of the Civil Code was seen as a solution for at least one of the most critical issues of the Japanese private law system: the lack of codified property law.

The discussion on K. Kōno and S. Shimada's bill started just before 6:00 pm and lasted about 40 minutes with a small break. S. Shimada spoke up, trying to convince the postponement faction to allow for the partial entry into force of the Civil Code. After providing comprehensive explanations of the bill, the Chairman ordered a vote on postponing the entry into force of part of the Civil Code. Overall, 281 members of the House of Representatives took part in it: 107 of them voted in favour, 152 against and two abstained.[118] According to the legislative procedure, the outcome of voting on two bills was the following: (1) the House of Representatives negatively assessed the entry into force of the Civil Code concerning the Property Law (the least controversial part of the Code), (2) T. Murata's bill providing for postponing the date of entry into force of the Civil Code and the Commercial Code remained in force, including a clause allowing the entry into force of parts of the Codes that would be considered amended.

Since there were no objections to the voting process, T. Hoshi closed the legislative path of the House of Representatives, confirming the adoption of M. Murata's bill and the rejection of K. Kōno and S. Shimada's bill. Japanese scholars agree that this decision marked the end of the Civil Code and the Commercial Code Controversy in the Imperial Diet.[119] After three years of fierce political and legal dispute, the postponement faction persuaded both houses of parliament to postpone the entry into force of the Civil Code and the Commercial Code to provide comprehensive amendments to them. However, the delay in introducing both Codes was not indefinite, as according to T. Murata's bill, if the Imperial Diet did not approve amended Codes by 31 December 1896, they were to immediately enter into force in their initial shape.[120]

6.7. The Cabinet's reaction to the end of the Controversy

The Imperial Diet's third (extraordinary) meeting ended on 14 June 1892. Under the legislative path adopted in the Constitution of Japan, T. Murata's bill was processed to the cabinet, which was obliged to submit it to the emperor to obtain the emperor's sanction necessary for publication. As Y. Ōkubo and Y. Takahashi argued,

[118] Record of the House of Representatives voting on K. Kōno and S. Shimada's bill, 10 June 1892.

[119] Hironaka, 2020, p. 10; Ōkubo, Takahashi, 1999, p. 301; Ōkubo, 1977, p. 181; Kawaguchi, 2014, p. 266; Kumagai, 1955, p. 215; Iwata, 1943, p. 17; Nakagawa, 2015, pp. 364–365.

[120] Record of the House of Peers deliberations on submitting T. Murata's bill, 16 May 1892.

during the official meeting on 18 June, the cabinet's reaction to the decisions taken by both houses of parliament was ambiguous. By 27 June, F. Tanaka submitted two legal opinions to Prime Minister M. Matsukata: one on the bill postponing the entry into force of the Civil Code and the Commercial Code and the other on the proposal to establish the Revision Committee for the Civil Code and the Commercial Code. In the first opinion, the Minister of Justice emphasized that there is a possibility of halting the further legislative path of T. Murata's bill. As an argument, he mentioned Article 6 of the Constitution, imposing a duty on the emperor to promulgate each legal act, and Article 32 of the Parliament Law (Gi'inhō), which required submitting a "report to the throne" after the Imperial Diet passed the bill to obtain the emperor's sanction necessary for publication. The cabinet was faced with accepting the parliament's will and thus admitting that the Codes had flaws or petitioning the emperor to pursue the policy of introducing the Civil Code and the Commercial Code against the democratically made decisions.[121]

At a historic moment for Japanese legislation, the unexpected event weakened the still insecure position of M. Matsukata's cabinet, forcing him to abandon plans to overturn the Imperial Diet's bill on the Codes. On 20 June, F. Tanaka resigned as Minister of Justice due to the ministry's gambling scandal (rōka jiken), which was publicly disclosed on 30 April by the newspaper *Tōkyō Nichinichi*.[122] His petition was accepted on 23 June, and on the same day, the Minister of Agriculture, Togama Kōno, temporarily replaced him.[123] Despite the extraordinary reshuffle, Prime Minister M. Matsukata struggled with personal problems in the cabinet in the following month, especially in the ministerial positions of the armed forces. This crisis finally made him resign on 30 July.[124]

On 8 August 1892, H. Itō formed his second cabinet. Former Prime Minister A. Yamagata was appointed Minister of Justice. Subsequently, the issue of securing the emperor's sanction for the bill on postponing the date of entry into force of the Civil Code and the Commercial Code led to the creation of two factions in H. Itō's cabinet, both of which had a different vision of legislative policy. To complete the further proceedings concerning T. Murata's bill, on 7 October 1892, the Prime Minister established the Research Committee for the Entry into Force of the Codes (Hōten Shikō Torishirabe I'inkai).[125] The role of chairman was given to Prince Kim'mochi Saionji, one of the leading political activists of Meiji-era Japan and a graduate

[121] Ōkubo, Takahashi, 1999, pp. 300–301.

[122] *Tōkyō Nichinichi Shimbun*, 30 April 1892.

[123] *Kanhō Shimbun*, 23 June 1892

[124] After only three weeks, T. Kōno also took over the Home Ministry, replacing M. Matsukata himself. *Kanhō Shimbun*, 14 July 1892.

[125] Ōkubo, Takahashi, 1999, p. 303; Shichinobe, 2009a, pp. 40–42.

of the Faculty of Law of the University of Paris. Apart from him, the Research Committee consisted of 12 members, six jurists each from the postponement and decisive faction. The first group was represented by Y. Hozumi, H. Kinoshita, T. Matsuno, T. Murata, U. Obata and M. Tomii, while the second by Takashi Hasegawa, T. Kishimoto, B. Kumano, K. Motō, K. Ume and K. Yokota.[126] Additionally, on 8 October, during a cabinet meeting, H. Itō announced the Research Committee tasks:

> [it should] not decide on the entry into force or postponement of the entry into force of the Civil Code and the Commercial Code, but to identify possible obstacles related to their partial entry into force, as well as to determine the resulting potential profits and losses.[127]

From 8 to 13 October, the Research Committee focused on analysing the existing proposals for the entry into force of the Civil Code and the Commercial Code, and from 21 October to 21 November, it discussed amendments to the Commercial Code that could lead to its partial entering into force in accordance with T. Murata's bill.

While the Research Committee was mainly consistent regarding the general changes to the Commercial Code and the possibility of its earlier entry into force, two divergent opinions were drawn up regarding the Civil Code. One of them, presented by six decisive faction representatives, suggested the entry into force of part of the Civil Code, excluding 13 Personal and Succession Law chapters. The second opinion, prepared by six postponement faction representatives, underlined the need to postpone the entry into force of the entire Civil Code to introduce comprehensive amendments. Despite a significant difference in views, the Research Committee members unanimously supported the opinion rejecting the entry into force of the entire Civil Code in its original shape.[128]

As noted by T. Arichi, the Research Committee deliberations were dominated by a discussion between M. Tomii and K. Ume. It was a natural continuation of the dispute between the postponement and decisive factions and testimony of distant views on drafting the Codes by two recognized French School jurists. Their arguments were, in fact, the same opinions that were presented during the Civil Code Controversy. Therefore, the discussion ended without binding resolutions.[129]

Since the Research Committee reached a balance of votes between the supporters of two opinions, K. Saionji could decide on the further fate of the Civil Code as the Chairman with the decisive voice. Although he openly supported the decisive faction during the Controversy and after the Imperial Diet's resolution, he took no

126 Hironaka, 2020, p. 11.

127 Ōkubo, Takahashi, 1999, pp. 303–305.

128 Ōkubo, Takahashi, 1999, p. 307.

129 Arichi, 1971, pp. 98–103.

unequivocal stand then. On 13 October, when both opinions on the Civil Code were drafted, he informed the cabinet informally of his intention to abstain from voting. On 22 November, just after completing the plan of amendments to the Commercial Code, K. Saionji submitted the Research Committee's final report to the cabinet, which confirmed no binding decisions regarding the Civil Code. Having additional time to solve the stalemate, the cabinet independently chose to uphold T. Murata's bill and postpone the date of entry into force of the Civil Code by 8 November.[130] On 23 November, H. Itō secured the emperor's sanction for the postponement bill, which was officially published the following day. The Civil Code Controversy was officially over.[131]

130 The cabinet decided to uphold T. Murata's bill despite some of its ministers advocating the partial entry into force of the Civil Code. Among the biggest supporters of this solution were Minister of Justice A. Yamagata and Minister of Communications and Transport K. Kuroda. A moderate stance in favour of the Civil Code was taken by Treasury Minister Kunitake Watanabe, Minister of Education T. Kōno and Minister of Foreign Affairs Mutsumune Mutsu. Prime Minister H. Itō was more inclined to the postponement faction postulates. Nobuoka, 1892.

131 Meiji 25-nen 11-gatsu 24-nichi Hōritsu Dai-8 Gō: Mimpō oyobi Shōhō Shikō Enchō Hōritsu.

CHAPTER SEVEN

SUMMARY OF THE CIVIL CODE CONTROVERSY

Abstract

The last chapter summarizes the Controversy by presenting the most important research conclusions. The attached table gathers all the arguments and responses used by both factions during the Controversy. The chapter explains the reasons for the failure of the Civil Code by presenting the most essentials factors with the commentary. The book ends with a conclusion based on analysed legal opinions and events in parliament.

Keywords: Civil Code Controversy, Meiji Civil Code, Meiji Japan

"The old Japanese family law system is [nothing more than] *a traditional misunderstanding."*

—Kenjirō Ume's opinion on the customary Japanese family law

7.1. Objections and responses of both factions during the Civil Code Controversy

The Civil Code Controversy concluded with the victory of the postponement faction, which secured its primary demand to delay the date of entry into force of the Old Civil Code to revise the criticized provisions thoroughly. During more than three years of dispute, which became one of the most appealing subjects of public debate in legal journals and the Imperial Diet, both sides presented numerous arguments related to the assessment of the Civil Code and the possible consequences of its entry into force in its original form on 1 January 1893. Based on the legal opinions cited in this book and discussions in the Imperial Diet's lower and upper houses in 1890–1892, the postponement faction's most critical objections can be grouped into a few categories and investigated. Those allegations were the main reason for the decisive faction choosing to oppose the criticism and defend the Civil Code by formulating diversified comments to the adversary. Published and publicly spoken opinions on the Civil Code were primarily factual and encouraged the exchange of opposing thoughts. Yet, some Japanese jurists were also inclined to present non-substantive methods of argumentation, including mutual accusations of hidden motives or lack of proper competence. Personal attacks were used by both sides in the Controversy, which at the turn of the year 1891/1892 went far beyond the legal debate, becoming one of the most crucial issues in the domestic politics of the Empire of Japan.

Table 3 presents the most critical objections and responses of the postponement and decisive factions in the Civil Code Controversy, shown as individual legal opinions in legal journals or statements in the Imperial Diet. Directional arrows indicate the original objection (O), followed by the answer (or several answers) of the other party (A).

Table 3: The Civil Code Controversy objections (O) and answers (A) presented by the postponement and decisive factions.

Postponement Faction		Decisive Faction
O: The Civil Code falsely declares that it refers to domestic customary law.	→	**A1:** The Civil Code refers to favourable domestic customs; in the remaining scope, the customs were rejected due to their complicated, ambiguous or inconsistent nature. **A2:** Following the Meiji Restoration, the Japanese elites decided to abolish the customary law system, one of the most significant factors of legal, political, economic and social backwardness of Japan during the shogunate period.
O: The Civil Code is mainly a copy of the French Civil Code.	→	**A1:** The drafting of the Civil Code was based on the proven and recognized French Civil Code; the project was supplemented with favourable amendments from other legal systems and Japanese customary law. **A2:** Contrary to the common law system, the Japanese legal system does not have sufficiently documented historical judicial decisions, so it must be based on uniform statutory law. **A3:** There are no codes in the common law system, so the French Civil Code was the only reasonable choice.
O: The Civil Code promotes individualism and egalitarianism, values contrary to the Japanese legal tradition. **A1:** There are no universally recognized values in law due to natural evolution of society, and the law development direction results from specific regional characteristics.	→ ←	**A/O:** The Civil Code promotes the values commonly recognized in the civilized world and aims to remove legal particularism and feudalism, elements that are characteristic of the old customary law system.

Postponement Faction		Decisive Faction
O: The Civil Code contains procedural and substantive law provisions, which is why it has a low practical value and little importance for the legal system.	→	**A:** The Civil Code should be examined in a broader context: within the legal act and the whole legal system.
O: The Civil Code has an archaic and illogical internal systematic.	→	**A:** The Civil Code is a universal masterpiece of global jurisprudence; its systematics is accepted and instinctively understood in many countries.
O: The Civil Code contains provisions incomprehensible to the average citizen.	→	**A1:** The Civil Code does not contain incomprehensible provisions and it must be examined as part of the entire legal act. **A2:** The postulate of legibility in law, particularly the comprehension of law by the average citizen, is impossible to implement in the legislation development era. **A3:** The interpretation of the law should be the duty of a group of professional lawyers.
A: The Constitution and the Criminal Code are public law acts addressed to state institutions.	←	**O:** The Constitution and the Criminal Code also contain complex legal terminology, yet no one questions their value.
O: There is a fundamental contradiction between the legal norms of the Civil Code and the Constitution.	→	**A1:** There is no contradiction between the Civil Code and the Constitution's legal norms. **A2:** Extensive guarantees of the private rights of every citizen should be a paramount consideration to the protection of the entire nation.
O: The Civil Code contains many editorial errors and mistakes.	→	**A:** The Civil Code may be amended by the Imperial Diet at any time.
O: The Civil Code was promulgated in a rush without its content being made available for public debate.	→	**A:** The Civil Code has been the subject of legislation for the last 20 years, and there is no need for further debate on its content.
O: The Civil Code has been largely drafted by a foreigner who does not understand the Japanese legal history and its unique character.	→	**A1:** The Civil Code is based on the universal principles of law that shape civilized nations. **A2:** Japanese jurists also participated in drafting the Civil Code and prepared a significant part on their own.

Postponement Faction		Decisive Faction
O: Only Japanese jurists from the French School participated in the drafting of the Civil Code.	→	**A1:** Selecting jurists from the French School was a natural consequence of entrusting the drafting of the Civil Code to G. Boissonade. **A2:** At the time of the decision to draft the Civil Code, the French law school jurists were the only group of Japanese jurisprudence with sufficient competence.
O: After the proclamation of the Constitution in 1889, it is the Imperial Diet that should decide about the adoption of the Civil Code.	→	**A:** The cabinet acted within the limits of its competencies; the Imperial Diet had not passed earlier codes.
O: In its initial shape, the Civil Code will have harmful social effects.	→	**A1:** The lack of Civil Code is the most harmful social effect. **A2:** It cannot be unequivocally assessed that the Civil Code will have adverse social effects.
O: The Civil Code will be an ineffective statutory law due to all the indicated defects.	→	**A:** Without the implementation of the Civil Code, one cannot speak of any effectiveness of law.
A: English School jurists thoroughly research judicial decisions and statutory law, deriving from the traditional English legal positivism.	→	**O:** English School jurists should not participate in the discussion about the Civil Code since they are lawyers who only have expert knowledge of common law.
A: The Civil Code should come into force in a form that will not expose Japan and its emperor to the risk of reputation and image loss.	←	**O:** The Civil Code should come into force in line with social expectations and for the sake of the emperor's prestige.
A: The English School is not opposed to the codification of the Japanese legal system but desires the best possible Civil Code to come into force.	←	**O:** The postponement faction, mainly comprising the English School jurists, opposes codification, and completely rejects the idea of the Civil Code.
O: The French School wants to deny the old private law system and totally ignores Japanese history.	→	**A/O:** The English School overestimates the traditional Japanese legal system and ignores current political events, accepting a partial loss of sovereignty and the threat of foreign powers' intervention.
A: Revision of the unequal treaties is not a sufficient reason for the coming into force of the imperfect Civil Code, which primarily should positively impact internal affairs.	←	**O:** The Civil Code must come into force to help the cabinet revise the unequal treaties.

Objections and answers from both factions expressed in the Controversy can be divided into three main categories of arguments:

1) ideological principles and the content of legal norms – substantive aspect,
2) legal act's language and systematics – formal aspect,
3) publication method and pressure for a rash entry into force – procedural/legislative policy aspect.

The most significant category of objections to the Civil Code concerned its substantive aspect. The postponement faction's criticism resulted from the fact that the authors of the Japanese Civil Code adopted the French Civil Code (and consequently the natural law doctrine) as a model for their project. This decision was derived from two main factors. Firstly, in the early years after the restoration of imperial rule, the Meiji government positively evaluated the French legal system, especially private law and the judiciary's effectiveness. Secondly, based on this assessment, the Ministry of Justice employed G. Boissonade to draft the Civil Code, cutting off the discussion on Japan's role model in private law. Even though the English School already existed in Japan at the end of the 1870s, the Ministry of Justice, dominated by the French School jurists, did not consider revising the plan for the reception of French private law. Besides personal and professional ties within the French School, the selection of G. Boissonade also had some profound practical rationale. Within a few years, he prepared a draft of the amended Criminal Code and an entirely new draft of the Code of Criminal Procedure. In both projects, he adopted the comparative law method, and the value of his work was soon favourably assessed by Japanese jurisprudence. Hence, the Ministry of Justice believed that G. Boissonade, having appropriate support from Japanese jurists, was sufficiently competent to prepare a complete draft of the Civil Code after a decade of fruitless efforts made by his predecessors.

The part of the Civil Code related to Personal Law, particularly criticized by the postponement faction, was independently prepared by Japanese jurists, the French School graduates. Family law's most critical principles were based on the natural law doctrine, considered by opponents of the Civil Code as highly progressive in Japanese social reality. The postponement faction stated that foreign legal doctrine went against the Japanese customary law. In contrast, the decisive faction argued that the Civil Code did not fully implement the natural law theory and preserved all favourable norms of customary law. Although they agreed with the statement that the Civil Code was mainly based on the French Civil Code, they did not perceive it as a negative occurrence. From their perspective, the postponement faction's ideas, which advocated retaining a significant part of domestic customary law, were too conservative and contradictory to the current Japanese social development policy.

While the postponement faction representatives made critical comments on the anachronistic nature of a few Property Law norms, the book related to Personal Law influenced the general negative assessment of the entire Civil Code. To meet the expectations of the postponement faction, the decisive faction had to carry out a comprehensive revision of the Civil Code. However, in the early 1890s, the supporters of the Civil Code rigidly rejected the prospect of any substantial changes, emphasizing numerous difficulties encountered and successfully solved in the past 20 years.

The second group of the postponement faction's objections against the Civil Code concerned its formal aspect. The systematics of the Civil Code resulted from early decisions made by G. Boissonade, who was the unquestionable leader of the drafting team. His idea to distinguish two additional books, thus modifying the old systematics of Gaius' *Institutiones*, did not protect him from repeating the imperfections of the French Civil Code. According to opponents of the Japanese Civil Code, it was tough to read and understand due to its impractical systematics. In response, the Code supporters argued that many legal systems successfully adopted the traditional systematics. They also claimed that understanding the Civil Code required the reader to carefully analyse the entire legal act and open the mind to complex theoretical concepts.

Subsequently, the postponement faction representatives indicated that the Civil Code contained many norms of procedural law. The decisive faction representatives initially denied this, yet they eventually admitted that their adversary was correct on some points. The criticism of the Civil Code's legal language was a vital element of the allegations concerning the formal sphere. The postponement faction representatives tried to prove it was too abstract and artificial, causing a high risk of "an average citizen" misinterpreting the content of the Code. The decisive faction representatives noticed the complicated nature of the code's provisions but did not consider it its major flaw. They were convinced that no state could implement the postulate of universal comprehensibility of law; law as a field of knowledge had evolved to such an extent that only professional jurists with appropriate higher education and legal training were qualified to interpret it. Considering R. Mitsukuri's initial difficulties translating the French Civil Code into Japanese, the decisive faction was proud to develop the Japanese private law terminology from scratch. By making a spiteful remark, they argued that if experienced jurists have spent over 20 years drafting one code in their native language, the idea of all citizens understanding the legal act was pure fiction.

The decisive faction representatives recognized certain formal inaccuracies in the Civil Code. Still, they did not consider them a reason for postponement. In their opinion, Japanese jurisprudence could jointly amend the Civil Code through the ordinary parliamentary procedure. By contrast, the postponement faction disagreed with an incomprehensible and erroneous legal act coming into force. They also rejected the vision of its subsequent revision, fearing it would diminish the importance of the Civil Code in the legal system. Regardless of the different views on the code's formal aspect, it should be noted that an ad hoc amendment before its entry into force was impossible and required applying a more complicated legal procedure.

The third category of objections against the Civil Code concerned the procedural sphere and the broadly understood legislative policy. The postponement faction alleged that A. Yamagata's cabinet had deliberately accelerated the publication of the Civil Code despite being aware that according to the Constitution, the decision on its adoption should be made by the Imperial Diet. Additionally, they highly criticized the excessive haste of the Ministry of Justice during the legislative procedure (including the Chamber of Elders and Privy Council analysis), which bypassed a public debate on the Civil Code with the other two schools of legal scholarship. They also raised the concern that entrusting the drafting of the Civil Code to a French lawyer and an elite group of Japanese jurists from the French School had a negative impact on its substantive and formal spheres. In response, the decisive faction argued that the codification process of private law had lasted over 20 years, too long compared to other legislative initiatives. They claimed that without the Civil Code, the effectiveness of the Constitution would be limited due to significant shortcomings in the Japanese system of statutory law. At the same time, they warned that without the Civil Code, the Japanese judiciary was based on an individual, often highly different, assessment of the equity principle by judges. According to them, the rush in the publication of the Civil Code resulted solely from the concern for the efficient functioning of state authorities and the introduction of the guarantees of private law rights for all citizens. They also proved that the cabinet did not ignore separate opinions and was open to discussion by setting the protracted interim period of the entry into force of the Civil Code.

A separate issue within the procedural sphere and legislative policy was the impact of the entry into force of the Civil Code on the revision of unequal treaties. The decisive faction argued that establishing a complete system of statutory law was crucial in abolishing the jurisdiction of consular courts, the unilateral most-favoured-nation clause, and special tariffs that undermined Japan's sovereignty. The postponement faction questioned the connection between the entry into force of the Civil Code and the revision of unequal treaties, arguing that there were several other factors behind the international order and that Japanese society should not be a victim of the cabinet's foreign policy. They negatively assessed the Civil Code through the prism of all its spheres, trying to prevent its entry into force in its original shape by all means. The decisive faction did not agree with the harsh criticism, failing to understand the flaws that could be the reason for postponing the entry into force of the Code. From the beginning until the end of the Controversy, both factions did not seek a compromise of partial revision of the Code during the long period between the publication and 1 January 1893.

7.2. Reasons for the postponement faction's victory

7.2.1. Impact of legal opinions

Having analysed the Civil Code Controversy, it is difficult to identify the unequivocal cause of the postponement faction's victory. The changing nature of the dispute, which escalated well beyond the exchange of views between the two groups of Japanese jurisprudence and was finally settled by the Imperial Diet, shows that it was a significant legal, political and social issue. Nevertheless, most of the time, the discussion on the Civil Code was held by Japanese jurists, who presented numerous opinions on its advantages and disadvantages. For this reason, the postponement faction's arguments should be mentioned first.

Japanese scholars do not identify a single legal opinion that influenced the rejection of the Civil Code. From the point of view of the entire Japanese society, Y. Hozumi's article, emphasizing the negative impact of the new law on exceptionally valued family relations, provoked a stir and was later cited in other publications. In addition, the arguments of the opponents of the Civil Code were presented to a broad audience in a synthetic form by *The Jurisprudence News* editorial team. Despite the cabinet censorship of *Hōri Seika* in July 1890, the publishing and academic activity of the postponement faction made it possible to break the monopoly of the French School on the interpretation and evaluation of the Code. Regular publication of legal articles by *Hōri Seika* in the first period of the dispute allowed the opponents to consolidate around a recognized group of jurists, graduates of the former University of Tokyo/Imperial University. By encouraging the adversaries to express their opinions, the postponement faction's journal did not let the topic be ignored by the decisive faction, which had strong connections with the Ministry of Justice and could shape independent legislative policy.

Among the legal opinions quoted in this work, attention should also be paid to C. Egi's article concerning errors and omissions in Property Law and criticizing the inclusion of procedural law in the Book on Evidence. While most of the postponement party's allegations focused on issues related to family law and derived from ideological disputes, C. Egi also presented practical flaws in the Civil Code that potentially could have a negative impact on its effectiveness in terms of economic relations and the application of the law by the judiciary.

The victory of the postponement faction during the Imperial Diet's first meeting regarding the postponement of the entry into force of the Commercial Code was undoubtedly secured by N. Hozumi and his oratorical skills and broad legal argumentation experience. According to T. Hoshino, the postponement faction won the critical vote at the House of Peers related to the postponement of the entry into force of the Civil Code and the Commercial Code in May 1892 thanks to M. Tomii, H. Katō and H. Kinoshita. For him, all three House of Peers members used only arguments based on rational premises and undeniable facts in their speeches, in contrast to the decisive faction representatives who presented a more emotional standpoint against the threat of rejection of both Codes.[132] Although the Japanese press highly criticized H. Katō for his nationalist statements in the debate with Minister of Education T. Ōki on natural human rights, M. Tomii's speech was of crucial importance, especially considering he was a famous French School jurist. He presented a specific plan for a comprehensive revision of the Civil Code within a limited time, avoiding the accusation that the postponement party had an implicit intention to keep Japanese private law in its uncodified form. M. Tomii not only convinced the House of Peers members who had not taken an unequivocal position so far but also made some supporters of the Codes change their minds and support the postponement plan. Y. Shigematsu also noted that the adoption of T. Murata's bill by the vast majority of the House of Peers had a decisive impact on the further course of events in the House of Representatives, ensuring the final victory of the postponement faction.[133]

Both factions focused on the key issue related to the influence of legal opinions on resolving the Civil Code Controversy. According to T. Nakagawa, the postponement faction focused on proving that the Civil Code Controversy was an important national issue (*kokka no daiji*) and also tried to reach the broadest possible group of influential personalities (*asano no meishi*).[134]

Based on the analysis of both parties' activities, it can be concluded that the decisive faction representatives considered the issue of the entry into force of the Civil Code a crucial matter for all citizens. Still, they failed to influence the public and neutral members of the Japanese elites. The actions of the supporters of the Codes resulted, to a large extent, from the conviction of the rightness to promote legal egalitarianism and the introduction of extensive guarantees of private law rights, which should automatically have overwhelming support in society. Contrary to the decisive faction's legal opinions, which were addressed to

[132] Hoshino, 1943, p. 136.

[133] Shigematsu, 2007, p. 126. Shigematsu noted that before the vote, the postponement faction had managed to gather 114 supporters of T. Murata's project in the House of Peers, even though prior to this, his supporters usually did not exceed 70 out of all 160 present house members. Eventually, 123 of the House of Peers members supported the postponement of the entry into force of the Civil Code and Commercial Code, which proves the importance of the critical debate in the upper house.

[134] Nakagawa, 2015, p. 374.

an unspecified recipient, the postponement party adjusted its message to a more specific audience. By presenting possible losses related to the entry into force of the Codes, they gained the support of a group of wealthy entrepreneurs in the House of Representatives.[135] This kind of activity could be perceived as an element of a larger and long-term strategy to create a postponement faction-oriented electorate among future members of the Imperial Diet.

7.2.2. Influence of the Civil Code's guiding principles

Undoubtedly, the lack of support for the guiding principles of the Civil Code was one of the most important reasons for the victory of the postponement faction. However, looking through the prism of the social reforms promoted by the Meiji government, it should be noted that the delay in the coming into force of the Codes was an appalling defeat for the decisive faction. Its representatives should have taken the opportunity to demonstrate the advantages of the Civil Code and Commercial Code for Japanese society and entrepreneurs. Their arguments mainly referred to complicated issues related to the theory and philosophy of law. Ironically, the positive practical aspects, which included the introduction of broad guarantees of individual private law rights and the liberalization of private law relations, were insufficiently presented and largely overlooked. The decisive faction tried to demonstrate the necessity to implement the Codes by stressing the benefits for the judiciary and the prestige in the international arena. Indeed, a fair and uniform judiciary and the revision of unequal treaties were significant political problems for the Empire of Japan in the early 1890s but did not reflect the real concerns of Japanese society and its influential group of entrepreneurs.

Based on the natural law doctrine, the Civil Code met significant opposition from the postponement faction since it promoted individualism, legal egalitarianism and social reformism. Although the Civil Code drafted by G. Boissonade and a team of Japanese jurists did not fully implement postulates of natural law doctrine, it was still too progressive for the Japanese political and social conditions at the end of the 19th century. Regardless of the reforms initiated in 1868, aimed at abolishing feudalism and introducing the rule of law, it must be admitted that most Japanese citizens, including the Meiji elites, still remembered the Edo era's feudalism. Individualism and legal egalitarianism apparently contradicted the traditional social order.[136] Any attempt to reform Japanese society required the authors of the Civil Code to replace at least part of the customary law with the

[135] Due to the property qualification, only the wealthiest citizens of Japan, including a group of influential entrepreneurs, could run in the elections to the House of Representatives.

[136] Ōkubo, 1977, pp. 185–186.

statutory law system. The decisive faction was aware that reshaping the Japanese private law system could not entail revolutionary changes and expressed concern about maintaining "favourable customs" during the Controversy. This statement was crucial for understanding the decisive faction's notion: to reform the Japanese private law system yet reach a social compromise. Despite the clearly outlined policy, the French School jurists shared negative views of Japanese customary law, often described as "disdain for lawlessness". They considered old provisions as feudal-era relics, a source of social injustice, and the main reason for Japan's backwardness and lagging behind colonial superpowers. Comparing the analogous solutions adopted in Europe during the 19th century to the Japanese customary family law system, K. Ume sadly depicted the latter as *zokusetsu gokai* – a traditional misunderstanding.[137] Nevertheless, the Civil Code drafters kept some customary law norms contrary to a negative assessment of their principles. This ploy, however, did not meet with a positive reaction from the postponement faction, which saw the desire to change domestic customary law, especially concerning family relations, as an attempt to Westernize, or even Christianize, Japan in areas where it should retain its original legal culture.

Since both parties of the dispute supported contradictory ideas, it was impossible to compromise on the Civil Code.[138] Having used the conservative views of most of Japanese society and the elites, the postponement faction skilfully defended customary law against significant modification and also successfully raised arguments of nationalist and chauvinist nature. The radical views were reflected in claims that Japanese culture was superior to Western culture. G. Boissonade's legal competencies were even denied at some point because of his non-Japanese nationality. This argument could also be assessed as deliberate manipulation since the Japanese jurists independently drafted the most controversial part of the Civil Code.

One should agree with W.N. Yeremin that the history of Japan, including the codification of the private law system, did not include revolutionary leaps in social development. Even the Meiji-era reforms, which introduced the "compressed revolution" in Japan, did not radically change the existing social order. Looking at the same aspect from the perspective of legal reforms, the new system was based on the foundations of the previous one, which strengthened the old traditions during the process.[139]

137 K. Ume, 1910, pp. 742–764.

138 The decisive faction eventually admitted that the Civil Code was mostly based on the French Civil Code but saw no negative impact of this fact on the Japanese private law system. Hoshino, 1943, p. 142.

139 Yeremin, 2010, pp. 22–24.

7.2.3. Contradiction between Civil Code and Meiji Constitution principles

Another reason for the victory of the postponement faction was the contradiction of the Civil Code's guiding principles with the general provisions of the Meiji Constitution. The Meiji government, aspiring to reform Japan in the spirit of a modern state with a codified legal system, finally adopted a mixed Prussian-British constitutional monarchy model at the end of the 1880s. Although the Meiji Constitution, promulgated in 1889, formally introduced a system of representative democracy and a guarantee of civil rights, these were façade provisions overshadowed by the dominant role of the emperor. Pursuant to Article 4 of the Meiji Constitution, the emperor was not only the head of state but also the embodiment of national sovereignty with the right to exercise it within limits specified by law. The rejection of the concept of sovereignty related to the nation had far-reaching consequences for the Constitution, which introduced the duty to subordinate citizens to the emperor's dominant position. Consequently, Japanese public law granted administrative authorities more competencies to exercise executive power on behalf of the emperor.

Drafted by G. Boissonade and a group of Japanese jurists, the Civil Code adopted ideas of a democratic state of law, also predominantly republican, with the dominant role of the nation (understood as all citizens). Since the Civil Code was primarily based on the French Civil Code, it also implemented the fundamental postulates of the bourgeoisie during the French Revolution: abolition of feudalism and the guarantee by the state of personal freedom, inviolability of private property, and freedom of contract. Although the Civil Code did not fully adopt the natural law principles, the limited individualism and progressivism contradicted collectivism and the traditional concept of national sovereignty established by the Meiji Constitution. This inconsistency drew the attention of the postponement faction representatives, who expressed the anxiety that the Civil Code, in particular private law rights, would undermine the authority of public administration and, thus, the emperor's authority. Due to the hierarchy of the Constitution in the legal system, the Civil Code was perceived as an essential but supplementary legal act that must not collide with the basic law norms. Even though the English School jurists also saw the need to codify the system of Japanese private law, they believed that the judiciary based on provisional law and judicial decisions was a better solution than the entry into force of the defective Civil Code, which would call into question the vital points of the imperial system established by the Meiji Constitution.

Moreover, it is worth mentioning that the Meiji Constitution remained a significant obstacle to the liberalization and modernization of the Japanese legal system for the next few decades. It was not until the defeat of the Empire of Japan in the Pacific War that an entirely new Constitution was adopted in 1946, establishing a democratic rule of law and extensive guarantees of civil rights. In December 1947, the Meiji Civil Code was thoroughly amended by introducing fundamental changes to family law and succession law to harmonize their principles with a democratic society.[140]

7.2.4. Practical flaws of the Civil Code

Although the decisive faction claimed that thorough knowledge of the Civil Code could help understand its principles, the overall Code contained articles replicating the same regulations. Additionally, some norms were inconsistent within the Code and the legal system (Meiji Constitution, Penal Code, Commercial Code and Code of Civil Procedure). The Code also included anachronistic legal definitions (including the right to property, division of real rights, etc.) and numerous procedural law provisions that should be part of the Code of Civil Procedure.

Unfortunately for the decisive faction, the Civil Code Controversy coincided with the drafting of an analogous Civil Code in Germany and a heated discussion on its provisions. Japanese jurists were active observers of German legislative actions. While in the 1870s and 1880s, they mostly agreed with adopting the systematics of Gaius' *Institutiones*,[141] the tangible advantages of the pandectic systematics suddenly came to light in 1892. At first sight, it differed from the French School's ideas based on logical division into classic *personae-res-actiones* scheme, yet it was also partly based on old Roman law (Justinian's *Institutiones*) and had numerous practical advantages. Looking from the perspective of Japanese legislative issues, new systematics provided a clear separation of family law from the Book on Personal Law, and Succession Law from the Book on Property Law.

Although the decisive faction firmly supported the entry into force of the Civil Code in its original shape, it eventually also noticed its apparent flaws. Even G. Boissonade expressed dissatisfaction with the result of the drafting process, especially preserving the eldest son's exclusive succession.[142] The decisive faction, trying to avert the threat of a complete amendment of the Civil Code, advocated the initial date of coming into force and insisted on continuing the discussion on amendments in the Imperial Diet through the ordinary legislative procedure.[143]

[140] Kokuritsu Kōbunshokan: Ref. 御 30627100: Mimpō no Ichibu o Kaitei Suru Hōritsu, Goshomei Gempa, Shōwa 22-nen, Hōritsu Dai 222-Gō.

[141] The shortcomings of the system based on Gaius' *Institutiones* were noticeable in Europe already at the beginning of the 19th century. Górnicki, 2012, p. 128.

[142] G. Boissonade felt that the eldest son's exclusive succession was a typical institution of feudalism permanently embedded in Japanese customary law. Toshitaka, Toshitani, 1975, p. 50.

[143] K. Ume recognized many of the flaws of the Civil Code and supported the general idea to amend them after the Civil Code would come into force. Hoshino, 1943, pp. 537–545.

Once they publicly admitted that the Civil Code was far from perfection, they lost many supporters who recognized the urgent need to improve it.

7.2.5. Weakened political position of the cabinet and the Ministry of Justice

The codification of Japanese private law in 1879–1892 was part of the broader legislative policy of the cabinet, supervised directly by the Ministry of Justice. Described as the decisive faction "nest", the Ministry of Justice coordinated the drafting of the Civil Code and advised on complex legal matters most of the time. In the initial period of the dispute, however, it did not foresee a significant threat from the postponement faction. This mistake resulted in the astonishing postponement of the Commercial Code during the Imperial Diet's first meeting in 1890. Minister of Justice A. Yamada – whom K. Ume called *hōten haku*, the Count of the Codes,[144] who zealously fought for their entry into force[145] – was then unable to take advantage of the superior position in the executive to rebut the bill passed by parliament. The seemingly harmless postponement of the entry into force of the Commercial Code positively influenced the postponement faction morale and led to its further consolidation in the fight to challenge the Codes.

Although the Civil Code was not discussed during the Imperial Diet's second meeting due to the political crisis and the dissolution of the House of Representatives, the events at the end of 1891 showed that the relations between M. Matsukata's cabinet and the lower house were nothing more than mutual distrust. The struggle for the political position was exacerbated by the unsuccessful attempt to intervene in the second general elections to the House of Representatives, which weakened the cabinet's prestige in the eyes of the Imperial Diet's new members. Despite the increased activity of the decisive faction in early 1892, following A. Yamada's resignation as Minister of Justice, the cabinet lost the will to fight for the Codes. At the beginning of the Imperial Diet's third meeting, only three ministers were dedicated and active advocates of the entry into force of the Codes in their original shape and date. In contrast, the rest of the ministers, led by Prime Minister M. Matsukata, passively observed the developments, and did not take the initiative to defend the Codes. The weakness of the Ministry of Justice was reflected in T. Ōki's speeches, who as the Minister of Education was the main and the only dangerous opponent for the postponement faction during the discussion in the House of Peers.

It cannot be unequivocally stated whether a more active attitude of the cabinet would have led to the rejection of T. Murata's bill. Still, the lack of support from

[144] Ume, 1894, pp. 77–86.

[145] Nihon Daigaku (ed.), 1963, pp. 922–923. The authors claimed that A. Yamada fought for the rapid entry into force of the Codes because he believed they could help to revise unequal treaties.

Prime Minister M. Matsukata and Minister of Justice F. Tanaka resulted in the loss of some decisive faction supporters in the longer term. A. Yamada could not influence the outcome of the vote on delaying the entry into force of the Commercial Code during the Imperial Diet's first meeting. This defeat, however, essentially resulted from the decisive faction's inaction in the first stage of the dispute. The Ministry of Justice led by F. Tanaka was undoubtedly more aware of the potential threats during the Imperial Diet's third meeting. Yet, the political events in early 1892 strongly influenced the cabinet's approach towards domestic affairs, with the cabinet ultimately losing the determination to fight for the Codes.[146]

The victory of the postponement faction during the Imperial Diet's third meeting raised the issue of challenging T. Murata's bill on delaying the date of entry into force of the Civil Code and Commercial Code. However, the plan developed by F. Tanaka was abandoned due to the collapse of M. Matsukata's cabinet and the establishment of H. Itō's second cabinet. Further proceedings with T. Murata's bill, still awaiting the emperor's sanction needed for publication and entry into force, were among the most critical matters to decide on. It was a difficult task, as the new cabinet ministers shared different opinions on the Civil Code Controversy. After all, Prime Minister H. Itō – described by some Japanese newspapers as *kuromaku*: "grey eminence" of the postponement faction[147] – decided to delay the entry into force of the Civil Code and the Commercial Code. Indeed, he was more inclined to the postulates of the opponents of the Codes, yet he also respected the Imperial Diet's and the Research Committee's decisions. Following K. Saionji's reluctance to resolve the balance of votes in the Research Committee and thus the future of the Code, H. Itō acceded to the option that respected the initial Imperial Diet decision.

The events leading to the postponement of the entry into force of the Civil Code and the Commercial Code proved that the cabinet lost its undisputed supreme position in Japanese political life and had to consider opposition in the Imperial Diet. The postponement party skilfully used the Meiji Constitution to win the Controversy and protect the rule of law in Japan. However, it should be noted that the decisive faction's idea to use the cabinet to rebut the Imperial Diet's decision was treated as a necessary evil to push through a more critical objective: completion of the codification process.

[146] Hironaka, 2020, p. 10. The author claims that Minister of Justice F. Tanaka also tried to fight for the Codes by developing a plan to jeopardize the procedure of obtaining the emperor's sanction for the postponement bill. Given the cabinet's past problems in February 1892 (intervention in the House of Representatives elections), his proposal did not receive sufficient support.

[147] Arichi, 1971, p. 120.

7.3. Drafting of the revised Civil Code and completion of the codification

The publication of T. Murata's bill on postponing the entry into force of the Civil Code and the Commercial Code in November 1892 marked a formal end to the Civil Code Controversy. According to the Imperial Diet's decision, both Codes were to be comprehensively revised by 31 December 1896. Considerations regarding the plan for drafting the revised Civil Code began after the end of the Imperial Diet's fourth meeting, which lasted from 29 November 1892 to 28 February 1893. On 21 March 1893, Prime Minister H. Itō, backed by Prince K. Saionji, organized a meeting with jurists at the cabinet's official residence. They selected the new Civil Code drafting team members and discussed the most critical issues regarding revising the Codes.[148] On 25 March, Imperial Edict No. 11 established the Codes Investigation Committee (Hōten Chōsa Kai) with Prime Minister H. Itō as the Chairman and Prince K. Saionji as the Deputy.[149]

On 27 April 1893, the cabinet issued Ordinance No. 3 on the detailed internal regulations of the Codes Investigation Committee, confirming the status of the Chairman and Deputy and electing 20 research members (Shusa I'in) and 30 revision members (Satei I'in).[150] Additionally, among the research members, the cabinet selected the Drafting Committee (Kisō I'in) comprising K. Ume, M. Tomii and N. Hozumi, who were to draft the revised Civil Code. The composition of the Drafting Committee was not a pure coincidence. Besides the fact that K. Ume, M. Tomii and N. Hozumi were all recognized jurists who greatly influenced the Civil Code Controversy, their affiliation with schools of legal jurisprudence and both factions guaranteed a balance in future proceedings.[151] Even though N. Hozumi and M. Tomii were postponement faction representatives, M. Tomii, as a French School graduate, tried to secure a thread of understanding between the natural law and the historical law doctrines. It should also be mentioned that N. Hozumi, who soon became the leader of the Drafting Committee, was an English and German School graduate. Therefore, all three schools of legal scholarship in Japan were represented in the most prominent part of the Codes Investigation Committee.

The victory of the postponement faction in the Civil Code Controversy was a symbolic end of the French School's domination in Japanese jurisprudence. For over 25 years, the French School had educated two generations of Japanese jurists who

[148] Ōkubo, 1977, p. 194. The author wrote that the two basic conclusions were related to the necessity to carry out a thorough revision of the Civil Code and the adoption of pandectic systematics.

[149] Kokuritsu Kōbunshokan: Ref. 御01349100, Hōten Chōsa Kai Kisoku, Go Shomei Gembon, Meiji 23-nen, Chokurei Dai 11-Gō.

[150] The emperor approved the establishment of the Codes Investigation Committee much earlier, on 22 February. Kokuritsu Kōbunshokan: Ref. 類 00637100, Hōten Chōsa Kai Kisoku o Sadamu.

[151] Shichinobe, 2009a, pp. 40–41.

failed to introduce all the most important natural law principles into the Japanese legal system. Paradoxically, the postponement of the entry into force of the Civil Code and the Commercial Code did not result in the English School's domination. Despite preserving the domestic customary law system, the English School's legal thought and professional skills, mainly based on the Anglo-American common law system, played a secondary role in revising the Civil Code. The unexpected beneficiary of the Civil Code Controversy turned out to be the German School, which promoted conservative views on family relations and the collective vision of a society based on the nation's leading role. However, the German School did not replace the French School as a dominant force since Japanese jurisprudence shifted towards researching domestic statutory law rather than German codes. Nevertheless, the German School's influence on the revised Civil Code remains visible today.[152]

The first Codes Investigation Committee plenary meeting occurred on 28 April 1893, followed by the first meeting of the research members five days later. The Japanese jurists prepared a preliminary opinion, confirming the previous findings on revising the Civil Code. The most critical decision was related to adopting pandectic systematics. Its implementation soon became one of the main Drafting Committee tasks. While drafting the new Civil Code, the Codes Investigation Committee was reorganized under Imperial Edict No. 30 of 27 March 1894.[153] The status of the research member and the revision member was unified and replaced with the regular member (I'in). The number of committee members was reduced from 50 to 35, excluding those with the lowest meeting attendance. Due to the status unification, the separate plenary sessions for the research and revision members were combined into one general committee session.[154]

Despite great effort to prepare the comprehensive draft of the Code, the Codes Investigation Committee faced many legal issues in the following years. It was not until 30 December 1895 that the drafts of the first three Books – *General Principles (Sōsoku), Real Rights (Bukken)* and *Obligations (Saiken)* – were approved by the Imperial Diet and then promulgated by the emperor on 27 April 1896.[155] However, difficulties related to the drafting of Books on *Relatives* (*Shinzoku*) and *Succession (Sōzoku)* forced parliament to pass on 29 December 1896 an act on extending the deadline for the revised Civil Code by another two years.[156] Eventually, Books Four

152 Ikeda, 2011, p. 66.

153 T. Hironaka, *Mimpōten hensanshi*..., p. 32.

154 K. Shichinobe, *Genkō Mimpōten... Jōron*, p. 41.

155 Meiji 29-nen 4-gatsu 27-nichi, Hōritsu Dai 89-Gō.

156 Meiji 29-nen 12-gatsu 29-nichi, Hōritsu Dai 94-Gō.

and Five were promulgated on 21 June 1898, and the revised Civil Code, better known as the Meiji Civil Code, entered into force on 16 July 1898.[157]

What may seem peculiar is that the entry into force of the Meiji Civil Code did not mark the end of the codification process in Japan. In fact, the end did not come until the end of February 1899, when the Imperial Diet's thirteenth meeting approved the revised Commercial Code, before it was then officially promulgated on 9 March 1899 and entered into force on the same day.[158] The Codes Investigation Committee's crucial contribution to delivering two missing Codes took six years, two years longer than M. Tomii initially declared during his landmark speech at the House of Peers on 27 May 1892.

The postponement of the entry into force of the Civil Code and the Commercial Code had no impact on Japanese foreign policy, which refrained from strictly following the "Western doctrine" principle. In 1894, H. Itō's second cabinet made a breakthrough in revising unequal treaties. On 16 July, the Empire of Japan and the United Kingdom signed the Treaty of Trade and Navigation (Nichiei Tsūshō Kōkai Jōyaku). The British renounced the unilateral most-favoured-nation clause, the right to the jurisdiction of consular courts and partially withdrew from lowered customs tariffs.[159] Even though the treaty was to enter into force in the next five years, it proved that after four decades of struggle to preserve sovereignty, Japan had become an equal partner with the Western powers.[160] Notably, during the negotiations with the British, the Japanese legal system was still not fully codified. Some Meiji politicians expressed concern that foreign diplomats would exploit this argument to advocate colonial policy towards Japan. However, the British did not question the effectiveness of the Japanese legal system and recognized the revised Civil Code and Commercial Code even during their drafting process. After all, before the Anglo-Japanese Treaty of Trade and Navigation entered into force, the Japanese jurists established a complete system of statutory law, which soon became a role model not only for Asian but also for some European nations.

[157] Meiji 31-nen 6-gatsu 21-nichi, Hōritsu Dai 11-Gō.

[158] Meiji 32-nen 3-gatsu Kokonoka, Hōritsu Dai 48-Gō

[159] Teikoku to Dai Buriten Koku to no Tsūshō Kōkai Jōyaku; Takayanagi, 1931, p. 11.

[160] In the following months, the Japanese cabinet also revised other unequal treaties with other Western powers. Japanese historians claim that the end of the period of revision of unequal treaties was marked by the signing of the US–Japan Treaty of Commerce and Navigation (Nichibei Tsūshō Kōkai Jōyaku) on 21 February 1911, which replaced the treaty of 22 November 1894.

CHAPTER EIGHT

CONCLUSIONS

The Civil Code Controversy had a decisive influence on the codification of Japanese private law. The discussion on the draft of the Civil Code, begun by the Association of Jurists in April 1889, initially did not get a response from the cabinet. The Japanese executive pursued the "Western doctrine" principle and published the Civil Code in two parts in 1890. However, the postponement party's criticism became the subject of a heated debate in a short time. Japanese jurisprudence was divided into supporters and opponents of the entry into force of the Civil Code in its original form on 1 January 1893. In less than two years, the Civil Code Controversy went beyond academic discussion in legal journals. It escalated into one of the most important political and legal issues, which had to be solved by the Imperial Diet. During the House of Representatives and the House of Peers sessions, the speakers directly engaged in the dispute and cited the arguments of supporters and opponents of the Civil Code. Based on analysis of the events in 1889–1892, it should be stated that the legal controversy became the rationale for parliament to postpone entry into force of the Civil Code (and Commercial Code) to provide their thorough revision. Ironically, if A. Yamagata's cabinet had decided to establish a shorter interregnum, the postponement party's arguments would probably not have reached such a broad audience. Therefore, the Civil Code would have entered into force in its original shape. A hypothetical dispute in this alternate scenario would be entirely different, focusing on issues related to a potential revision of the legal act in force.

The reception of the French Civil Code, regardless of the scope of the changes introduced in family and succession law, proved impossible in Japan's legal, political and social conditions at the end of the 19th century. Thorough reform of the private law system by promoting individualism and egalitarianism, advocated by the decisive faction, especially the French School, was unacceptable to Japanese society and a significant part of the elites, which saw the Civil Code as a potential threat to the state. Opponents of the Civil Code were aware of their legal tradition and culture, believing it was one of the essential sources of Japanese national identity. Despite supporting the abolition of feudalism, they did not agree that Japan's underdevelopment compared to Western countries derived from the anachronistic private law system. The plan to introduce the Civil Code based on the French legal model was established by a small group of Japanese jurists in the early stages of codification. Two decades later, it met unexpected opposition as an initiative threatening the state and society, promoting foreign legal and cultural patterns. Speaking of foreign legal influences, even old Chinese administrative and penal codes, initially unknown and incomprehensible, were successfully adopted into the Japanese legal system throughout the ages and constituted its natural part in the 19th century. However, according to the postponement faction, there was no way the Civil Code could overcome regional differences. As they emphasized, there was also no time to learn its interpretation from scratch. Undoubtedly, the Civil Code Controversy rejected the reception of the French civil law model, which promoted progressive social values from the Japanese point of view. The code drafted by G. Boissonade and a team of Japanese jurists was replaced by a code based on comparative law methodology, formally flawless but far more conservative.

Furthermore, the Civil Code Controversy led to the consolidation of all schools of legal scholarship in Japan. Apart from a few exceptions, the French School graduates supported the decisive faction, while the English School graduates joined the postponement faction. Significant differences between the two factions of Japanese jurisprudence, visible even before the Civil Code Controversy, became even more apparent during the fight over two entirely contradictory visions of the Japanese private law system. In addition to the ideological aspects, the consolidation of the schools of legal scholarship was also significantly influenced by personal factors, such as the superiority complex and the sense of unity, repeatedly mentioned in legal opinions and speeches in parliament. The German School did not form a separate faction, but its existence and influence on Japanese jurisprudence were noticed during the dispute. The English School contributed to the promotion of the German School to the role of the third research centre, a natural counterbalance to French School domination in statutory law. Looking at the German struggles with drafting the civil code for a unified country, the postponement party wanted to prove that Japan should not speed up the process of passing the controversial Civil Code unless all schools of legal scholarship agreed on its content.

Looking from a broader perspective, the Civil Code Controversy considerably impacted the development of Japanese legal scholarship, especially the research on private law, theory and philosophy of law, and the legal history of domestic common law and foreign systems. The participants of fierce discussions on the Civil Code needed to meticulously study the other party's position and prepare legal arguments. Therefore, the French School representatives became more familiar with the Anglo-American common law system and German statutory law, broadening their horizons with new, previously unknown legal systems. At the same time, the English School and the German School representatives studied French civil law to prove the shortcomings of the Civil Code. The exchange of views and experiences between jurists lasted for over three years. It resulted in the publication of many legal texts that significantly bolstered the Japanese jurisprudence of the Meiji era.

This book is the first attempt in Western legal scholarship to present the codification of Japanese private law in 1869–1892. The Civil Code Controversy was the most crucial part of this process, yet it should not be separated from the Ministry of Justice projects from the 1870s, which failed due to legal and linguistic reasons. Western scholars have failed to present the real role of G. Boissonade and the team of Japanese jurists in drafting two separate parts of the Civil Code. This fact is sometimes also not well underlined in Japan, as a few legal historians omitted the circumstances of drafting the family and succession law, often exaggerating G. Boissonade's role.

The Controversy invaluably influenced the shape and the nature of Japanese private law. The dispute between the two factions of Japanese jurists resulted in the establishment of the Codes Research Committee, which drafted the revised Civil Code in 1893–1898. It was no longer a modified copy of French law but a product of comparative jurisprudence based on German private law principles. Despite the significant delay in the legislative plans of the cabinet, the Meiji Civil Code entered into force on 16 July 1898, two years before the renowned German *Bürgerliches Gesetzbuch*.

The Civil Code Controversy in Japan should be compared to the famous dispute between A. Thibaud and C. von Savigny concerning similar issues related to the codification of law in Germany in the first half of the 19th century. Unfortunately, contrary to the heated discussion of the historical school of law and the positivist school in Germany, landmark events in the Far East in 1889–1892 were not profoundly researched in Europe throughout the 20th century.

The analysis should be supplemented with the conclusion related to significant differences in the codification process of private law between the Japanese model (presented in this book) and the French-Germanic model, which dominated European legal scholarship in the 19th century. By employing a foreigner as a project team leader, the Japanese model initially resembled the Romano-Germanic model since drafting the Civil Code was entrusted to a small group of jurists. However, public discussion on the project and the bill promulgated by A. Yamagata's cabinet allowed Japanese jurisprudence to express their views. In 1889–1892, deliberations on the Civil Code were not held between selected jurists during official meetings but among three distinctive schools of legal scholarship, which formed two competing factions. At the turning point of the dispute (1891–1892), politicians, educational activists, entrepreneurs and journalists actively joined the debate, remarkably influencing the final political decision. When the Imperial Diet voted to postpone the date of entry into force of the Civil Code to carry out its thorough revision, it was apparent that drafting of the new code could not remain a public matter. To draft the Civil Code reconciling the expectations of all three schools of legal jurisprudence, H. Itō's cabinet reverted to the French-Germanic model. In 1893–1898,

K. Ume, N. Hozumi and M. Tomii, members of the Drafting Committee, played a crucial role in preparing the new Civil Code. All three jurists actively participated in the Civil Code Controversy and represented the three most prominent schools of legal scholarship. Japanese jurisprudence unanimously recognized them as highly competent lawyers with outstanding intellectual abilities. In contrast to Japan, 19th-century European jurisprudence did not experience such large-scale public discussion on law codification. Despite consulting lawyers from various academic centres during the drafting process, schools of legal scholarship never gained such a unique position in the French-Germanic model that forced the European legislators to find a middle ground to reconcile their postulates.

Besides studying jurists' legacy and past views, researching Japanese legal history would not be possible without understanding the social attitudes of both Meiji elites and ordinary people whose lives served as a bridge between the feudal and modern state. As shown in this book, the desire to introduce epoch-making reforms and elevate the country to a superpower could just as well be considered a deadly threat to the nation as a transition into foreign culture patterns. Even though the Old Civil Code and Meiji Civil Code were passed more than 100 years ago, and the reformed Civil Code of 1946 partially refers to decisive faction principles, the Controversy remains the subject of lively discussion among Japanese researchers. The Japanese experience can teach us in the 21st century that fierce ideological deliberations were and will be integral to the legislative process. Yet, the free exchange of thoughts under the protective umbrella of the rule of law can save entire nations from enforced radical changes that could have been catastrophic, despite their promulgators' best intentions. For my own part, as an author and a jurist, I regard the rule of law as a fundamental safeguard for liberal democracy that sometimes, as seen in the example of Japan, could also become a negative factor, slowing down the introduction of progressive social values. This final observation is still valid in the case of many countries using democracy as a convenient tool to oppress minorities with the majority's views.

ILLUSTRATIONS

Tokugawa Ieyasu (徳川家康) – (1543–1616), one of the three great "fathers of unified Japan", the first shogun from the Tokugawa family, who marked the beginning of the Edo era, lasting over 200 years. A painting by Tan'yū Kanō, one of the most recognized Japanese painters of the Edo era, court artist of the Tokugawa family. The painting is currently in the collection of the Osaka Castle Museum.

A Japanese drawing showing the arrival of the "black ships" – the US Navy fleet under the command of Commodore M. Perry, which forced Japan to open its borders.

A poster from Yokohama promoting the slogan "revere the Emperor, expel the barbarians" (尊王攘夷, sonnō jōi). It shows a sumo wrestler who defeats a foreign newcomer in front of other Western observers. The political activity of Emperor Kōmei and the presence of foreign residents in Japanese cities led to societal incidents against foreigners, who were blamed for economic crises and natural disasters. Ultimately, this movement was suppressed by Emperor Meiji, who promoted opening to contact with the West.

Tokugawa Yoshinobu (徳川慶喜) – (1837–1913), the last shogun from the Tokugawa family, who took power in 1866. His goal was to maintain the central position in the state by reaching a compromise with the imperial party and carrying out thorough reforms. However, his double game led to a civil war (Boshin War), which ended with the victory of Emperor Meiji's faction. After Yoshinobu's resignation, the Edo era ended. Despite the complete defeat, he avoided punishment for disobedience. He grew old age as one of the former daimyōs, yet without any real influence on internal politics.

Mutsuhito, known as Emperor Meiji (明治天皇, Meiji Ten'nō) – (1852–1912), the 122nd emperor of Japan since 1867, who initiated the reform of the country and its opening to the world. At the beginning of the 20th century, Japan became one of the world's superpowers in the final years of his rule.

Photo of the members of the so-called Iwakura Mission (岩倉使節団, Iwakura Shisetsudan), which visited the United States and Europe in 1871–1873 to establish cordial diplomatic contacts between Japan and the leading superpowers and find patterns to modernize the country based on about Western models. The photo was taken in 1872 in London. Iwakura Tomomi sits in the middle, the only one wearing a traditional Japanese kimono and with his hair tied in a bun.

Etō Shimpei (江藤新平) – (1834–1874) a Japanese politician, the first Minister of Justice, a supporter of the modernization of Japan by codifying law based on a European model while maintaining Japanese customary law norms. Disagreement with the Meiji government led to his resignation from the Ministry of Justice and subsequent support for a rebellion in the former Hizen Domain (now Saga Prefecture in Kyushu) against the emperor and his advisors. After crushing the uprising and being captured, he was sentenced to death for treason and then executed.

Mitsukuri Rinshō (箕作麟祥) – (1846–1897) – a Japanese jurist, politician and academic who was the first to translate French codes into Japanese in 1869–1871 independently. His fluent knowledge of the so-called Western sciences (蘭学, rangaku) and foreign languages made him one of the undisputed legal authorities. During his public activity, he held, among others, the function of Deputy Minister of Justice and member of the Council of Elders and the House of Peers. He was a famous French School of legal scholarship graduate and the decisive faction representative. As one of the few Japanese jurists, he participated in the codification process from the beginning until its end (over 30 years).

Georges H. Bousquet – (1845–1937) was a French jurist and advisor to the Meiji government and the Ministry of Justice from 1872 to 1876. He participated in the first stage of codifying Japanese law while teaching at the Law School of the Ministry of Justice. He supported the modernization of Japanese private law, especially family and succession law. He returned to France after losing his position in the Ministry of Justice to the more experienced G. Boissonade.

Ōki Takatō (大木喬任) – (1832–1899) – a Japanese jurist, politician, and Minister of Justice in 1873–1880 and 1881–1883. As a politician responsible for codifying Japanese law for almost 10 years, he was one of the most zealous representatives of the decisive faction in the Civil Code Controversy.

Gustave Émile Boissonade de Fontarabie – (1825–1910), a French jurist, advisor to the Meiji government and the Ministry of Justice, an academic teacher at various Japanese law schools and the leading drafter of the Old Civil Code. He initially came to Japan in 1873 under a contract lasting only a few years. However, he prolonged his stay for over two decades as an international, criminal and private law expert. He was a declared supporter of the coming into force of the Old Civil Code despite its flaws. After the defeat of the decisive faction in the Civil Code Controversy, he returned to France in 1895. Today, he is considered one of the fathers of modern Japanese civil law.

Itō Hirobumi (伊藤博文) – (1841–1909), a Japanese politician, the first Prime Minister of Japan in 1885–1888 and three times in 1892–1896, 1898 and 1900–1901. His political activities focused on adopting the Meiji Constitution, creating a modern state of law, revising unequal treaties, and establishing the foundations of the Empire of Japan as one of the world's superpowers. He opposed the adoption of the codes at all costs since he believed that too haste legislation might be ineffective and incomprehensible to Japanese society. H. Itō was murdered at a train station by a Korean independence activist, An Jung-geun, as a result of the Japanese imperial policy towards Korea and plans of annexation.

Yamada Akiyoshi (山田顕義) – (1844–1892) a Japanese jurist, Minister of Justice in 1883–1891, a zealous supporter of the hasty codification of the Japanese legal system. Nicknamed "Count of Codes", Yamada sought to implement the Western doctrine by publishing all missing codes and revising unequal treaties. His explosive personality and unyielding attitude towards the postponement party led to a cabinet crisis and eventually his removal from the position. The absence of Yamada during crucial debates in the Imperial Diet in May and June 1892 was one of the reasons for the decisive faction defeat in the Civil Code Controversy.

Isobe Shirō (磯部四郎) – (1851–1923) a Japanese jurist, French school graduate and the decisive faction representative, one of the primary drafters of the books on family and succession law of the Old Civil Code.

Hozumi Yatsuka (穂積八束) – (1860–1912) a Japanese jurist and academic teacher. Nobushige's younger brother. The German school and the postponement party representative. His pieces regarding the harmful nature of the Old Civil Code had a significant impact on Japanese jurisprudence and were one of the reasons for the postponement party's victory in the Civil Code Controversy.

Egi Chū (江木衷) – (1858–1925) a Japanese jurist, the English school and the postponement party representative. The decisive faction representatives also appreciated his opinions regarding the Book on Property Law and the unintuitive systematics of the Civil Code.

Ume Kenjirō (梅謙次郎) – (1860–1910) a Japanese jurist and academic teacher. The French school and the decisive faction representative. One of the drafters of the revised Civil Code. Even his rivals from the postponement party considered Ume a genius with unlimited intellectual potential.

Tanaka Fujimaro (田中不二麿) – (1845–1909) a Japanese political and educational activist. Minister of Justice in 1891–1892. During that time, the Civil Code Controversy was resolved to the detriment of the cabinet and the decisive faction.

Prince Saionji Kim'mochi (西園寺公望) – (1849–1940) a Japanese jurist and political and educational activist. The French law and the decisive faction representative. Despite his positive views on the Old Civil Code and the Commercial Code, he respected the parliament's decision and supported the plan to revise both codes.

The famous photo showing all three fathers of the revised Civil Code and members of the Drafting Team (民法起草委員, Mimpō Kisō I'in). From left to right: Masaakira Tomii (富井政章), Ume Kenjirō (梅謙次郎) and Hozumi Nobushige (穂積陳重).

BIBLIOGRAPHY

1. Archive documents

1.1. National Archives (Kokuritsu Kōbunshokan)

a) Civil Code legislative analysis documents

Ref. 単01937100: Genrōin Kaigi Hikki (Chamber of Elders Meeting Records), Summary Volume for the Preliminary Analysis Carried from 24 January to 7 March 1889, Project of Law No 614.

Ref. 単01937100: Genrōin Kaigi Hikki (Chamber of Elders Meeting Records), Summary Volume for the Civil Code Approval Carried from 24–27 July 1889, Project of Law No 614.

Ref. 単01751100: Genrōin Gitei Jōsoan: Hōrei, Jinji Hen, Zaisan Shutoku Hen (Chamber of Elders Report: Introductory Provisions, Books on Personal Law and Acquiring Property, August 1890).

Ref. 類00527100: Mimpō Hensan Kyoku Jōshinan (Draft Report of the Civil Law Codification Department on the Civil Code Draft, Book on Property Law).

Ref. 御30627100: Mimpō no Ichibu o Kaitei Suru Hōritsu, Goshomei Gempa, Shōwa 22-nen, Hōritsu Dai 222-Gō (Act Amending Part of the Civil Code, Version with Original Signatures, the 22nd Year of the Shōwa era, Law No. 222).

Ref. 類00528100: Mimpō Zaisan Hen, Zaisan shutoku Hen, Saiken Tampo Hen, Shōko Hen Hōritsu Torishirabe I'inkai Jōshinan (Report of the Legal Research Committee on the Civil Code: Book on Property Law, Acquisition of Property, Security and Evidence, December 1888).

Ref. 類00529100: Mimpōchū Zaisan Hen, Zaisan Shutoku Hen, Saiken Tampo Hen, Shōkohen o Sadamu, Sore San (Introducing Final Amendments to the Civil Code: Books on Property Law, Acquiring Property, Security and Evidence, Part 3).

Ref. 類00531100: Mimpōchū Zaisan Hen, Zaisan Shutoku Hen, Saiken Tampo Hen, Shōkohen o Sadamu, (Final Amendments to the Civil Code: Books on Property Law, Acquiring Property, Security and Evidence, End of March 1890).

Ref. 類00532100: Mimpōchū Zaisan Hen, Zaisan Shutoku Hen, Saiken Tampo Hen, Shōkohen o Sadamu, (Final Amendments to the Civil Code: Books on Property Law, Acquiring Property, Security and Evidence, End of March 1890).

Ref. F00035100: Sūmitsuin Ketsugi (Privy Council Resolution on the Approval of the Civil Code: Books on Property Law, Acquiring Property, Security and Evidence, 11–25 March 1890).

b) Materials related to the Civil Law Codification Department (Establishment, Organization, Members, Statute, Financial Matters, Minutes of Meetings):

Ref. 太00712100, Ref. 太00713100, Ref. 太00750100, Ref. 太00780100;

Ref. 公02926100, Ref. 公02927100, Ref. 公03023100, Ref. 公03179100, Ref. 公03180100, Ref. 公03294100, Ref. 公03402100, Ref. 公03424100, Ref. 公03426100, Ref. 公03426100, Ref. 公03428100, Ref. 公03429100, Ref. 公03430100, Ref. 公03431100, Ref. 公03437100, Ref. 公03439100, Ref. 公03510100, Ref. 公03528100, Ref. 公03646100, Ref. 公03647100, Ref. 公03648100, Ref. 公03650100, Ref. 公03651100, Ref. 公03655100, Ref. 公03657100, Ref. 公03658100, Ref. 公03660100, Ref. 公03737100, Ref. 公03846100, Ref. 公03847100, Ref. 公03878100, Ref. 公03879100, Ref. 公03881100, Ref. 公03882100, Ref. 公03883100, Ref. 公03884100, Ref. 公03885100;

Ref. 記00577100, Ref. 記00588100, Ref. 記00609100, Ref. 記00641100.

c) Materials related to the Law Research Committee (Establishment, Organization, Members, Statutes):

Ref. 類00289100, Ref. 類00291100.

d) Materials related to G. Boissonade (Contractual, Professional and Payroll Issues):

Ref. 太00717100, Ref. 太00838100;

Ref. 公02571100, Ref. 公02692100;

Ref. 纂00034100;

Ref. 記00570100;

Ref. 別00007100.

e) Codes Investigation Committee documents:

Ref. 御01349100, Hōten Chōsa Kai Kisoku, Go Shomei Gembon, Meiji 23-nen, Chokurei Dai 11-gō (Regulations of the Codes Investigation Committee, Original Signatures, Meiji Year 23, Imperial Edict No. 11).

Ref. 類00637100, Hōten Chōsa Kai Kisoku o Sadamu (Provisions on the Statute of the Codes Investigation Committee).

Ref. 類00637100, Hōten Chōsa Kai Kisoku o Kaisei Su (Amendment of the Statute of the Codes Investigation Committee).

1.2. National Diet Library (Kokuritsu Kokkai Toshokan)

1) Minutes of meetings and reports of the Law Research Committee

a) Preliminary examination of the part on Property Law (3 December 1887 – 25 September 1888):

Mimpō Sōan Giji Hikki, Dai 1–5 Kai (Record of the Meeting on the Civil Code Draft, 1st–5th Meeting on 2, 5, 6, 12, 13 December 1887), Ref. XB300 N2-2a-1, https://dl.ndl.go.jp/info:ndljp/pid/1367415/5, (access: 10.04.2021).

Mimpō Sōan Giji Hikki, Dai 6–10 Kai (Record of the Meeting on the Civil Code Draft, 6th–10th Meeting on 19, 20, 23, 26, 27 December 1887), Ref. XB300 N2-2a-2, https://dl.ndl.go.jp/info:ndljp/pid/1367416/3, (access: 10.04.2021).

Mimpō Sōan Giji Hikki, Dai 11–16 Kai (Record of the Meeting on the Civil Code Draft, 11th–16th Meeting on 9, 10, 16, 17, 21, 23 January 1888), Ref. XB300 N2-2a-3, https://dl.ndl.go.jp/info:ndljp/pid/1367417/3, (access: 10.04.2021).

Mimpō Sōan Giji Hikki, Dai 17–22 Kai (Record of the Meeting on the Civil Code Draft, 17th–22nd Meeting on 24, 25, 31 January, 1, 6, 7 February 1888), Ref. XB300 N2-2b-1, https://dl.ndl.go.jp/info:ndljp/pid/1367418/3, (access: 10.04.2021).

Mimpō Sōan Giji Hikki, Dai 23–28 Kai (Record of the Meeting on the Civil Code Draft, 23rd–28th Meeting on 8, 13, 14, 15, 20, 21 February 1888), Ref. XB300 N2-2b-2, https://dl.ndl.go.jp/info:ndljp/pid/1367419/3, (access: 10.04.2021).

Mimpō Sōan Giji Hikki, Dai 29–34 Kai (Record of the Meeting on the Civil Code Draft, 29th–34th Meeting on 22, 27, 28, 29 February, 5, 6 March 1888), Ref. XB300 N2-2b-3, https://dl.ndl.go.jp/info:ndljp/pid/1367420/3, (access: 10.04.2021).

Mimpō Sōan Giji Hikki, Dai 35–37 Kai (Record of the Meeting on the Civil Code Draft, 35th–37th Meeting on 7, 12, 13 March 1888), Ref. XB300 N2-2b-4, https://dl.ndl.go.jp/info:ndljp/pid/1367421/3, (access: 10.04.2021).

Mimpō Sōan Giji Hikki, Dai 38–41 Kai (Record of the meeting on the Civil Code Draft, 38th–41st Meeting on 14, 19, 26, 27 March 1888), Ref. XB300 N2-2b-5, https://dl.ndl.go.jp/info:ndljp/pid/1367422/3, (access: 10.04.2021).

Mimpō Sōan Giji Hikki, Dai 42–44 Kai (Record of the Meeting on the Civil Code Draft, 42nd–44th Meeting on 28 March, 2, 4 April 1888), Ref. XB300 N2-2c-1, https://dl.ndl.go.jp/info:ndljp/pid/1367423/3, (access: 10.04.2021).

Mimpō Sōan Giji Hikki, Dai 45–48 Kai (Record of the Meeting on the Civil Code Draft, 45th–48th Meeting on 9, 10, 16, 17 April 1888), Ref. XB300 N2-2c-2, https://dl.ndl.go.jp/info:ndljp/pid/1367425/3, (access: 10.04.2021).

Mimpō Sōan Giji Hikki, Dai 49–52 Kai (Record of the Meeting on the Civil Code Draft, 49th–52nd Meeting on 23, 24, 26, 30 April, 1 May 1888), Ref. XB300 N2-2c-3, https://dl.ndl.go.jp/info:ndljp/pid/1367426/5, (access: 10.04.2021).

Mimpō Sōan Giji Hikki, Dai 53–58 Kai (Record of the Meeting on the Civil Code Draft, 53rd–58th Meeting on 7, 8, 14, 15, 21, 22 May 1888), Ref. XB300 N2-2c-4, https://dl.ndl.go.jp/info:ndljp/pid/1367427/3, (access: 10.04.2021).

Mimpō Sōan Giji Hikki, Dai 59–65 Kai (Record of the Meeting on the Civil Code Draft, 59th–65th Meeting on 28, 29 May, 4, 5, 11, 12, 18 June 1888), Ref. XB300 N2-2c-5, https://dl.ndl.go.jp/info:ndljp/pid/1367428/3, (access: 10.04.2021).

Mimpō Sōan Giji Hikki, Dai 66–71 Kai (Record of the Meeting on the Civil Code Draft, 66th–71st Meeting on 19, 25, 26 June, 9, 10 16 July 1888), Ref. XB300 N2-2c-6, https://dl.ndl.go.jp/info:ndljp/pid/1367429/3, (access: 10.04.2021).

Mimpō Sōan Giji Hikki, Dai 72–76 Kai (Record of the Meeting on the Civil Code Draft, 72nd–76th Meeting on 17, 23, 24, 30, 31 July 1888), Ref. XB300 N2-2d-1, https://dl.ndl.go.jp/info:ndljp/pid/1367430/3, (access: 10.04.2021).

Mimpō Sōan Giji Hikki, Dai 77–81 Kai (Record of the Meeting on the Civil Code Draft, 77th–81st Meeting on 3, 4, 10, 11, 17 September 1888 r.), Ref. XB300 N2-2d-2, https://dl.ndl.go.jp/info:ndljp/pid/1367431/3, (access: 10.04.2021).

Mimpō Sōan Giji Hikki, Dai 82–84 Kai (Record of the Meeting on the Civil Code Draft, 82nd–84th Meeting on 18, 24, 25 September 1888), Ref. XB300 N2-2d-3, https://dl.ndl.go.jp/info:ndljp/pid/1367432/3, (access: 10.04.2021).

b) Re-examination of the Book on Property Law (3 July 1888 – 28 December 1888):

Mimpō Sōan Saichōsa Giji Hikki, Dai 1–6 Kai (Record of the Meeting Regarding the Re-examination of the Civil Code Draft, 1st–6th Meeting on 3, 4, 7, 14, 21, 28 July 1888), Ref. XB300 N2-6a-1, https://dl.ndl.go.jp/info:ndljp/pid/1367433/24, (access: 10.04.2021).

Mimpō Sōan Saichōsa Giji Hikki, Dai 7–10 Kai (Record of the Meeting Regarding the Re-examination of the Civil Code Draft, 7th–10th Meeting on 1 August, 1, 2, 4, 5, 8 October 1888), Ref. XB300 N2-6a-2, https://dl.ndl.go.jp/info:ndljp/pid/1367434/3, (access: 10.04.2021).

Mimpō Sōan Saichōsa Giji Hikki, Dai 11–13 Kai (Record of the Meeting Regarding the Re-examination of the Civil Code Draft, 11th–13th Meeting on 9, 13, 15, 16 October 1888), Ref. XB300 N2-6a-3, https://dl.ndl.go.jp/info:ndljp/pid/1367435/3, (access: 10.04.2021).

Mimpō Sōan Saichōsa Giji Hikki, Dai 14–17 Kai (Record of the Meeting Regarding the Re-examination of the Civil Code Draft, 14th–17th Meeting on 20 October, 12, 13, 14 November 1888), Ref. XB300 N2-6b-1, https://dl.ndl.go.jp/info:ndljp/pid/1367436/3, (access: 10.04.2021).

Mimpō Sōan Saichōsa Giji Hikki, Dai 18–21 Kai (Record of the Meeting Regarding the Re-examination of the Civil Code Draft, 18th–21st Meeting on 16, 17, 19, 20 November 1888), Ref. XB300 N2-6b-2, https://dl.ndl.go.jp/info:ndljp/pid/1367437/3, (access: 10.04.2021).

Mimpō Sōan Saichōsa Giji Hikki, Dai 22–25 Kai (Record of the Meeting Regarding the Re-examination of the Civil Code Draft, 22nd–25th Meeting on 21, 22, 26, 27 November 1888), Ref. XB300 N2-6b-3, https://dl.ndl.go.jp/info:ndljp/pid/1367438/3, (access: 10.04.2021).

Mimpō Sōan Saichōsa Giji Hikki, Dai 26–44 Kai (Record of the Meeting Regarding the Re-examination of the Civil Code draft, 26th–44th Meeting on 28, 29, 30 November, 3, 4, 5, 8, 10, 11, 12, 13, 15, 17, 18, 19, 21, 22, 24, 25 December 1888), Ref. XB300 N2-6c-2, https://dl.ndl.go.jp/info:ndljp/pid/1367440/3, (access: 10.04.2021).

c) Preliminary examination of the Book on Personal and Succession Law

Mimpō: Hōrei, Jinji Hen, Zaisan Shutoku Hen Hōritsu Torishirabe I'inkai Jōshinan (Report of the Law Research Committee on the Re-examination of the Civil Code: Introductory Law, Books on Personal Law, Acquiring Property, December 1889), Ref. XB300 H1-3, https://dl.ndl.go.jp/info:ndljp/pid/1367498, [access: 10.04.2021].

2) Examination of proposed amendments of the Chamber of Elders regarding Property Law

Mimpō Sōan Saichōsa Giji Kikki (Record of the Meeting regarding the Examination of Proposed Amendments of the Chamber of Elders on 13–23 July 1889), Ref. XB300 N2-5, https://dl.ndl.go.jp/info:ndljp/pid/1367447/108, (access: 10.04.2021).

3) G. Boissonade's opinion on the comments of the Chamber of Elders

Mimpō Hensan ni kansuru Zassho (vol. 1–2), Boasonaado-shi Mimpō Sōan Shūsei ni kansuru Iken Hikki, Dai 1–13 Kai (Mr. Boissonade's Written Opinion on the Amendments to the Civil Code Draft, Part 1–13), Ref. XB300 N2-14, XB300 N2-15, XB300 N2-16, https://dl.ndl.go.jp/info:ndljp/pid/1367521, (access: 10.01.2021).

4) Cabinet's approval of the Book on Personal and Succession Law

Mimpō Jinji Hen Naikaku Shūseian (Draft of the Cabinet's Amendments to the Civil Code's Book on Personal Law, September 1890), Ref. XB300 H1-3B, https://dl.ndl.go.jp/info:ndljp/pid/1367503, [access: 10.04.2021].

2. Legal acts, legal act drafts and treaties

G. Boissonade, *Projet de Code Civil pour l'Empire du Japon accompagné d'un commentaire, Tome premier: Des droits réels*, Tokyo 1882.

G. Boissonade, *Projet de Code Civil pour l'Empire du Japon accompagné d'un commentaire, Tome deuxième: Des droits personnel ou obligations*, Tokyo 1883.

G. Boissonade, *Projet de Code Civil pour l'Empire du Japon accompagné d'un commentaire, Tome troisième: Des moyens d'acquérier les biens*, Tokyo 1888.

G. Boissonade, *Projet de Code Civil pour l'Empire du Japon accompagné d'un commentaire, Tome quatrième: Des sûretés ou garanties des créances ou droits personnels*, Tokyo 1889.

G. Boissonade, *Projet de Code Civil pour l'Empire du Japon accompagné d'un commentaire, Tome cinquième: Des preuves et de la prescription*, Tokyo 1889.

Chizaihō Meiji 13-nen Daijōkan Fukoku Dai 37-gō (Code of Criminal Procedure, Daijōkan's Decree No 37 of 13th Year of the Meiji era), http://dl.ndl.go.jp/info:ndljp/pid/787960/80, [access: 04.03.2020].

Daijōkan Nikki, Keiō 4-nen kan 1-2 (Daijōkan Diaries, 4th Year of the Keiō era, vol. 1–2), Tokyo 1876, https://dl.ndl.go.jp/info:ndljp/pid/787614/39 [access: 12.10.2020].

Dai Nippon Teikoku Kempō (The Constitution of the Empire of Japan), https://www.digital.archives.go.jp/DAS/pickup/view/detail/detailArchives/0101000000/0000000001/00, [access: 12.11.2020].

Haihan Chiken no Mikotonori, in: Meiji Shōchokushū (Collection of Emperor Meiji's decrees), Tokyo 1893, https://dl.ndl.go.jp/info:ndljp/pid/759506/18 [access: 14.10.2020].

Hōrei Zenshō Keiō 3-nen (Comprehensive Set of Laws, 3rd Year of the Keiō era), https://dl.ndl.go.jp/info:ndljp/pid/787948/9, [access: 12.10.2020].

Ikokusen Uchiharairei (Foreign Ship Deterrence Act), http://archives.pref.yamaguchi.lg.jp/user_data/upload/File/ags/3-3-6-010.pdf, [access: 25.09.2020].

Jinshin Koseki, in: http://www.archives.go.jp/ayumi/kobetsu/m04_1871_02.html, [access: 12.11.2020].

Jōi Chokumei (The Order to Expel Barbarians), bakumatu.727.net/bakumatu/tuushi-b3-kamogyoko.htm#taikyo, [access: 21.02.2019].

Keihō Meiji 13-nen Daijōkan Fukoku Dai 36-gō (Criminal Code, Daijōkan's Decree No 36 of 13th Year of the Meiji era), http://dl.ndl.go.jp/info:ndljp/pid/787960/80, [access 04.03.2020].

Kosekihō o Seitei Su (Introduction of Family Registration Law) http://www.archives.go.jp/ayumi/photo.html?m=8&pm=1 [access: 12.10.2020].

Meiji 8-nen Daijōkan Fukoku Dai 103 Gō (Daijōkan's Decree No 103 of 8th year of the Meiji era), https://dl.ndl.go.jp/info:ndljp/pid/787955/125, [access: 02.10.2020].

Meiji 23-nen Hōritsu Dai-28 Gō (Act No. 28, 23rd Year of the Meiji era), https://dl.ndl.go.jp/info:ndljp/pid/787979/35, [access: 12.11.2020].

Meiji 23-nen Hōritsu Dai-29 Gō (Act No. 29, 23rd Year of the Meiji era), https://dl.ndl.go.jp/info:ndljp/pid/2945291/67, [access: 12.11.2020].

Meiji 23-nen Hōritsu Dai-98 Gō (Act No. 98, the 23rd Year of the Meiji era), https://dl.ndl.go.jp/info:ndljp/pid/787979/517, [access: 12.11.2020].

Meiji 23-nen 12-gatsu 27-nichi Hōritsu Dai 108-gō: Shōhō oyobi Shōhō Shikō Jōrei Shikō Kigen Kōritsu (Act No. 108, 27 December of the 23rd Year of the Meiji era: The Act on the Date of Entry Into Force of the Commercial Code and the Provisions on Entry Into Force of the Commercial Code), https://hourei.ndl.go.jp/simple/detail?lawId=0000001730&current=-1, [access: 24.01.2021].

Meiji 25-nen 11-gatsu 24-nichi Hōritsu Dai-8 Gō: Mimpō oyobi Shōhō Shikō Enchō Hōritsu (Act No. 8, 24 November of the 25th Year of the Meiji era: The Act on the Postponement of the Date of Entry Into Force of the Civil Code and the Commercial Code), https://hourei.ndl.go.jp/simple/detail?lawId=0000002265&current=-1, [access: 12.02.2021].

Meiji 29-nen 4-gatsu 27-nichi, Hōritsu Dai 89-Gō (Act No. 89, 27 April of the 29th Year of the Meiji era), https://hourei.ndl.go.jp/simple/detail?lawId=0000003534&current=-1, [access: 27.03.2021].

Meiji 29-nen 12-gatsu 29-nichi, Hōritsu Dai 94-Gō (Act No. 94, 29 December of the 29th year of the Meiji era), https://hourei.ndl.go.jp/simple/detail?lawId=0000003896&current=-1, [access: 28.03.2021].

Meiji 31-nen 6-gatsu 21-nichi, Hōritsu Dai 11-Gō (Act No 11, 21 June of the 31st Year of the Meiji era), https://hourei.ndl.go.jp/simple/detail?lawId=0000004759&current=-1, [access: 28.03.2021].

Meiji 32-nen 3-gatsu kokonoka, Hōritsu Dai 48-Gō (Act No. 48, 9 March of the 32nd Year of the Meiji era), https://hourei.ndl.go.jp/simple/detail?lawId=0000005222&current=-1, access: 28.03.2021].

Mimpō Kari Hōsoku – Zen (Provisional Civil Law Provisions – the Whole Version), https://dl.ndl.go.jp/info:ndljp/pid/2937518/2?__lang=jp, [access: 12.11.2020].

Mimpō Sōan: Dai 1–2 Hen (Draft of the Civil Code, Book 1–2), https://dl.ndl.go.jp/info:ndljp/pid/904057, [access: 15.11.2020].

Mimpō Ketsugi, Dai 1–2 (Resolution on the Civil Code, Part 1–2), https://www.sagalibdb.jp/komonjo/detail/?id=20740, [access: 12.11.2020].

Mimpō Sōan: Dai 3 Hen (Draft of the Civil Code: Book 3), https://dl.ndl.go.jp/info:ndljp/pid/904058, [access: 15.11.2020].

Mimpō Sōan Jinji Hen (Draft of the Civil Code, Book on Personal Law), https://dl.ndl.go.jp/info:ndljp/pid/1367490/4, [access: 12.11.2020].

Mimpō Sōan Kakutoku Hen Dai Ni Bu Riyūsho (Draft of the Civil Code, Book on Ownership Acquisition Part 2 with Written Introduction), https://waseda.repo.nii.ac.jp/?action=pages_view_main&active_action=repository_view_main_item_detail&item_id=30954&item_no=1&page_id=13&block_id=21, [access: 12.11.2020].

Nichibei Washin Jōyaku (Japan–US Treaty of Peace and Amity), https://www.ndl.go.jp/modern/img_t/002/002-003tx.html [access: 24.10.2020].

Nihonkoku-Meriken Gasshūkoku Shūkō Tsūshō Jōyaku (Treaty of Amity and Commerce between Japan and the United States), in: Hōrei Zenshū (Set of laws), vol. Keiō 3-nen, Tokyo 1912.

Nichiei Shūkō Tsūshō Jōyaku (Anglo-Japanese Treaty of Amity and Commerce), in: Hōrei Zenshū (Set of Laws), vol. Keiō 3-nen, Tokyo 1912.

Nichifutsu Shūkō Tsūshō Jōyaku (Treaty of Amity and Commerce between France and Japan), in: Hōrei Zenshū (Set of laws), vol. Keiō 3-nen, Tokyo 1912.

Nichiran Shūkō Tsūshō Jōyaku (Treaty of Amity and Commerce between the Netherlands and Japan), in: Hōrei Zenshū (Set of laws), vol. Keiō 3-nen, Tokyo 1912.

Nichiro Shūkō Tsūshō Jōyaku (Treaty of Commerce and Navigation between Japan and Russia), in: Hōrei Zenshū (Set of laws), vol. Keiō 3-nen, Tokyo 1912.

Tokugawa Ieyasu Sei'i Taishōgun Bunin no Senji (Written Emperor's Order to Appoint Ieyasu Tokugawa as Shogun), Inscription in Nikkō Tōshōgū.

Tokugawa Naibu Taisei Henjō no Sōgi Keiō 3-nen (The Act of Resignation of the Supreme Minister, the 3rd Year of the Keiō era), https://www.kodomo.go.jp/yareki/theme/theme_05.html, [access: 12.10.2020].

Shihōshō (ed.), *Boasonaado-shi Kisō Saietsu Mimpō Sōan Seijō Bukken Jinken Zen* (*Re-examined Draft of the Civil Code Based on Mr. Boissonade's Version – All real rights and Obligations*), https://dl.ndl.go.jp/info:ndljp/pid/1367384, [access: 17.11.2020].

Shihōshō (ed.), *Boasonaado-shi Kikō Mimpō Sōan Shūseibun. Ji 501-jō shi 1502-jō* (*The Corrected Text of the Civil Code Draft Based on Mr. Boissonade's Version – from Articles 501 to 1502*), https://dl.ndl.go.jp/info:ndljp/pid/1367399, [access: 17.11.2020].

Shinritsu Kōryō (Outline of the New Law), https://dl.ndl.go.jp/info:ndljp/pid/1366244 [access: 12.11.2020].

Shiritsu Hōritsu Gakkō Tokubetsu Kantoku Jōki (Special Ministerial Regulation on Supervision of Private Law Schools), 13 November of 19th year of the Meiji era, https://www.chuo-u.ac.jp/uploads/2018/10/shiryoshu00010004.pdf? 1553126400062, [access: 21.11.2020].

Teikoku to Dai Buriten Koku to no Tsūshō Kōkai Jōyaku (Anglo-Japanese Treaty of Commerce and Navigation), https://dl.ndl.go.jp/info:ndljp/pid/2946617/1, [access: 13.03.2021].

3. Cabinet announcements and press

"Tōkyō Asahi Shimbun", 6 November 1886.

"Tōkyō Nichinichi Shimbun", 30 April 1892.

"Kanhō" Newspaper, 19 September 1887, https://dl.ndl.go.jp/info:ndljp/pid/2944503, [access: 21.11.2020].

"Kanhō" Newspaper, 23 June 1892, https://dl.ndl.go.jp/info:ndljp/pid/2945960/14, [access: 21.02.2021].

"Kanhō" Newspaper, 14 July 1892 r, https://dl.ndl.go.jp/info:ndljp/pid/2945978/8, [access: 21.02.2021].

"Kanhō" Newspaper, 8 August 1892, https://dl.ndl.go.jp/info:ndljp/pid/2945999/8, [access: 21.02.2021].

Cabinet Announcement on the Resignation of the Home Minister, Yajirō Shinagawa, in: Cabinet Bulletin of 11 March 1892, https://dl.ndl.go.jp/info:ndljp/pid/2945871/6, p. 6, [access: 31.01.2021].

4. Records of speeches in the House of Representatives and the House of Peers

a) House of Peers

Record of the House of Peers session on 13 February 1891, https://dl.ndl.go.jp/info:ndljp/pid/1621993/152, [access: 24.01.2021].

Record of the House of Peers session on 26 May 1892 regarding the draft act on the postponement of the date of entry into force of the Civil Code and the Commercial Code, https://dl.ndl.go.jp/info:ndljp/pid/1621993/820, [access: 05.02.2021].

Record of H. Katō's speech during the House of Peers session on 26 May 1892, https://dl.ndl.go.jp/info:ndljp/pid/1621993/821, [access: 05.02.2021].

Record of K. Torio's speech during the House of Peers session on 26 May 1892, https://dl.ndl.go.jp/info:ndljp/pid/1621993/822, [access: 05.02.2021].

Record of T. Ōki's speech during the House of Peers session on 26 May 1892, https://dl.ndl.go.jp/info:ndljp/pid/1621993/823, [access: 05.02.2021].

Record of R. Mitsukuri's speech during the House of Peers session on 26 May 1892, https://dl.ndl.go.jp/info:ndljp/pid/1621993/825, [access: 05.02.2021].

Record of T. Tani's speech during the House of Peers session on 27 May 1892, https://dl.ndl.go.jp/info:ndljp/pid/1621993/827, [access: 05.02.2021].

Record of R. Mitsukuri's, F. Tanaka's, and S. Okauchi's speeches during the House of Peers session on 27 May 1892, https://dl.ndl.go.jp/info:ndljp/pid/1621993/828, [access: 05.02.2021].

Record of T. Murata's and H. Katō's speeches during the House of Peers session on 27 May 1892, https://dl.ndl.go.jp/info:ndljp/pid/1621993/828, [access: 05.02.2021].

Record of M. Tomii's speech during the House of Peers session on 27 May 1892, https://dl.ndl.go.jp/info:ndljp/pid/1621993/832, [access: 05.02.2021].

Record of T. Hachisuki's speech during the House of Peers session on 27 May 1892, https://dl.ndl.go.jp/info:ndljp/pid/1621993/832, [access: 05.02.2021].

Record of the debate during of the House of Peers session on 28 May 1892, https://dl.ndl.go.jp/info:ndljp/pid/1621993/837, [access: 09.02.2021].

Record of the results of the vote on the approval of the second reading of the draft act on the postponement of the date of entry into force of the Civil Code and the Commercial Code during the House of Peers session on 28 May 1892, https://dl.ndl.go.jp/info:ndljp/pid/1621993/838, [access: 09.02.2021].

Record of the voting results on T. Murata's project and the introduction of amendments during the House of Peers session on 28 May 1892, https://dl.ndl.go.jp/info:ndljp/pid/1621993/839, [access: 09.02.2021].

Record of the discussion on U. Obata's proposal to establish the Revision Committee for the Civil Code and the Commercial Code during the House of Peers session on 6 and 7 June 1892, https://dl.ndl.go.jp/info:ndljp/pid/1621993/872, https://dl.ndl.go.jp/info:ndljp/pid/1621993/879 [access: 09.02.2021].

Record of approval of U. Obata's proposal on the establishment of the Revision Committee for the Civil Code and the Commercial Code during the House of Peers session on 8 June 1892, https://dl.ndl.go.jp/info:ndljp/pid/1621993/881, [access: 09.02.2021].

Record on the information about the announcement of U. Obata's project on establishing the Revision Committee for the Civil Code and the Commercial Code during the House of Peers session on 9 June 1892, https://dl.ndl.go.jp/info:ndljp/pid/1621993/883, [access: 09.02.2021].

Record on the announcement of the results of the vote in the House of Peers during the House of Representatives session on 30 May 1892, https://dl.ndl.go.jp/info:ndljp/pid/1621993/1017, [access: 09.02.2021].

b) House of Representatives

Record of the House of Representatives session on 15 December 1890 regarding the change of the date of entry into force of the Commercial Code, https://dl.ndl.go.jp/info:ndljp/pid/1621993/272, [access: 23.01.2021].

Record of R. Mitsukuri's speech during the House of Representatives session on 15 December 1890, https://dl.ndl.go.jp/info:ndljp/pid/1621993/258, [access: 24.01.2021].

Record of the House of Representatives session on 10 December 1891 regarding the entry into force of part of the Commercial Code, https://dl.ndl.go.jp/info:ndljp/pid/1621993/698, [access: 31.01.2021].

Record of the House of Representatives session on 17 December 1891 regarding the entry into force of part of the Commercial Code, https://dl.ndl.go.jp/info:ndljp/pid/1621993/743, [access: 31.01.2021].

Record of the House of Representatives session on 22 December 1891 regarding the draft budget for 1892, https://teikokugikai-i.ndl.go.jp/#/detail?minId=000213242X02018911222, pp. 8–10, [access: 31.01.2021].

Record of the House of Representatives session on 24 May 1892, https://dl.ndl.go.jp/info:ndljp/pid/1621993/977, [access: 09.02.2021].

Record of the House of Representatives session of 27 May 1892, https://dl.ndl.go.jp/info:ndljp/pid/1621993/999, [access: 09.02.2021].

Record of the appointment of the Special Committee during the House of Representatives session on 3 June 1892, https://dl.ndl.go.jp/info:ndljp/pid/1621993/1055, [access: 09.02.2021].

Record of the appointment of members of the Special Committee during the House of Representatives session on 4 June 1892, https://dl.ndl.go.jp/info:ndljp/pid/1621993/1055, [access: 09.02.2021].

Record of the confirmation of the appointment of the Chairman and Chairman of the Board of the Special Committee during the House of Representatives session on 6 June 1892, https://dl.ndl.go.jp/info:ndljp/pid/1621993/1077, [access: 09.02.2021].

Record of the first reading of the Murata's draft during the House of Representatives session on 10 June 1892, https://dl.ndl.go.jp/info:ndljp/pid/1621993/1109, [access: 09.02.2021].

Record of F. Tanaka's speech during the House of Representatives session on 10 June 1892, https://dl.ndl.go.jp/info:ndljp/pid/1621993/1109, [access: 09.02.2021].

Record of I. Abei's, K. Misaki's, and K. Suematsu's speeches during the House of Representatives session on 10 June 1892, https://dl.ndl.go.jp/info:ndljp/pid/1621993/1111, [access: 09.02.2021].

Record of S. Shimada's, M. Watanabe's, K. Miyagi's, and M. Katō's speech during the House of Representatives session on 10 June 1892, https://dl.ndl.go.jp/info:ndljp/pid/1621993/1112, [access: 09.02.2021].

Record of approval of the first reading of T. Murata's draft during the House of Representatives session on 10 June 1892, https://dl.ndl.go.jp/info:ndljp/pid/1621993/1114, [access: 09.02.2021].

Record of the voting results on T. Murata's draft during the House of Representatives session on 10 June 1892, https://dl.ndl.go.jp/info:ndljp/pid/1621993/1114, [access: 09.02.2021].

Record of voting results on K. Kōno's and S. Shimada's during the House of Representatives session on 10 June 1892, https://dl.ndl.go.jp/info:ndljp/pid/1621993/1118, [access: 09.02.2021].

Record of informing about T. Murata's draft during the House of Peers session on 16 May 1892, https://dl.ndl.go.jp/info:ndljp/pid/1621993/820, [access: 09.02.2021].

5. Legal opinions

S. Aō (ed.), *Hōten Hensan ni kansuru Hōgakushikai no Iken* (*Association of Jurists' Opinion on the Compilation of Codes*), https://dl.ndl.go.jp/info:ndljp/pid/786137/2, [access: 10.11.2020].

C. Egi, *Mimpō sōan zaisan hen hihyō* (*Criticism of the book on property law in the draft of the Civil Code*), "Hōri Seika" 1889, Vol. 4 (Issue 19), pp. 1–10, https://dl.ndl.go.jp/info:ndljp/pid/1493304, [access: 12.11.2020].

C. Egi, *Mimpō sōan zaisan hen hihyō* (*Criticism of the book on property law in the draft of the Civil Code*), "Hōri Seika" 1889, Vol. 4 (Issue 21), pp. 1–5, https://dl.ndl.go.jp/info:ndljp/pid/1493306, [access: 12.11.2020].

C. Egi, *Mimpō sōan zaisan hen hihyō* (*Criticism of the book on property law in the draft of the Civil Code*), "Hōri Seika" 1889, Vol. 4 (Issue 22), pp. 1–6, https://dl.ndl.go.jp/info:ndljp/pid/1493307, [access: 12.11.2020].

K. Handa, *Wagakuni hōritsu-jō no kanshū ni tsuite* (*About native customs from a legal point of view*), "Hōchi Kyōkai Zasshi" 1891, Issue 1, pp. 38–43.

T. Hanai, *Aa Mimpō shōko hen* (*Ah, this book on evidence in the Civil Code ...*), "Hōri Seika" 1889, Vol. 4 (Issue 20), https://dl.ndl.go.jp/info:ndljp/pid/1493305, pp. 15–18, [access: 12.11.2020].

T. Hanai, *Hōten to jōyaku kaisei* (*Codes and revision of unequal treaties*), "Hōgaku Shimpō" 1892, Issue 14, pp. 58–61.

S. Hirayama, *Eihōgakusha ha shinhōten o dō sukebiya?* (What should English law school's jurists do with the new code[s]?), "Nihon no Hōritsu" 1890, Vol. 2 (Issue 6), pp. 11–15.

Y. Hozumi, *Kokkateki Mimpō* (*National Civil Code*), "Hōgaku Shimpō" 1891, Issue 1, pp. 8–10.

Y. Hozumi, *Mimpō Idete, Chūkō Hōfu* (*The entry into force of the Civil Code is the death of loyalty and filial devotion*), *Hōgaku Shimpō* 1891, Issue 5, pp. 8–13.

Y. Hozumi, Yasokyō Izen no Oūshū Iesei (*European Family System before Christianity*), "Kokka Gakkai Zasshi" 1891, Vol. 5 (Issue 54), pp. 2–5.

Hōchi Kyōkai (ed.), *Hōten Jisshi Dankō no Iken* (*Opinion on the Immediate Entry Into Force of the Codes*), "Hōritsu Zasshi" 1892, Issue 883, pp. 110–118.

Hōchi Kyōkai (ed.), *Hōten Jisshi Dankō no Iken* (*Opinion on the Immediate Entry Into Force of the Codes*) "Hōritsu Zasshi" 1892, Issue 884, s. 166–172.

Hōchi Kyōkai (ed.), *Hōten Jisshi Dankō no Iken, Shōzen* (*Opinion on the Immediate Entry Into Force of the Codes, Continuation*) "Hōritsu Zasshi" 1892, Issue 885, pp. 228–234.

Hōchi Kyōkai Zasshi (ed.), *Kankō no ji to tomoni ni Hōchi Kyōkai no shugi kōryō o akiraka ni su* (*Explaining the most important ideological assumptions of the Association of Constitutionalists related to the publication of the journal*), "Hōchi Kyōkai Zasshi" 1891, Issue 1, pp. 1–5.

Hōgaku Shimpō (ed.), *Hōgaku Shimpō Hakkō no Shu Omomuki* (*The Main Importance of Publishing the Jurisprudence News*), "Hōgaku Shimpō" 1891, Issue 1, pp. 1–3.

Hōgaku Shimpō (ed.), *Hōten Jisshi Enki Iken* (*Opinion on the Postponement of the Date of Entry Into Force of the Code[s]*), "Hōgaku Shimpō" 1892, Issue 14, pp. 1–35.

Hōri Seika (ed.), *Meiji 22-nen no hōritsu shakai oyobi Hōri Seika* (*Hōri Seika and the Legal Community in the 22nd Year of the Meiji era*), "Hōri Seika" 1890, Vol. 5 (Issue 25), https://dl.ndl.go.jp/info:ndljp/pid/1493309, pp. 1–7, [access: 17.11.2020].

Hōri Seika (ed.), *Shin hōten gaihyō* (*Commentary on the new codes*), "Hōri Seika" 1890, Vol. 6 (Issue 35), https://dl.ndl.go.jp/info:ndljp/pid/1493319, pp. 1–8, [access: 17.11.2020].

Hōri Seika (ed.), *Shin hōten gaihyō* (*Commentary on the new codes*), "Hōri Seika" 1890, Vol. 6 (Issue 36), https://dl.ndl.go.jp/info:ndljp/pid/1493320, pp. 1–27, [access: 17.11.2020].

Hōri Seika (ed.), *Shōkohō ron* (*Discussion on evidence law*), "Hōri Seika" 1890, Vol. 5 (Issue 25), https://dl.ndl.go.jp/info:ndljp/pid/1493309, pp. 8–31, [access: 17.11.2020].

Hōritsu Zasshi (ed.), *Dai san gikai to Shihōshō* (*Third Imperial Diet session and the Ministry of Justice*), "Hōritsu Zasshi" 1892, Issue 881, pp. 1–6.

Hōritsu Zasshi (ed.), *Waga saigo no kesshin* (*Our final determination*), "Hōritsu Zasshi" 1892, Issue 885, pp. 213–216.

M. Inoue, *Hōritsu hensan no kahi* (*Advantages and disadvantages of law codification*), "Hōsei Shigyō" 1890, pp. 103.

S. Isobe, *Hōri Seika o yomu* (*Reading Hōri Seika*, "Hōsei Shigyō" 1890, Issue 99.

S. Isobe, *Hōten shikō no hitsuyō* (*The necessity for the code[s] to enter into force*), "Hōchi Kyōkai Zasshi" 1892, Issue 10.

H. Itō, *Kon'in yūkō no jōken ni kansuru ichi gimon* (*One doubt about the law on the validity of marriage*), "Nihon no Hōritsu" 1890, Vol. 2 (Issue 11), pp. 29–33.

T. Kishimoto, *Hōten Happu ni tsuite* (*About the Promulgation of the Codes*), "Hōsei Shigyō" 1890, Issue 107.

R. Masujima, *Hōgakushi Kai no iken o ronzu* (*Discussing the opinion of the Jurists Association*), "Hōri Seika" 1889, Vol. 2 (Issue 12), https://dl.ndl.go.jp/info:ndljp/pid/1493297, pp 28–38, [access: 16.12.2020].

Meihō Shisō (ed.), *Meihō Kai setsuritsu mokuteki oyobi kai'in* (*Purpose of establishing the Meihō Association and its members*), *Meihō Shisō* 1892, Issue 1, pp. 67–80.

K. Miyagi, *Hōten iji-ron wa eihō gakusha yori okoru* (*The doctrine of protecting the codes has its origins in the English law school representatives*), "Hōchi Kyōkai Zasshi" 1891, Issue 5.

H. Morozumi, *Shinten no Happu ni tsuite* (*About the Promulgation of the new Codes*), "Hōsei Shigyō" 1890, Issue 107.

K. Nakamura, *Hōten Igen-ron* (*Discussion on the Gravity of the Codes*), *Nihon no Hōritsu* 1890, Vol. 2 (Issue 6), pp. 15–20.

Nihon no Hōritsu (ed.), *Dōtokusha no Hinan = Hōritsuka no Reishō* (*Criticism of Moral Persons = Lawyers' Mockery*), *Nihon no Hōritsu* 1890, Vol. 2 (Issue 5), pp. 87–88.

Nihon no Hōritsu (ed.), *Hōten Hensan Yoroshiku Dankō Subeshi* (*The Codification of the Codes Must Be Carried out Properly*), *Nihon no Hōritsu* 1890, Vol. 2 (Issue 1), pp. 84–85.

Nihon no Hōritsu (ed.), *Jōken Ronsha no Sōzoku Setsu* (*The Feminist Activists Theory of Succession*), *Nihon no Hōritsu* 1889, Vol. 1 (Issue 22).

Nihon no Hōritsu (ed.), *Ki Mata Ki* (*Odd and Peculiar*), *Nihon no Hōritsu* 1890, Vol. 2 (Issue 5), p. 90.

Nihon no Hōritsu (ed.), *Shoshi no sei ni tsuite Ozaki-shi no iken* (*Mr. Ozaki's opinion on the status of illegitimate children*), "Nihon no Hōritsu" 1890, Vol. 2 (Issue 3), pp. 97–98.

Y. Nobuoka, *Hōten Shikō Torishiarabe I'inkai o ronjite gen naikaku ni oyobu* (*Impact of the dispute in the Codes Enforcement Study Committee on the cabinet*), "Nihon no Hōritsu" 1892, Vol. 4 (Issue 11).

K. Okano, *Eihō no tame ni mida o bensu* (*Response to allegations against the English law school*), "Hōri Seika" 1889, Vol. 3 (Issue 14), https://dl.ndl.go.jp/info:ndljp/pid/1493299, pp. 24–27, [access: 16.12.2020].

T. Okuda, *Jinji hen no teishoku oyobi jūfuku* (*Repetitions and contradictions in the book on personal law*), "Hōgaku Shimpō" 1892, Issue 13, pp. 33–36.

T. Okuda, *Mitsukuri Shihō Jikan no enshū o bunseki seyo* (*Let us analyse the speech of the Deputy Minister of Justice, R. Mitsukuri*), "Hōri Seika" 1889, Col. 3 (Issue 15), pp. 4–10, https://dl.ndl.go.jp/info:ndljp/pid/1493300, [access: 16.12.2020].

K. Ōi, *Waga Teikoku ni okeru hōten rigai ika?* (*What are the advantages and disadvantages of codes in our empire?*), "Hōchi Kyōkai Zasshi" 1891, Issue 2, pp. 3–7.

M. Shirome (S. Koshino), *Hōten to jōyaku kaisei* (*Codes and revision of [unequal] treaties*), "Hōchi Kyōkai Zasshi" 1891, Issue 5, pp. 40–48.

K. Takahashi, *Hōten jisshi dankō ronsha no jihaku* (*Confession of the supporters of the theory of the immediate entry into force of the codes*), "Hōgaku Shimpō" 1892, Issue 14, pp. 50–52.

T. Torii, *Hōritsu no gakushi Isobe no Shirō Daisensei no go giron o hyōsu* (*Judging five arguments of the great professor and jurist Shirō Isobe*), "Hōri Seika" 1890, Vol. 5 (Issue 26), https://dl.ndl.go.jp/info:ndljp/pid/1493310, pp. 1–7, [access: 21.12.2020].

T. Torii, *Hōritsu no gakushi Isobe no Shirō Daisensei no go giron o hyōsu* (*Judging five arguments of the great professor and jurist Shirō Isobe*), "Hōri Seika" 1890, Vol. 5 (Issue 27), https://dl.ndl.go.jp/info:ndljp/pid/1493311, pp. 1–5, [access: 21.12.2020].

T. Torii, *Hōritsu no gakushi Isobe no Shirō Daisensei no go giron o hyōsu* (*Judging five arguments of the great professor and jurist Shirō Isobe*), "Hōri Seika" 1890, Vol. 5 (Issue 28), https://dl.ndl.go.jp/info:ndljp/pid/1493312, pp. 25–29, [access: 21.12.2020].

Z. Tsuboya, *Hōgakushi Kai, hōten hensan o hinan su* (*Jurists Association and criticism of the compilation of codes*), "Nihon no Hōritsu" 1889, Vol. 1 (Issue 17).

Z. Tsuboya, *Mimpō no jinji hen ni tsuite* (*About the book on personal law in the Civil Code*), "Nihon no Hōritsu" 1891, Vol. 3 (Issue 7).

K. Ume, *Hōten jisshi iken* (*Opinion on the entry into force of the code[s]*), "Meihō Shisō" 1892, Issue 1, pp. 1–21.

K. Ume, *Hōten ni kansuru jukkai* (*Thoughts on the code[s]*), in: T. Hoshino, *Meiji Mimpō...*, pp. 537–545.

K. Ume, *Hōten ni tsuite* (*About the codes*), "Kokka Gakkai Zasshi" 1894, Vol. 8 (Issue 84), s. 77–86.

Wafutsu Hōritsu Gakkō Kōyūkai (ed.), *Hōten jisshi dankō iken* (*Opinion on the immediate entry into force of the code[s]*), "Hōritsu Zasshi" 1892, Issue 884, pp. 166–172.

Wafutsu Hōritsu Gakkō Kōyūkai (ed.), *Hōten jisshi dankō iken* (*Opinion on the immediate entry into force of the code[s]*), "Hōritsu Zasshi" 1892, Issue 885, pp. 228–234.

6. Monographs and articles

T. Abe, J. Rejaunier, *Japan's Hidden Face: A Call for Radical Change in Japanese Society & Commerce*, Philadelphia 1998.

H. Akiyama, *Mimpō seitei katei ni okeru kazoku seido: dai ichi sōan, Kyūmimpō, Meiji Mimpō o megutte* (*Family system dispute during the drafting of the Civil Code: first draft, Old Civil Code, and Meiji Civil Code*), "Kōbe Jogakuin Daigaku Ronshū" 1974, vol. 20 (n. 3), pp. 65–83.

I. Amano, *Daigaku no tanjō. <jō> Teikoku daigaku no jidai* (*The birth of universities <part 1> The era of the Imperial University*), Tokyo 2004.

Y. Amino (ed.), *Nihon chūseishizō no saikentō* (*Re-evaluation of the Japanese Middle Ages*), Tokyo 1988.

Y. Arano, *Kindai Nihon ni oite gaikokujin hanzaisha wa dō yō ni sabakarete ita ka?: Meiji jidai ni okeru ryōji saibanken no rekishiteki zentei no sobyō* (*How were foreign criminals tried in modern Japan? Initial historical outline of consular jurisdiction in the Meiji period*), "Shien" 2009, Vol. 9, pp. 158–172.

T. Arichi, *Meiji Mimpō kisō no hōshin nado ni kansuru jakkan no shiryō to sono kentō* (*Fragments of materials regarding the Meiji Civil Code drafting plan and their analysis*), "Hōsei Kenkyū" 1971, Vol. 37 (Issue 1–2), pp. 95–123.

T. Asada, *Sakoku seisaku ka no Nihon bōeki* (*Japanese trade during the sakoku policy*), "Meidai Shōgaku Rongyō" 2000, Vol. 82 (Issue 1), pp. 27–46.

K. Asaji, *17-seiki Ōsutoria kizoku ni totte no "Ōsaka-zu byōbu" no nedan (The price of the "Osaka byōbu" according to a 17th-century Austrian aristocrat)*, in: *Kokusai shimpojiumu hōkokusho: shinhakken "Toyotomi ki Ōsaka-zu byōbu" no miryoku (The charm of the newly discovered "Osaka byōbu of the Toyotomi period", a record of an international symposium)*, Osaka 2009.

H. Asako, T. Itō, N. Ueda, F. Jimbo (ed.), *Nihon hōseishi (History of Japanese Law)*, Tokyo 2010.

H. Asakuro (ed.), *Meiji Kansei Jiten (Dictionary of Meiji State Institutions)*, Tokyo 1969.

G. Barratt, *Russia in Pacific Waters: 1715–1825*, Toronto 1981.

G. M. Beckmann, *The Making of the Meiji Constitution. The Oligarchs and the Constitutional Development of Japan, 1868–1891*, Kansas 1957.

J. Bentham, *General View of a Complete Code of Laws*, in: J. Bowring (ed.), *The Works of Jeremy Bentham, vol. 3*, London 1843.

P. Van den Berg, *Politics of codification in Meiji Japan (1868-1912): Comparative perspective of position of customary law in Japanese civil code*, "Osaka University Law Review" 2018, Vol. 65, pp. 69–87.

H. Bocken, *Recht en wet in Japan*, "Rechtskundig Weekblad" 1985, Vol. 50 (Issue 2), pp. 81–144.

G. Boissonade, *Réponse à la question: « L'homme est-il naturellement bon ou mauvais ?»*, in: Revue française du Japon: publiée sous le patronage de la Société de langue française, Tokyo 1892, pp. 65–73.

G. Bousquet, *Le Japon de nos jours et les échelles de l'extrême Orient*, Tome 2, Paris 1877.

J. Chen, *Chinese Law: Context and Transformation: Revised and Expanded Edition*, Boston 1966.

M. Cooper, *Rodrigues The Interpreter: An Early Jesuit in Japan and China*, New York 1974.

L.M. Cullen, *A History of Japan: 1582–1941*: Internal and External Worlds, Cambridge 2003.

Dai Nippon Suisan Kai (ed.), *Murata Suisan okina tsute (Biography of the honorable gentleman Murata)*, Tokyo 1919.

M. Dean, *Japanese Legal System*, London 2002.

J. Denney, *Respect and Consideration: Britain in Japan 1853–1868 and Beyond*, Leicester 2011.

R. Domingo, *El Código Civil Japonés, un Código a la Europea*, "Boletín de la Facultad de Derecho" 2003, Vol. 21, pp. 263–279.

R.R. Ellis, *The Best Thus Far Discovered: The Japanese in the Letters of Francisco Xavier*, "Hispanic Review" 2003, Vol. 71 (Issue 2), pp. 155–169.

W.W. Farris, *Sacred Texts and Buried Treasures: Issues in the Historical Archaeology of Ancient Japan*, Honolulu 1998.

M. Frolík, *Funkce hlavy rodiny v Japonsku v 1. polovině 20. stol.*, LLM thesis defended at the Faculty of Philosophy of the Charles University, Prague 2009.

Fujiwara, *Bowasonādo teitōhō no kenkyū (Boissonade's mortgage studies)*, Kobe 1995.

M. Fujiwara, *Nihon Hōritsu Gakkō to Tokubetsu Ninka Gakkō Kisoku (Japanese Law School and Special School Licensing Regulation)*, "Kyōikugaku Zasshi: Nihon Daigaku Kyōiku Gakkai Kiyō" 1987, pp. 14-22.

M. Fukushima, *Nihon shihonshugi no hatten to shihō (The development of Japanese capitalism and private law)*, Tokyo 1988.

M. Fukushima, T. Yoshii (ed.), *Fukushima Masao chosakushū dai 1 kan: Nihon kindai hōshi (Masao Fukushima Works, vol. 1: Modern Japanese Legal History)*, Tokyo 1993.

L. Górnicki, *Kodyfikacja prawa prywatnego*, in: M. Safjan (ed.), *System Prawa Prywatnego, t. 1, Prawo cywilne – część ogólna*, 2nd edition, Warsaw 2012, pp. 77–155.

G. Górski, *Konstytucja Cesarstwa Japonii z 1889 roku*, "Roczniki Nauk Prawnych" 2003, Vol. 13 (Issue 1), pp. 43–52.

S. Grzybowski, *Dzieje prawa. Opowieść, refleksje, rozważania*, Wroclaw 1981.

J. Hammer, *Yokohama Burning: The Deadly 1923 Earthquake and Fire that Helped Forge the Path to World War II*, New York-Toronto-London-Sydney 2006.

P. Hein, *How the Japanese became foreign to themselves: the impact of globalization on the private and public spheres in Japan*, Berlin 2009.

J. C. Hepburn, *A Japanese and English dictionary: with an English and Japanese index*, Osaka 1887.

K. Hirai, K. Murakami (ed.), *Isobe Shirō Kenkyū: Nihon kindai hōgaku no kyohaku* (*A study of Shirō Isobe: father figure of contemporary Japanese jurisprudence*), Tokyo 2007.

J.C. Hall, *The Tokugawa Legislation*, Yokohama 1910.

J.W. Hall (ed.), *The Cambridge history of Japan, vol. 4: Early Modern Japan*, Cambridge 1988.

K. Harada, *Nihon Mimpōten no shiteki sobyō* (*Historical outline of the Japanese Civil Code*), Tokyo 1954.

G. Haruhara (ed.), *Meiji shoki no hōgaku kōgi* (*Lectures on law in the early Meiji period*), Osaka 1965.

K. Hatoyama, *The Civil Code of Japan Compared With the French Civil Code*, "The Yale Law Journal" 1902, Vol. 11 (Issue 7), pp. 354–370.

T. Hayashi, *Roman Law Studies and the Civil Code in Modern Japan: System, Ownership, and Co-ownership*, "Osaka University Law Review" 2008, Vol. 55, pp. 15–26.

T. Hayashi, *El derecho romano y el Código Civil en el Japón moderno. Sistemática, propiedad y copropiedad*, "Revista Chilena de Derecho" 2009, Vol. 36 (Issue 1), pp. 9–21.

I. Higashibaba, *Christianity in Early Modern Japan: Kirishitan Belief and Practice*, Boston & Cologne 2002.

Y. Hirano, *Nihon shihonshugi no kikō to hōritsu* (*The law and mechanisms of Japanese capitalism*), Tokyo 1948.

T. Hironaka, *Mimpōten hensanshi no kenkyū* (*Research on the history of the drafting of the Civil Code*), Tokyo 2020.

T. Honderich (ed.), *The Oxford Companion to Philosophy*, Oxford 1995.

Y. Horie, *L'influence du Code Napoleon sur Le Code Civil japonais*, "Comparative Legilinguistics" 2014, Vol. 19, pp. 49–59.

T. Hoshino, Matsuyama Daigaku Hogakubu (ed.), *"Mimpōten ronsō shiryōshū" (Fukkoku zōhoban) no gendaiteki igi: Shimpojiumu*, (*Contemporary meaning of the "Collection of materials concerning the Civil Code Controversy": Symposium (supplemented edition)*), Tokyo 2014.

T. Hoshino, *Meiji Mimpō Hensan Kenkyūshi* (*The history of research on the codification of the Meiji Civil Code*), Tokyo 1943.

T. Hoshino, *Mimpōten Ronsōshi* (*History of the Civil Code Controversy*), Tokyo 1944.

T. Hoshino, *Mimpō Ronsōshi: Meiji Kazokuhō Ronsōshi* (*The history of the Civil Code Controversy: the history of the dispute over the Meiji family law*), Tokyo 1949.

Hōseishi Gakkai Hen (ed.), *Tokugawa kinreikō* (*The idea of legal prohibitions of the Tokugawa period*), separate volume, Tokyo 1961.

Hōsei Daigaku (ed.), *Hōsei Daigaku 80-nen shi* (*Hōsei University's 80-Year History*), https://dl.ndl.go.jp/info:ndljp/pid/9583799, [access: 12.11.2020].

H. Hōyō, S. Miyahira, *Nihon kindai keihō no seiritsu katei* (*The process of establishing modern Japanese criminal law*), "Ryūkei Hōgaku" 2009, Vol. 9, (Issue 1), pp. 13–57.

N. Hozumi, *Hōsō yawa* (*Night talks about law*), Tokyo 1980.

N. Hozumi, *Hōtenron* (*The theory of codes*), Tokyo 1890.

N. Hozumi, *Shinzokuhō* (*Family law*), Tokyo 1933.

N. Hozumi, *The new Japanese civil code: As material for the study of comparative jurisprudence*, Tokyo 1912.

Iezusu Kai (ed.), *Nippo Jisho* (*Japanese-Portuguese dictionary*), Nagasaki 1603.

R. Igeta, E. Yamanaka, H. Ishikawa (ed.), *Nihon kindai hōshi* (*History of modern Japanese law*), Kyoto 1982.

M. Ikeda, *Bowasonaado to sono Mimpō* (*Boissonade and his Civil Code*), Tokyo 2011.

K. Ikuta (ed.), *Zenkoku minji kanrei ruishū* (*Nationwide collection of various customs of civil law*), Tokyo 1880, https://dl.ndl.go.jp/info:ndljp/pid/786945/1 [access: 12.11.2020].

I. Imai, Y. Setani, M. Bitō, *Nihon shisō taikei (53) Mito gaku* (*An Outline of Japanese Thought (53) Mito School*), Tokyo 1973.

K. Imamura, *Kainan* (*Interpretation difficulties*), Tokyo 1890.

K. Inoue, *Bakumatsu–Ishin* (*Bakumatsu Revolution*), Tokyo 2006.

K. Inoue, *Nihon no Rekishi, kan 20: Meiji Ishin* (*History of Japan, Vol. 20: the Meiji Revolution*), Tokyo 2006

R. Ishii, *Mimpōten no hensan* (*Compilation of the Civil Code*), Tokyo 1979.

S. Ishii, *Nihon shisō taikei (21) Chūsei seiji shakai shisō* (*An outline of Japanese ideologies (21) Medieval socio-political thought*), vol. 1, Tokyo 1972.

T. Ishii, *Nihon kaikokushi* (*The history of Japan's opening to the world*), Tokyo 2010.

M. Itō (ed.), *Iwanami kōza gendaihō <14> Gaikokuhō to Nihonhō* (*Iwanami's lectures on contemporary law <14> Foreign law and Japanese law*), Tokyo 1966.

H. Iwamura (ed.), *Hōseishi nyūmon* (*Introduction to the history of law*), Tokyo 1996.

S. Iwao, *Nihon no rekishi <14> Sakoku* (*History of Japan <14> Isolation*), Tokyo 2005.

A. Iwata, *Mimpō kisō to Nihon seishin: Ume sensei no "jōri" o chūshin to shite* (*Civil Code drafting and the Japanese spirit: around Professor Ume's 'Principles of Equity'*), Tokyo 1943.

A. Iwata, *Nihon mimpōshi: Mimpō o tsūjite mitaru Meiji Taishō shisōshi* (*History of Japanese civil law: A history of the ideas of the Meiji and Taishō period as seen through civil law*), Tokyo 1928.

B. Jaluzot, *Les origines du Code civil japonais*, "Zeitschrift für japanisches Recht: zugleich DJJV-Mitteilungen" 2015, Vol. 20 (Issue 40), pp. 121–146.

M. Jansen, *The Making of Modern Japan*, Harvard 2000.

J.M. Jehle, V. Lipp, K. Yamanaka (ed.), *Rezeption und Reform im japanischen und deutschen Recht, Zweites Rechtswissenschaftliches Symposion Göttingen-Kansai*, Göttingen 2008.

B. Jelonek, *XIX-wieczne procesy tworzenia Japońskiego Kodeksu Cywilnego*, "Wrocławskie Studia Erazmiańskie = Studia Erasmiana Wratislaviensia" 2014, vol. 8. *Rozprawa o metodzie prawa i polityki*, pp. 253–267.

S. Kanamori, *German influences on Japanese Pre-war Constitution and Civil Code*, "European Journal of Law and Economics" 1999, Vol. 7, pp. 93–95.

C. Kanda, *Shimabara no ran* (*Shimabara Rebellion*), Tokyo 2005.

Kansai Hōritsu Gakkō no Kōgiroku (Kansai Law School lecture transcript), https://dl.ndl.go.jp/info:ndljp/pid/1614786?tocOpened=1, [access: 12.11.2020].

Y. Kashimi, *Meijiki ni okeru hōten hensan jigyō to jōyaku kaisei ni tsuite: Mimpō o chūshin to shite* (*About the codification and revision of unequal treaties during the Meiji period: around the Civil Code*), "Hōsei Riron" 2014, Vol. 46 (Issue 3), pp. 106–139.

T. Karaś, T. Suzuki (ed.), *Prawo japońskie*, Warsaw 2008.

T. Katada, *Doitsu Gakkyōkai Gakkō Senshūka: aru hōgakkō no rekishi* (*Specialist course at the School of the German Academic Association: the history of a certain school of law*), "Doku Kyōhōgaku" 1995, Vol. 3, pp. 35–69.

Y. Katayama, *Komura Jutarō*, Tokyo 2011.

M. Kawahara, *Nishi Amane to Doitsu Gakkyōkai Gakkō no sōsetsu* (*Amane Nishi and founding of the School of the German Academic Association*), "Kyōikugaku Zasshi" 2000, vol. 34, pp. 33–45.

Y. Kawaguchi, *Nihon kindai hōseishi* (*The history of modern Japanese law*), Tokyo 2014 (2nd edition).

T. Kawashima, N. Toshitani, *Mimpō ue: Hōtaisei jumbiki* (*Civil law, part 1: Period of adaptation of the legal system*), in: N. Ukai, M. Fukushima, T. Kawashima, K. Tsuji (ed.), *Kōza, Nihon kindai hō hattatsushi <5>* (*Lectures on the history of the development of modern Japanese law <5>*), Tokyo 1958.

R. Keene, *Emperor of Japan: Meiji and His World: 1852–1912*, New York 2002.

Kengaku no kokorozashi to yūjō: yonin no sōritsusha (*Friendship and ambition to found a school: the four founders*), https://www.senshu-u.ac.jp/history/founder.html, [access: 12.12.2020].

T. Kimura, *Nihon ni okeru jōyaku kaisei no ikisatsu* (*Circumstances of the revision of treaties in Japan*), "Waseda Jimbu Shizen Kagaku Kenkyū" 1891, Issue 19, pp. 1–18.

H. Kishigami, *Nihon Mimpōgaku koto shikō: Boassonaado to rippōsha ishi* (*The thought of the Japanese science of civil law: the Boissonade's and the legislator's ideas*), "Nagoya Hōgaku" 1996, Vol. 30 (Issue 4), pp. 7–37.

C. Kitabatake, *Jinnō Shōtōki* (*Chronicle of the Authentic Line of Divine Emperors*), http://www.j-texts.com/chusei/rek/jinno.html, [access: 26.09.2020].

K. Kobayakawa, *Zoku Meiji hōsei sōkō* (*Considerations about the successful Meiji legislation*), Kyoto 1944.

Kokugakuin Daigaku (ed.), *Kokugakuin Daigaku 85-nen shi* (*85 years of history of Kokugakuin University*), Tokyo 1970–1979.

A. Kość, *Filozoficzne podstawy prawa japońskiego w perspektywie historycznej*, Lublin 2001.

K. Koyanagi, *Kokufuron taikei no rekishi to riron* (*History and theory of the "Wealth of Nations" system*), Tokyo 1981.

G. Köbler, T. Satō (ed.), *Doitsu hōshi* (*History of German law*), Tokyo 1999.

K. Kumagai, *Mimpō – Kazokuhō* (*Civil law – Family law*), "Juristo" 1968, Issue 400.

K. Kumagai, *Nihon kindaihō no seiritsu* (*The Creation of Modern Japanese Law*), Tokyo 1955.

J. Kurimoto, *Akatsuki mado tsuiroku* (*Travel notes*), Tokyo 1868.

T. Kuryū, *Kon'in rippō ni okeru ni shugi no kōsō* (*Opposition to two doctrines in matrimonial legislation*), Kyoto 1928.

L. Leszczyński, *Prawo japońskie*, in: W. Barbasiewicz (ed.), *Główne kultury prawne współczesnego świata*, Warsaw 1995, pp. 160–182.

M. Luković, *Valtazar Bogišić and the General Property Code for the Principality of Montenegro: Domestic and Foreign Associates*, "Balcanica" 2008, Vol. 39, pp. 175–188.

E. Makino, *Hōrigaku, dai ikkan* (*Jurisprudence, vol. 1*), Tokyo 1949.

L.R. Marković, R.M. Đurović, *Pravni sistem Japana*, Belgrade 2016.

B. Martin, P. Wetzler, *The German Role in the Modernization of Japan – The Pitfall of Blind Acculturation*, "Oriens Extremus" 1990 vol. 33 (n. 1), pp. 77–88.

H.P. Martuschke, *Einführung in das japanische Recht*, Munich 2009.

T. Matsudaira, *Edo jidai seido no kenkyū* (Research on the Edo era's system), Tokyo 1919, pp. 1–3.

T. Matsumoto, *Kindai Nihon ni okeru kazokuhō no tenkai* (*The development of family law in contemporary Japan*), Tokyo 1975.

H. Matono, *Etō Nampaku, ge* (*Nampaku Etō, vol. 2*), Tokyo 1914.

A. de La Mazelière, *M. Gustave Boissonade: Sa vie, sa mission au Japon (1874–1894)*, "Société franco-Japonaise de Paris" 1991, Issue 21, pp. 127–134.

Meiji Daigaku (ed.), *Meiji Daigaku 60-nen shi* (*60-year history of Meiji University*), Tokyo 1940.

Meiji Hōritsu Gakkō setsuritsu no shushi (*The Importance of Establishing the Meiji Law School*), Meiji University Online Materials, [access: 12.11.2020].

M. Metzler, *Lever of empire: the international gold standard and the crisis of liberalism in prewar Japan*, Los Angeles 2006.

M. Medzini, *French Policy in Japan during the Closing Years of the Tokugawa Regime*, Cambridge 1971.

R. Mitsukuri, *Furansu Hōritsusho: Keihō* (*French statutory law: Criminal law*), Tokyo 1870.

R. Mitsukuri, *Furansu Hōritsusho: Mimpō* (*French statutory law: Civil law*), Tokyo 1874.

R. Mitsukuri, *Furansu Hōritsusho, Mimpō: Genmei – Kōdo Naporeon* (*French statutory law, Civil law: Original work – Napoleon's Code)*, Tokyo 1871.

G. Miyahara, *Gyōsei shoshi: Ronkō* (*Notary profession: dissertation*), Tokyo 2010.

K. Miyakawa, *Kyūmimpō to Meiji Mimpō <1>* (*Old Civil Code and Meiji Civil Code <1>*), "Rikkyō Keizaigaku Kenkyū" 1962, Vol. 15 (Issue 4), pp. 261–288.

K. Miyakawa, *Kyūmimpō to Meiji Mimpō <2>* (Old Civil Code and Meiji Civil Code <2>), "Rikkyō Keizaigaku Kenkyū" 1962, Vol. 16 (Issue 2), pp. 191–220.

K. Miyakawa, *Kyūmimpō to Meiji Mimpō <3>* (Old Civil Code and Meiji Civil Code <3>), "Rikkyō Keizaigaku Kenkyū" 1962, Vol. 16 (Issue 4), pp. 109–140.

K. Miyakawa, *Kyūmimpō to Meiji Mimpō <4>* (*Old Civil Code and Meiji Civil Code <4>*), "Rikkyō Keizaigaku Kenkyū" 1963, Vol. 17 (Issue 1), pp. 201–228.

K. Miyakawa, *Kyūmimpō to Meiji Mimpō <5>* (*Old Civil Code and Meiji Civil Code <5>*), "Rikkyō Keizaigaku Kenkyū" 1963, Vol. 17 (Issue 2), pp. 195–224.

K. Miyakawa, *Kyūmimpō to Meiji Mimpō <6>* (*Old Civil Code and Meiji Civil Code <6>*), "Rikkyō Keizaigaku Kenkyū" 1964, Vol. 17 (Issue 4), pp. 185–214.

K. Miyakawa, *Kyūmimpō to Meiji Mimpō <7>* (*Old Civil Code and Meiji Civil Code <7>*), "Rikkyō Keizaigaku Kenkyū" 1964, Vol. 18 (Issue 2), pp. 175–207.

A.P. Morriss, *Codification and Right Answers*, "Chicago-Kent Legal Review" 1999, Issue 74, pp. 355–370.

K. Mukai, *Meihōryō Mimpō sōan hensan katei no ichi kōsatsu* (*Considerations on the Compilation Process of the Meihōryō Civil Code*), "Waseda Daigaku Hōgaku Kai" 1982, Vol. 57 (Issue 3), pp. 41–62.

K. Murakami, *Nihon kindai hōgaku no yōran to Meiji Hōritsu Gakkō* (*The cradle of contemporary Japanese law science and the Meiji Law School*), Tokyo 2007.

K. Murakami, *"Nihon no Hōritsu" ni miru hōten ronsō kankei kiji (1)* (*"Nihon no Hōritsu" as seen in articles regarding the Civil Code Controversy, part 1*), "Hōritsu Rongyō" 2008, Vol. 80 (Issue 4–5), pp. 267–367.

K. Murakami, *"Nihon no Hōritsu" ni miru hōten ronsō kankei kiji (2)* (*"Nihon no Hōritsu" as seen in articles regarding the Civil Code Controversy, part 2*), "Hōritsu Rongyō" 2008, Vol. 81 (Issue 1), pp. 207–268.

K. Murakami, *"Nihon no Hōritsu" ni miru hōten ronsō kankei kiji (3)* (*"Nihon no Hōritsu" as seen in articles regarding the Civil Code Controversy, part 3*), "Hōritsu Rongyō" 2009, Vol. 81 (Issue 4–5), pp. 243–297.

K. Murakami, *"Nihon no Hōritsu" ni miru hōten ronsō kankei kiji (4)* (*"Nihon no Hōritsu" as seen in articles regarding the Civil Code Controversy, part 4*), "Hōritsu Rongyō" 2009, Vol. 81 (Issue 6), pp. 289–350.

K. Murakami, *"Nihon no Hōritsu" ni miru hōten ronsō kankei kiji (5)* (*"Nihon no Hōritsu" as seen in articles regarding the Civil Code Controversy, part 5*), "Hōritsu Rongyō" 2011, Vol. 83 (Issue 4–5), pp. 289–350.

K. Murakami, *"Nihon no Hōritsu" ni miru hōten ronsō kankei kiji (6)* (*"Nihon no Hōritsu" as seen in articles regarding the Civil Code Controversy, part 6*), "Hōritsu Rongyō" 2011, Vol. 83 (Issue 6), pp. 289–350.

K. Murakami, *Shihōshō Gakkō ni okeru hōgaku kōgi: Inoue Misao ni yoru 7-satsu no futsubun no nōto* (*Lecture on law at the School at the Ministry of Justice: Seven volumes of French memos by Misao Inoue*), "Meiji Daigaku Daigaku Shiryō I'inkai" 2006, Issue 10, pp. 2–4.

M. Nabatsu, *Les missions militaires françaises au Japon entre 1867 et 1889*, Paris 2018.

T. Nagamata, *Goseibai Shikimoku hensan no kisoteki kenkyū* (*Basic Goseibai Shikimoku compilation studies*), Tokyo 2017.

K. Nagamori (ed.), *Minji shūkan rui shū* (*Collection of civil law customs*), Tokyo 1877, https://dl.ndl.go.jp/info:ndljp/pid/787052/1 [access: 12.11.2020].

C. Nagumo, *Meijiki hōgakusha no hōritsuyōgo kan: Mimpōten no honyaku o megutte* (*A look at the legal terminology of the Meiji period jurists: around the translation of the Civil Code*), "Nihongogaku Ronshū" 2017, Vol. 13 (Issue 3), pp. 34–54.

K. Nakagawa, *Meiji hōten ronsō no naka no shiritsu hōritsu gakkō* (*Private law schools in the Civil Code Controversy*), "Meiji Daigaku Shiryō Sentaa Hōkoku" 2016, Vol. 37, pp. 35–60.

T. Nakagawa, *Meiji Hōten ronsō ni okeru enkiha no kiseki* (*Tracking the activity of the postponement party during the Meiji Code Controversy*), "Hōgaku Shimpō" 2015, Vol. 121 (Issue 9–10), pp. 349–380.

K. Nakamura, *Kindai Nihon no hōteki keisei: Jōyaku kaisei to hōten hensan* (*The legal system of contemporary Japan: Revision of treaties and codification of law*), Tokyo 1956.

K. Nakamura, *Meiji hōseishi, dai ikkan* (*Meiji law history, vol. 1*), Tokyo 1967.

K. Nakamura, *Tokugawa Ieyasu kōden* (*Ieyasu Tokugawa's Official Biography*), Tokyo 1965.

N. Nakamura, *Ōkuma Shigenobu*, Tokyo 1972.

K. Nakada, *Tokugawa jidai no bungaku to shihō* (*Literature and private law of the Tokugawa period*), Tokyo 1923.

Nihon Daigaku (ed.), *Yamada Akiyoshi den* (*Akiyoshi Yamada's biography*), Tokyo 1963.

M. Niida, *Kyūmimpō* (*Old Civil Code*), Tokyo 1943.

Y. Noda (ed.), *Introduction to Japanese Law*, Tokyo 1976.

Y. Noda, *La réception du droit français au Japon*, "Revue internationale de droit compare" 1963, Vol. 15 (Issue 3), pp. 543–556.

Y. Noda, *Meiji Shōnen ni okeru Furansuhō no Eikyō* (*The fame of French law in the first period of the Meiji era*), "Nichifutsu Hōgaku" 1961, Issue 1, pp. 3–59.

H. Oda, *Japanese Law*, Oxford 2009.

T. Oka, *Nihon ni okeru Mimpōten ronsō no igi to kongo no kadai* (*The significance of the Civil Code Controversy in Japan and subsequent issues*), "19-seki Gaku Kenkyū" 2014, Issue 8, pp. 37–48.

H. Okamoto, *Ansei kaisei mondai* (*The problem of revision of the Ansei Treaties*), Tokyo 2010.

Y. Ōkubo, *Bowasonaado: Nihon kindai hō no chichi* (*Boissonade: the father of modern Japanese law*), Tokyo 1977.

Y. Ōkubo, *La querelle sur le premier Code civil japonais et l'ajournement de sa mise en vigueur: le refus du législateur étranger?*, "Revue internationale de droit comparé" 1991, Vol. 43 (Issue 2), pp. 389–405.

Y. Ōkubo, Y. Takahashi, *Bowasonaado Mimpōten no hensan* (*Compilation of the Boissonade's Civil Code*), Tokyo 1999.

S. Ono, *Comparative Law and the Civil Code of Japan*, "Hitotsubashi Journal of Law and Politics" 1996, Issue 24, pp. 27–45.

T. Ōtsu (ed.), *Hōreisei Kenkyū Nyūmon* (*Introduction to the science of the statutory law system*), Tokyo 2011.

F. Ōtsuki, *Mitsukuri Rinshō kun den* (*Rinshō Mitsukuri's biography*), Tokyo 1907.

S. Ono, *Hōritsu shisōshi gaisetsu* (*A general outline of the history of legal thought*), Tokyo 1961.

E. Pałasz-Rutkowska, *Cesarz Meiji (1852–1912) Wizerunek władcy w modernizowanej Japonii*, Warsaw 2012.

M.A. Piegzik, *Rozwój szkół prawa w Japonii w okresie ery Meiji*, "Folia Iuridica Universitatis Wratislaviensis" 2016, Vol. 5 (Issue 1), pp. 69–84.

M.A. Piegzik, *Wczesne próby kodyfikacji japońskiego prawa cywilnego ery Meiji i ich kontekst historyczno-polityczny*, "Folia Iuridica Universitatis Wratislaviensis" 2018, Vol. 7 (Issue 1), pp. 137–159.

Z. Radwański, *Kodyfikacja Prawa Cywilnego*, in: "Ruch Prawniczy, Ekonomiczny i Socjologiczny", Rok LXXI (2009), Issue 2, pp. 131–142.

F.L. Ramaioli, *La genesi del Costituzionalismo giapponese nell'era Meiji*, "Ricerche giuridiche" 2015, Vol. 4 (Issue 2), pp. 443–469.

Ritsumeikan 100-nen shi: tsūshi dai ikkan (*100 Years of Ritsumeikan History: A General History, Vol. 1*), http://www.ritsumei.ac.jp/archives/common/file/publication/history-1-introduction.pdf, [access: 04.12.2020].

J. Robert, *Le role de la France dans l'enseignement du droit au Japon*, "Revue d'histoire des Facultés de Droit et de la Science Juridique" 1994, Vol. 15, pp. 49–62.

F.V. Rodríguez, *Codificación y recepción jurídicas en Japón: la importación de la modernidad a partir del derecho*, "Revista Mexicana de Historia del Derecho" 2012, Vol. 25, pp. 231–253.

F.V. Rodríguez, *Derecho y discurso en la creación del modelo de familia japonés ie*, "Estudios de Asia y Africa" 2011, Vol. 46 (Issue 1), pp. 97–126.

W. Röhl, *Die Einflüsse des deutschen Rechts auf Japan*, in: G. Krebs (ed.), *Japan und Preußen*, Munich 2002, pp. 185–207.

W. Röhl, *History of law in Japan since 1868*, Leiden-Boston 2005.

J.G. Ruiz de Medina, *Documentos del Japón: 1547–1557*, Rome 1990.

C. Saeki, Y. Kobayashi, *Keihōgaku shi* (pol. *History of the science of criminal law*), in: N. Ukai, M. Fukushima, T. Kawashima, K. Tsuji (ed.), *Kōza, Nihon kindai hō hattatsushi <11>* (*Lectures on the history of the development of contemporary Japanese law <11>*), Tokyo 1958.

K. Sakamoto, *Mimpō no hensan to Meiji ishin* (*Meiji revolution and codification of civil law*), Tokyo 2004.

S. Sasaki, *Ōkubo Toshimichi to Meiji ishin* (*Toshimichi Ōkubo and the Meiji Revolution)*, Tokyo 1998.

E. Satow, *A Diplomat in Japan*, Oxford 1968.

F. von Savigny, *O powołaniu naszych czasów do ustawodawstwa i nauki prawa*, Warsaw 1964.

Sawczuk, M. Konarski, *Pojęcie i rola kodyfikacji w systemie prawa – wybrane zagadnienia*, "Teka Komisji Prawniczej OL PAN" 2011, pp. 133–146.

H. H. Seiler, *Geschichte und Gegenwart im Zivilrecht: Ausgewählte Schriften*, Cologne 2005.

T. Sekiguchi, *Tsuyoi naikaku to kindai Nihon: kokusaku kettei no shudōken kakuho e* (*A strong cabinet and contemporary Japan: to guarantee the leading role of national politics*), Tokyo 2021.

Senshū Daigaku no enkaku (*Chronology of the Senshū University*), https://www.senshu-u.ac.jp/history/chronology.html, [access: 12.12.2020].

Senshū Gakkō Hōritsu Kōgi Hikki (*Records of law lectures at the Senshū School*), http://base1.nijl.ac.jp/infolib/meta_pub/G0037150meijisub_IA0034498, [access: 12.12.2020].

K. Shichinobe, *Genkō Mimpōten o tsukutta hitobito (1) Jōron: Sōsai, Fukusōsai: Itō Hirobumi, Saionji Kim'mochi* (*People who created the modern Civil Code (1) Introduction: Chairman, Vice-chairmen: Hirobumi Itō, Kim'mochi Saionji*), "Hōgaku Seminaa" 2009, n. 54/5, pp. 40–42.

K. Shichinobe, *Genkō Mimpōten o tsukutta hitobito (2) Sōsai, Fukusōsai: Matsukata Masayoshi, Kiyoura Keigo, Sone Arasuke* (*People who created the modern Civil Code (2) Chairman, Vice-chairmen: Masayoshi Matsukata, Keigo Kiyoura, Arasuke Sone*), "Hōgaku Seminaa" 2009, n. 54/6, pp. 78–80.

K. Shichinobe, *Genkō Mimpōten o tsukutta hitobito (3) Kisō I'in: Hozumi Nobushige, Tomii Masaakira, Ume Kenjirō* (*People who created the modern Civil Code (3) Members of the Drafting Committee Nobushige Hozumi, Masaakira Tomii, Kenjirō Ume*), "Hōgaku Seminaa" 2009, n. 54/7, pp. 64–66.

K. Shichinobe, *Genkō Mimpōten o tsukutta hitobito (4) Shusa I'in 1: Suematsu Kenchō, Itō Miyoshi* (*People who created the modern Civil Code (4) Members of the Research Committee 1: Kenchō Suematsu, Miyoshi Itō*), "Hōgaku Seminaa" 2009, n. 54/8, pp. 86–88.

K. Shichinobe, *Genkō Mimpōten o tsukutta hitobito (5) Shusa I'in 2: Mitsukuri Rinshō, Murata Tamotsu* (*The people who created the modern Civil Code (5) Members of the Research Committee 2: Rinshō Mitsukuri, Tamotsu Murata*), "Hōgaku Seminaa" 2009, n. 54/9, pp. 72–73.

K. Shichinobe, *Genkō Mimpōten o tsukutta hitobito (6) Shusa I'in 3: Kinoshita Hiroji, Kumano Binzō (People who created the modern Civil Code (6) Members of the Research Committee 3: Hiroji Kinoshita, Binzō Kumano)*, "Hōgaku Seminaa" 2009, n. 54/10, pp. 64–65.

K. Shichinobe, *Genkō Mimpōten o tsukutta hitobito (7) Shusa I'in 4: Yokota Kuniomi, Takagi Toyozō, gaiden 3 (People who created the modern Civil Code. (7) Members of the Research Committee 4: Kuniomi Yokota, Toyozō Takagi, supreme biography 3)*, "Hōgaku Seminaa" 2009, n. 54/11, pp. 67–69.

K. Shichinobe, *Genkō Mimpōten o tsukutta hitobito (8) Shusa I'in 5: Hatoyama Kazuo, Kikuchi Takeo, gaiden 4: Nihon saisho no bengoshi (People who created the modern Civil Code. (8) Members of the Research Committee 5: Kazuo Hatoyama, Takeo Kikuchi, supreme biography 4: the first Japanese attorneys)*, "Hōgaku Seminaa" 2009, n. 54/12, pp. 81–83.

K. Shichinobe, *Genkō Mimpōten o tsukutta hitobito (9) Shusa I'in 6: Motoda Hajime, Kikuchi Takeo, Misaki Kamenosuke, gaiden 5: nikai shiken (People who created the modern Civil Code (9) Research Committee Members 6: Hajime Motoda, Kamenosuke Misaki, Supplementary Biography 5: Double Examination)*, "Hōgaku Seminaa" 2010, n. 55/1, pp. 74–76.

K. Shichinobe, *Genkō Mimpōten o tsukutta hitobito (10) Shusa I'in 7: Tanabe Kaoru, Hasegawa Takashi, Motō Keizaburō, gaiden 6: Gyōsei saibansho no naifun (People who created the modern Civil Code (10) Research Committee Members 7: Taoru Kanabe, Takashi Hasegawa, Keizaburō Motō, Supplementary Biography 6: Internal Conflict in the Judicial Administration)*, "Hōgaku Seminaa" 2010, n. 55/2, pp. 74–76.

K. Shichinobe, *Genkō Mimpōten o tsukutta hitobito (11) Satei I'in 1: Yasushi Hijikata, Motono Ichirō (People who created the modern Civil Code (11) Members of the Revision Committee 1: Hijikata Yasushi, Ichirō Motono)*, "Hōgaku Seminaa" 2010, n. 55/3, pp. 68–70.

K. Shichinobe, *Genkō Mimpōten o tsukutta hitobito (12) Satei I'in 3, 4: Nambu Mikao, Nakamura Motoyoshi, gaiden 7: Rōkyū shihōkan no tōta (The people who created the modern Civil Code (12) Members of the Revision Committee 3, 4: Mikao Nambu, Motoyoshi Nakamura, supreme biography 7: The elimination of old officials of the Ministry of Justice)*, "Hōgaku Seminaa" 2010, n. 55/3, pp. 68–70.

K. Shichinobe, *Genkō Mimpōten o tsukutta hitobito (15) Satei I'in 9/10: Eki Chū, Hozumi Yasuka, gaiden 11 (People who created the modern Civil Code (15) Members of the 9/10 Revision Committee: Chū Eki, Yasuka Hozumi, supreme biography 11)*, "Hōgaku Seminaa" 2009, n. 55/7, pp. 56–58.

Y. Shigematsu, *Jiyūshugi tachi to Mimpō ronsō (Liberals and the Civil Code Controversy)*, "Soshio Saiensu" 2005, Issue 11, pp. 175–189.

Y. Shigematsu, *Ōki Takatō to "tempu jinken" – Mimpōten ronsō ni okeru Ōki Takatō no zekka jiken (Takatō Ōki and "natural human rights" – Takatō Ōki's verbal incident during the Civil Code Controversy)*, "Soshio Saiensu" 2007, Vol. 13, pp. 125–139.

H. Shimizu, Y. Shimizu, *Kirishitan kankei hōsei shiryō (Materials from the history of the law related to Christians)*, Hachiōji 2002.

J. Shingū, *Doitsu Gakkyōkai Gakkō no tenkan (Transformation of the School of the German Academic Association)*, http://jsmh.umin.jp/journal/58-2/58-2_133.pdf, [access: 12.12.2020].

Y. Shiraha, *Mimpō kisōsha: Hozumi Nobushige ron (People preparing the draft of the Civil Code: Nobushige Hozumi's theories)*, Tokyo 1995.

Shōyū Kurabu (ed.), *Kizokuin no kaiha kenkyūkaishi (History of the scientific association of the House of Peers' faction)*, Tokyo 1980.

S. Sogabe, *Nicchū ritsuryō ron (Debate on Sino-Japanese administrative and criminal law)*, Tokyo 1995.

C. Sokolowski, *Der so genannte Kodifikationenstreit in Japan*, Munich 2010.

J. L. Sourioux, *La pensée juridique de G. Boissonade: aspects de droit civil*, "Revue internationale de droit compare" 1991, Vol. 43 (Issue 2), pp. 357–366.

K. Sójka-Zielińska, *Wielkie kodyfikacje cywilne. Historia i współczesność*, Warsaw 2009.

C. Steenstrup, *Die Rezeption des deutschen Rechts im Japan der Meiji-Zeit*, "Oriens Extremus" 1990, Vol. 33 (Issue 1), pp. 37–47.

T. Sueki, *Dai 2-kai Shūgi'in giin senkyo no kekka to gikai un'ei, senkyo kanshō no yūkōsei bunseki* (*Results of the second elections to the House of Representatives and the composition of the parliament, analysis of the effectiveness of intervention in the elections*), "Senkyo Kenkyū" 2010, Vol. 26 (Issue 2), pp. 120–130.

T. Sueki, *Meiji 25-nen senkyo kanshō jiken to rikken seiji: keitōteki shireisetsu to bōhatsusetsu o megutte* (*The Meiji 25 election intervention incident and the constitutional government: a dispute over deliberate orders and the theory of accidental firearm incident*), "Kindai Nihon Kenkyū" 2015, Vol. 35, pp. 105–135.

T. Sueki, *Senkyo kanshō to rikken seiji* (*Intervention in elections and constitutional government*), Tokyo 2018.

N. Sugiyama, *Tomii danshaku tsuitō shu* (*Collection commemorating Baron Tomii*), Tokyo 1936.

J. Suzuki, "fukoku kyōhei", in: *Rekishigaku Jiten, kan 13* (*Dictionary of Historiography, Vol. 13*), Tokyo 2006, pp. 525–526.

K. Suzuki, *Meijiki Nihon ni okeru ryōji saiban to shōnin ryōji* (*Consular and commercial jurisdiction in Meiji period Japan*), materials of the Japanese Ministry of Justice on the history of diplomacy, March 2018, https://www.mofa.go.jp/mofaj/ms/da/page25_001383.html [access: 21.10.2020].

M. Suzuki, *Kindai Minji Soshōhōshi: Nihon* (*A History of modern Civil Procedure: Japan*), Tokyo 2004.

Y. Suzuki, J. Siemes, *Hermann Roesler und die Japanische Verfassung*, "Monumenta Nipponica" 1941, Vol. 4, (Issue 1), pp. 53–87.

W.S. Svetlov, *Proischożdienije kapitalisticzeskoj Japonij*, Moscow-Leningrad 1934.

Y. Takahashi, Fujiwara Akihisa cho *"Bowasonaado teitōhō no kenkyū"* (shohyō) (Review of Akihisa Fujiwara's book – *'Studies on the Boissonade's Mortgage'*), "Hōseishi Kenkyū" 1996, Vol. 46, pp. 191–196.

K. Takami, *Kōza tan'nin kara mita kempōgaku setsu no shosō – Nihon Kempōgakushi kenkyū jōsetsu* (*Various aspects of the theory of the science of constitutional law seen from the lecturer's perspective – introduction to the science of the history of Japanese constitutional law*), "Hokudai Hōgaku Ronshū" 2001, Vol. 52 (Issue 3), pp. 803–840.

S. Takanagi, *Tokugawa jidai keihō no gaikan* (*Overview of criminal law during the Tokugawa shogunate period*), Tokyo 1942.

N. Takase (ed.), *Kaneko Kentarō chosakushū, dai 1-shū* (*The collection of works by Kentarō Kaneko, part 1*), Tokyo 1995.

C. Takatani, Y. Koishikawa (ed.), *Nihon hōshi kara nani ga mieruka: hō to chitsujo no rekishi o manabu* (*What is visible through the prism of the history of Japanese law: learning the history of law and order*), Tokyo 2018.

K. Takayanagi, *Contact of the Common Law with the Civil Law in Japan*, "The American Journal of Comparative Law" 1955, Vol. 4 (Issue 1), pp. 60–69.

K. Takayanagi, *Reception and Influence of Occidental Legal Ideas in Japan*, in: I. Nitobe (ed.), *Western Influences in Modern Japan*, Chicago 1931, pp. 1–21.

M. Takayanagi, *T. Rizō (ed.), Kadogawa Nihonshi jiten (Kadogawa Dictionary of Japanese History)*, Tokyo 1995.

K. Takeshita, *Kansai Hōritsu Gakkō no sōsetsu to hōshisō* (*Founding of the Kansai Law School and its legal thought*), https://www.kansai-u.ac.jp/nenshi/issue/pdf/24-1.pdf, [access: 12.11.2020].

A. Tanaka, *Kindai ten'nōsei e no michionori* (*The road to the modern imperial system*), Tokyo 2007.

H. Tanaka (ed.), *The Japanese Legal System*, Tokyo 1976.

K. Tanaka, *Boassonaado no hōtesugaku: toku ni sono no shizenhō shisō ni oite (The philosophy of Boissonade's law: about his natural law views)*, in: K. Tanaka (ed.), Hōtetsugaku Ronshū, Dai 3 (*Collection of essays on the philosophy of law*, vol. 3), Tokyo 1952, pp. 109–155.

T. Taniguchi, *Furansu Mimpō I Jinjihō (French civil law I: personal law)*, Tokyo 1939.

T. Taniguchi, K. Ishida (ed.), *Shimpan chūshaku Mimpō (1) Sōsoku (1) Kaitei han (New edition of the commentary on civil law (1) General part (1), revised edition)*, Tokyo 2002.

M. Terasaki, *Tōkyō Daigaku no rekishi: daigaku seido no sakigake (History of the University of Tokyo: a pioneer of the higher education system)*, Tokyo 2007.

Y. Tezuka, *Meiji hōgaku kyōikushi no kenkyū (Meiji legal education study)*, Tokyo 1988.

Y. Tezuka, *Meiji Mimpōshi no kenkyū, jō-ge (Research on the history of the Meiji Civil Code, vol. 1–2)*, Tokyo 1990–1991.

Y. Tezuka, *Shihōshō hōgakkōshi (2): Zokuzoku Meiji hōsei shiryō zassan (Ministry of Justice Law School (2): Continuation of various historical materials from the Meiji legal system)*, "Hōgaku kenkyū: hōritsu, seiji, shakai" 1967, Vol. 40 (Issue 7), pp. 57–100.

S. Tokuda, *Kansai Daigaku no sōsetsu ni kakawatta hitobito: shōdai kōchō Ogura Hisashi no nokoshita arubamu kara (People related to the founding of Kansai University: The leftover album of the first director of Hisashi Ogura)*, https://www.kansai-u.ac.jp/nenshi/issue/pdf/23_1-1.pdf, [access: 12.11.2020].

I. Tokutomi, *Kōshaku Yamagata Aritomo den, shita kan (Prince Aritomo Yamagata's biography, part 2)*, Tokyo 1933.

M. Tomii, *Mimpō genron, dai 1 kan: Sōron (Civil law theory, vol. 1: General part)*, Tokyo 1922.

N. Tomita, *Shūgi'in Gi'in senkyo no shiteki bunseki ichi, Meijiki/Taishōki (Historical analysis of the election of MPs in the House of Representatives (1), the Meiji and Taishō period)*, "Senkyo Kenkyū" 1986, Vol. 1, pp. 66–93.

N. Toshitani, *Nihon no hō o kangaeru (Thinking about Japanese law)*, Tokyo 2013.

Tōkyō Kaisei Gakkō ichiran, Meiji 8-nen 2-gatsu (*Tokyo Kaisei School Review, February of 8th year of the Meiji era*), https://dl.ndl.go.jp/info:ndljp/pid/992865, [access: 10.12.2020].

S. Tōyama, *Mimpōten no seijishiteki kōsatsu (Considerations on the historical and political aspects of the Civil Code)*, "Hōgaku-shirin" 1951, Vol. 49 (Issue 1), p. 60.

K. Ume, *Hōten ni kansuru hanashi (Considerations related to code[s])*, "Kokkai Gakkai Zasshi" 1898, Vol. 20 (Issue 134), pp. 333–352.

K. Ume, *Kazokusei no shōrai o ronsu (Debating the future of the family system)*, in: R. Abe (ed.), *Hōgaku taika rombunshū, Mimpō no bu, gekan (Collection of legal experts' texts, part Civil law, vol. 2)*, Tokyo 1910.

N. Umetani, *Oyatoi gaikokujin (Employed foreigners)*, Tokyo 2007.

T. Ushiomi, N. Toshitani, *Nihon no hōgakusha (Japanese jurists)*, Tokyo 1975.

B.L. Walker, *Foreign Affairs and Frontiers in Early Modern Japan: a Historio-graphical Essay*, "Early Modern Japan: An Interdisciplinary Journal" 2002, Vol. 10 (Issue 2), pp. 44–62.

Waseda Daigaku (ed.), *Hanseiki no Waseda Daigaku (Half a Century of Waseda University)*, Tokyo 1932.

H. Yamamoto (ed.), *Totoyomi Hideyoshi no komonjo (Hideyoshi Toyotomi's Old Papers)*, Tokyo 2015.

H. Yamano, *"Kansai Hōritsu Gakkō Kisoku" o fukkoku suru (Reissue of the "Kansai Law School Charter")*, https://www.kansai-u.ac.jp/nenshi/issue/pdf/17-1.pdf, [access: 12.11.2020].

T. Yoshii, Igirisu Hōritsu Gakkō, Tokio Senmon Gakkō, "Nihonshi Daijiten, kan 1" (Great Encyclopaedia of Japanese History, vol. 1), Tokyo 1992.

W.N. Yeremin, *Istorija prawowoj sistiemy Japonii*, Moscow 2010.

N.P. Zarubina, *Czastnoje prawo Japonii*, Chabarowsk 2016.

INDEX

MIX
Papier | Fördert gute Waldnutzung
FSC® C083411

Kolibri 360 GmbH
Ferdinand-Jühlke-Straße 7
99095 Erfurt, Deutschland
produktsicherheit@kolibri360.de